HISTORY

Curriculum Bank

KEY STAGE TWO
SCOTTISH LEVELS C-E

HISTORY II

LIFE IN TUDOR TIMES **VICTORIAN BRITAIN**

BRITAIN SINCE 1930 **LOCAL HISTORY**

MARTIN FORREST WITH PENELOPE HARNETT

Published by Scholastic Ltd,
Villiers House,
Clarendon Avenue,
Leamington Spa,
Warwickshire CV32 5PR
Text © Martin Forrest and Penelope Harnett
© 1996 Scholastic Ltd
5 6 7 8 9 0   9 0 1 2 3 4 5

AUTHOR
MARTIN FORREST WITH PENELOPE HARNETT

EDITOR
JEAN COPPENDALE

ASSISTANT EDITOR
LIBBY WEAVER

SERIES DESIGNER
LYNNE JOESBURY

DESIGNER
SUE STOCKBRIDGE

ILLUSTRATIONS
PAT MURRAY (GRAHAM-CAMERON ILLUSTRATION)
LIZ SAWYER (SIMON GIRLING ASSOC.)

COVER ILLUSTRATION
JONATHAN BENTLEY

INFORMATION TECHNOLOGY CONSULTANT
MARTIN BLOWS

SCOTTISH 5–14 LINKS
MARGARET SCOTT AND SUSAN GOW

Designed using Aldus Pagemaker

British Library Cataloguing-in-Publication Data
A catalogue record for this book is available from the
British Library.

ISBN 0-590-53409-2

Contents

ACKNOWLEDGEMENTS

The publishers gratefully acknowledge permission to reproduce the following copyright material:

Ordnance Survey (Licence Number 82816M) for 1886 map of Somerset 25" County series 29/2 and 1989 map of Somerset Sheet ST65SE 1:10,000 © Crown Copyright; Lamport Hall Trust and Northamptonshire Records Office for the use of an extract from John Isham's Account Book; Bristol (Archives) Record Office for the use of an extract from Redland Court Tithe Records; Public Records Office for the census return of Henbury 1851 © Crown Copyright.

Every effort has been made to trace copyright holders for the works reproduced in this book and the publishers apologise for any inadvertent omissions.

Introduction

Scholastic Curriculum Bank is a series for all primary teachers, providing both an essential planning tool for devising comprehensive schemes of work as well as an easily accessible and varied bank of practical, classroom-tested activities with photocopiable resources.

Designed to help planning for and implementation of progression, differentiation and assessment, *Scholastic Curriculum Bank* offers a structured range of stimulating activities with clearly-stated learning objectives that reflect the programmes of study, and detailed lesson plans that allow busy teachers to put the ideas into practice with the minimum amount of preparation time. The photocopiable sheets that accompany many of the activities provide ways of integrating purposeful application of knowledge and skills, differentiation, assessment and record-keeping.

Opportunities for formative assessment are highlighted where appropriate within the activities. Ways of using information technology for different purposes and within different contexts, as a tool for communicating and handling information and as a method for investigating, are integrated into the activities where appropriate and more explicit guidance is provided at the end of the book.

The series covers all the primary curriculum subjects with separate books for Key Stages 1 and 2/Scottish Levels A–B and C–E. It can be used as a flexible resource with any scheme to fulfil National Curriculum and Scottish 5–14 requirements and to provide children with a variety of different learning experiences that will lead to effective acquisition of skills and knowledge.

SCHOLASTIC CURRICULUM BANK HISTORY

This *Scholastic Curriculum Bank History* is designed for teachers of Key Stage 2 History. It provides a range of activities which are closely linked to the requirements of the Programme of Study of the History National Curriculum. Scholastic's *Curriculum Bank History* Key Stage 2 is divided into two volumes, this book covers Study Units 2, 3 and 5; Study Units 1, 4 and 6 are covered in *Curriculum Bank History* Key Stage 2:I.

Aims of this book

Curriculum Bank History has been designed to help teachers plan, teach and assess history activities in the classroom. The lesson plans include background information and suggestions for developing children's historical skills and understanding. The lesson plans identify the Study Units and the Key Elements of the History Key Stage 2 Programme of Study. There are suggestions to help assess children's learning in relation to the History Attainment Target. Advice is provided on differentiation to take into account the children's abilities and stages of maturity at Key Stage 2.

The activities take into account the cross–curricular nature of the primary school curriculum and links with other subject areas are identified on page 160.

Curriculum Bank History also provides guidance for planning a scheme of work at Key Stage 2. Criteria are suggested for the selection of historical content. Planning for progression is also addressed and advice is given on record-keeping and monitoring National Curriculum History.

Using this book

The book can be used in a variety of ways. The grids on pages 13–16 provide a summary of the activities. They can be used to select activities most suitable for the particular historical focus being developed in the classroom. The main chapter headings are linked to the Study Units in the Key Stage 2 Programme of Study. In this book, *Curriculum Bank History* Key Stage 2: II, these are Study Unit 2 – **Life in Tudor times;** Study Unit 3a – **Victorian Britain;** Study Unit 3b – **Britain since 1930** and Study Unit 5 – **Local History.** The activities suggested for Study Unit 5 can be adapted to cover the different historical periods and societies mentioned within the unit. Make a simple recording sheet similar to the one shown below to enable you to keep a record of the activities which have been undertaken.

Name of child	Study Unit 2 Life in Tudor times: Activities						
	1	2	3	4	5	6	etc

Lesson plans

Detailed lesson plans are included for historical activities. They are designed to provide appropriate material for immediate implementation in the classroom. Some lesson plans are quite short, whereas others provide a basis for a sequence of learning activities. The structure for each lesson plan is as follows;

Activity title box

The information contained in the box at the beginning of each activity outlines the following key aspects:

▲ Activity title and learning objective – For each activity a clearly stated learning objective is given in bold italics. Reference is made to the Study Unit and particular Key Elements in the Programme of Study for History.

▲ Class organisation/Likely duration – Icons †† and ⏰ indicate the number of children involved in the activity and the approximate duration of the activity respectively. The book contains activities suitable for individual, paired, group and whole class work. Many activities involve whole class introductions prior to individual or group work. In this case only the latter class organisation size is stated. Some activities will need to be continued and extended over more than one lesson.

Previous skills/knowledge needed

Information is given here when it is necessary for the children to have experienced particular skills or acquired certain knowledge before undertaking the activity.

Key background information

This section provides information to extend the teacher's historical knowledge and awareness about the activity. It is designed to set the activity within a broader historical framework and to elaborate on the context and skills addressed by the activity.

Preparation

Advice on preparation needed prior to the lesson is provided. Preparation of particular materials and photocopiable sheets is included as well as the organisation of a display or similar stimulus.

Resources needed

All of the materials needed to carry out the activity are listed,

so that the pupils or the teacher can gather them together easily before the beginning of the teaching session.

What to do
Clear instructions are provided for carrying out the tasks. Specific questions to ask children are included and points to develop through discussion are identified.

Suggestion(s) for support/extension
Advice on how the activities might be adapted to meet children's different learning needs is included. Modifications for both the less and the more able are included. Sometimes suggestions for extension describe further aspects of the same topic.

Assessment opportunities
Key questions are provided which can be used to help assess children's learning in history.

Opportunities for IT
The icon ◇ indicates where the activity might be extended to include opportunities for children to include information technology in their work.

Display ideas
Diagrams and notes for display ideas are incorporated within the activity plans as appropriate.

Reference to photocopiable sheets
Where photocopiable sheets accompany an activity a small reproduction is included in the lesson plan together with guidance notes for their use, and where appropriate, suggested answers.

Cross curricular links
The History National Curriculum is closely linked with the English National Curriculum and provides many opportunities for developing children's speaking and listening, reading and writing abilities. Links with other curriculum areas are identified in the grid on page 160.

Photocopiable activity sheets
Many of the activities are accompanied by photocopiable activity sheets. These can be used to develop historical skills and concepts and to provide opportunities for children to record and communicate their historical knowledge and understanding. Some activity sheets can also be used as historical sources to provide the children with historical information. Others provide material for craft/colouring/painting or modelling activities designed to stimulate children's interest in the past. Certain activity sheets have been identified as appropriate for assessment purposes and would be useful as records to include in portfolios of children's work to monitor their progression in historical understanding.

NATIONAL CURRICULUM HISTORY KEY STAGE 2

Programme of Study
The focus statement which is set out at the beginning of the Programme of Study, underpins all the teaching at Key Stage 2 and should be used as the guide for planning and teaching. The historical content to be taught is outlined in the Study Units. The Key Elements describe ways of developing children's historical understanding.

History Study Units
Curriculum Bank History covers all the Key Stage 2 Study Units.

This book *Curriculum Bank History* Key Stage 2: II provides activities linked with:
▲ Study Unit 2 – Life in Tudor times;
▲ Study Unit 3a – Victorian Britain;
▲ Study Unit 3b – Britain since 1930;
▲ Study Unit 5 – Local History.
Curriculum Bank History Key Stage 2: I covers:
▲ Study Unit 1 – Romans, Anglo-Saxons and Vikings in Britain;
▲ Study Unit 4 – Ancient Greece;
▲ Study Unit 6 – A past non-European society.

Key Elements
The Key Elements act as a guide for planning work within the Study Units. The Key Elements may not be developed in all the Study Units, but should be covered by the end of Key Stage 2. Consequently, schools will need to consider where particular elements are going to be addressed in their curriculum plans and history schemes of work. For advice and points to consider in developing whole school plans see page 12.

Key Elements have been identified within all the Curriculum Bank activities. There are five Key Elements:
1. Chronology
2. Range and depth of historical understanding
3. Interpretation of history
4. Historical enquiry
5. Organisation and communication

Chronology
The ability to sequence events and place objects in order is important in the study of history. Across Key Stage 2 children need to develop a chronological framework so that they can place events and different periods within time, and also recognise the relationship of different events and periods with each other. Language is central for children to communicate their understanding and to describe the passage of time. Particular vocabulary and terms for Key

Stage 2 children to become familiar with would include different eras for example, Tudors or the Victorians and terms such as century and decade. Numerical skills are also important for more precise recording of time. Children need varied experiences to help them develop their language of time and to experience using numerical skills to locate past events. Such experience could include:

▲ providing opportunities for children to place objects or pictures in historical order – beginning with the oldest and finishing with the most recent;

▲ creating personal timelines for children to sequence their own experience and changes which have occurred in their life times;

▲ creating class timelines to show features of the different Study Units covered;

▲ maintaining a class timeline which the class starts in Year 3 and which they complete as they progress through years 4, 5 and 6, so that children can relate new historical experiences to more familiar ones.

Progression in Key Element 1 can be noted by children's increasing ability to sequence events and objects in the correct order. Children will progress from simple sequences employing terms such as yesterday/today, now/then, past/present, long ago, to using more complex vocabulary linked with the passage of time, including reference to particular dates, terms and periods of history.

Range and depth of historical knowledge and understanding

A broad range of historical knowledge and understanding is included within this Key Element. Such a range takes into account the beliefs, attitudes and ideas held in the past, and the experiences of different sections of society. Children will learn about different aspects of past societies, such as their cultural, social, religious and ethnic diversity. Key historical ideas such as identifying reasons behind events and explaining their effects, and recognising changes and similarities are incorporated within this Key Element. As children acquire knowledge of different periods of history they will be able to recognise some of the characteristic

features of particular periods of time. For example, features of Tudor architecture, styles of Elizabethan costume or sailing ships which Drake, Columbus or Cabot used.

Classroom experiences to develop the range and depth of children's historical knowledge and understanding would include:

▲ learning about different aspects of society and researching particular areas;

▲ discussing why things happened and why particular events occurred;

▲ comparing and contrasting different events and features of periods across time;

▲ providing opportunities to recognise similarities and differences between present and past ways of life. Why have some of the changes in our ways of life taken place?

Progression in Key Element 2 can be noted as children become able to recount more details and information about episodes and ways of life in the past. They will learn to recognise some characteristics of different periods and will be able to relate this understanding to knowledge which they have of other periods in time. Children will begin to recognise reasons for events in the past and to identify the results of main events and changes.

Interpretations of history

Children can learn about the past from many different sources. Essentially this Key Element emphasises the importance of secondary sources of information. These sources are dependent to some degree on interpretation: how the past has been perceived by people living at a later date. Artists' drawings and illustrations in history books provide examples of particular interpretations of history: how do artists know what to draw? Some parts may be based on historical evidence but some will be dependent on the artists' imaginations.

Children viewing films or TV programmes are looking at the producers' versions of the past. Are these accurate interpretations of events? The contents of museum displays are influenced by the available artefacts and also by the views of the museum curators who arrange the display.

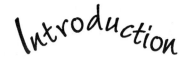

Introduction

This Key Element provides opportunities for children to question how historical knowledge and information about the past is handed down. In the classroom this Key Element can be developed through:

▲ encouraging children to question how we know about the past. Discuss the different sources of information available and encourage children to begin to identify whether the source is primary (drawn from a particular period of time) or secondary (that is an interpretation of an event/way of life which was created at a later date);

▲ discussing the sort of information which can be learned from different sources of information. Draw attention to the fact that some sources might be more reliable than others.

Progression in Key Element 3 will involve children recognising the different ways in which they can gain information about the past. They will begin to recognise that the past can be interpreted in different ways.

Historical enquiry

This Key Element emphasises the importance of primary source material as evidence for ways of life in the past. At Key Stage 2 such sources include documents and printed sources, artefacts, pictures and photographs, music, buildings and sites. Different Study Units will provide opportunities for children to engage with varied source material – for example the Study Units in *Curriculum Bank History* Key Stage 2:II provide many opportunities to work with written documents and pictures which illustrate themes in social history. In the classroom this Key Element can be developed through:

▲ encouraging children to raise questions and look for answers from a range of source material;

▲ organising collections of different objects for children to investigate and to handle. Such collections can include both original items and replicas of objects. Organise visits to local museums to view their collections; see if they operate a loan service. Pictures of objects from books and posters are also useful. Collections of old postcards and photographs can provide information about the locality;

▲ organising visits to different buildings and sites. Look for clues about past ways of life on short walks in the locality;

▲ providing examples of written sources of information, for example old maps of the locality, copies of the school log book. Older children enjoy trying to decipher old writing. Transcripts of some of the writing might also be helpful.

Progression in Key Element 4 can be noted as children identify the different sources they have used to find out about the past. Children progress from simple to more detailed observations of particular sources and develop skills in making generalisations and in drawing conclusions about life in the past from different sources.

Organisation and communication

This Key Element emphasises the importance of providing different opportunities for children to communicate their understanding. It also suggests ways for children to organise their understanding and includes particular terms for children to become familiar with. In the classroom you can develop understanding in this Key Element through:

▲ providing opportunities for children to talk and to share their historical understanding in class, group and paired discussions. Listen to their comments and ideas to develop your own awareness of their understanding;

▲ providing children with opportunities to record their understanding in a variety of ways: for example painting, drawing, modelling, collage, photography, using audio or video tape recorders;

▲ organising resources in the classroom to encourage role play activities to develop children's historical imagination;

▲ helping children plan structured accounts and narratives of the history which they have studied;

▲ providing opportunities to develop children's understanding of historical terms and to use them in appropriate contexts.

Progression in Key Element 5 could be noted as children begin to make some decisions on the best way of presenting the historical information which they have learned. They can structure their work and use dates and terms appropriately.

The History Attainment Target

The History National Curriculum has one Attainment Target to assess children's progress in historical knowledge and understanding. The level descriptions provide a means of recording children's progress in history throughout Key Stage 2 and are linked closely with the requirements for teaching history listed in the Key Elements. Children's progress is recorded by the level which provides the best description of their attainment at the end of Key Stage 2.

Curriculum Bank History has identified clear learning objectives within the classroom activities and assessment opportunities which relate closely to these learning objectives. The suggested questions in the activities can be used for both formative and summative assessment purposes.

Use the suggested assessment opportunities to acquire information about children's current skills, knowledge and understandings. The information gained from such assessments can help inform the planning of further learning activities designed to ensure children's progress in history. At the end of the key stage it will be necessary to ensure that enough information has been gathered concerning children's progress to make a summative assessment of their attainment. A grid, similar to the one shown below, can be designed to provide a record of children's progress and different historical experiences.

Child's name	
Activity Learning objectives	
Comments	
Activity Learning objectives	
Comments	

Curriculum Bank activities suggest a range of learning objectives and teachers can identify and select those which they wish to use for assessment purposes. Spaces have been provided on the grid for teachers to write down the learning objective together with the names of the children in their class. Teachers may like to devise their own coding system which relates to children's learning. For example, a scale ranging from A to E, describing children's understanding

from excellent, good, satisfactory, some to none. Space has also been left on the grid for any specific comments.

Teachers will not want to use all activities for summative assessment purposes. However, the grid provides opportunities to keep an ongoing record of selected activities which will provide a useful source of information for determining the level which provides the best description of children's attainment across Key Stage 2. Children will need to have acquired a range of historical knowledge for their attainment to be recorded on the higher level descriptions.

Ways of assessing history at Key Stage 2

Children's progress in history can be assessed in a variety of ways. Listening to children talking about the past and expressing their own points of view is important. *Curriculum Bank History* provides several activities where children are encouraged to talk about what they have found out and to express their opinions. Working with timelines provides opportunities to assess children's understanding of the passage of time and their ability to describe it with particular words and phrases. Modelling and painting activities can be helpful for assessing children's observational skills and to see what they consider are important features in the source materials from which they are working. Structured narratives and written accounts can enable assessments to be made on children's abilities to organise and communicate historical information.

Developing historical activities

The suggestions included here provide further guidance and ideas for extending children's historical experiences in the classroom.

Timelines

The concept of time is a very abstract one and timelines can provide opportunities for children to visualise the passage of time in less abstract ways. Organise timelines to include

different sources of information for example pictures, artefacts, children's own comments and research. In depth timelines can illustrate the chief events and features of a particular period. More extensive timelines covering a long period of time enable children to develop a broader chronological framework and help them to appreciate the relationship of different events with each other (for example, Exploring space, page 82). Timelines can provide a useful device for describing how different features have changed, for example, transport. Children will also need to consider how to depict continuity. For example, people have walked on foot and ridden horses from earlier times until the present. Comparison charts provide other means of comparing different periods of time. The coming of the railway in the 1840s marks a major change in the way people have travelled by land through the centuries. The invention of travel through the air marks a similarly dramatic watershed. Involve children in discussion on the scale of the timeline and what items to include.

Artefacts and pictures

Encourage children to look closely at different artefacts and pictures. Magnifying glasses are helpful for historical detective work. Placing an acetate sheet, divided into sections, over detailed pictures can be helpful to concentrate children's observations on particular areas. Children can be encouraged to make detailed drawings which involves careful observation of different sources material. Sometimes providing an outline for children to complete may help children record greater detail. Encourage children to recognise the significance of particular artefacts or pictures by relating them to other sources of information available during the same period as well as at other times. Begin by asking the children to explore the artefact/picture on their own. What questions do they raise? The diagram (right) suggests ways in which children's questioning skills could be developed further.

Children can be encouraged to review their current knowledge and to decide on what else they would like to know. This could be recorded on a form similar to that shown below.

LOOKING AT A PICTURE OF ELIZABETH I	
I have found out	I want to know

QUESTIONS TO CONSIDER WHEN USING ARTEFACTS OR PICTURES

Describe

▲ What can you see?
▲ What is happening in the picture?
▲ What is it made of ?
▲ What does it feel/smell like?
▲ How big is it?

Purpose and function

▲ Why was it made?
▲ What was it used for?

Evidence

▲ What does it tell us about life in the past?
▲ Similarities between then and now; then and other historical periods?
▲ Why has it survived?
▲ Is it unique?
▲ Is it complete?
▲ Why was it made?
▲ Is it authentic or is it a replica?
▲ Is it a reliable source of information?
▲ Were there many of them?
▲ What else would you like to know about it? (Relate to other sources of information, for example, oral testimony, documents, buildings etc.)

Time

▲ How old is the picture/object?
▲ How does it relate to other sources of information?

Using books in the classroom

Many fictional stories are set in the past and provide opportunities for children to learn about different ways of life and different values. Illustrations in picture books can also provide useful historical information for children.

There are many excellent historical reference books and children can be encouraged to examine the pictures for detail as well as the written text. Children can also extend their information-retrieval skills, by using contents pages and indices to find answers to their particular historical enquiries.

Role play in history

Role play can provide opportunities for children to imagine and to experience more fully what life might have been like in the past. Conflict resolution activities (for example the debate about the building of the Great Western Railway, page 40) enable children to explore different viewpoints and to use information to develop particular lines of argument. Children can all participate in such activities. Children can work in pairs and then join with another pair of children to share their points of view. Work can be extended from the two pairs of children working together to larger group work and finally whole class discussion. Historical re-enactments provide further opportunities to develop children's historical understanding, (for example the dissolution of the monasteries, page 22). Encourage children to consider what props they would need to re-enact such scenes and to research information from different sources.

Ranking activities

Such activities enable children to appreciate the importance and significance of particular events and changes. Different reasons and effects of particular events or changes can be recorded on separate pieces of card. Children can then be encouraged to rank them in a variety of ways, for example in order of importance; long term and short term effects; most important now contrasted with most important at the time.

Children can also rank their ideas in a triangular shape with the most important point at the top or they can use causation circles with a central main point and ripples representing less important features radiating out.

Planning the history curriculum at Key Stage 2

'The most effective teaching at Key Stage 2 was characterised by careful planning and clearly defined learning objectives related to the Attainment Targets.' (Report from the Office of Her Majesty's Chief Inspector of Schools. *History Key Stages 1, 2 and 3* Second Year, 1992–1993, page 7)

Curriculum Bank History aims to aid planning and the identification of clear learning objectives. In planning the history National Curriculum, decisions will need to be made both at whole school and classroom levels.

At school level consideration will need to be given to:

Whole school curriculum
▲ the allocation of time to cover the different study units;
▲ the links with other subject areas and themes being developed in the school;
▲ the records of children's historical experiences across Key Stage 2.

Historical content
▲ the selection of study units to be made, for example Victorian Britain or Britain since 1930;
▲ the choice of a past non-European society to be studied in study unit 6;
▲ the relationship of the Local History study unit 5 with content of other study units;
▲ the sequence in which the study units are to be taught across Key Stage 2;
▲ the historical perspectives which can be developed through different study units; for example, political, economic, technological and scientific, social, religious, cultural and aesthetic;
▲ the coverage of the different key elements within the study units at Key Stage 2.

Children's learning
▲ the assessment and recording of children's progress in history;
▲ the progression of children's historical understanding from Key Stage 1 and into Key Stage 3;
▲ differentiation to meet children's different needs and abilities.

Resources
▲ the resources available within the school and the community.

In the classroom
Teachers will need to consider:
▲ the selection of activities which cover the content of the study units and provide opportunities for children to experience the key elements;
▲ the ways in which children's historical language and vocabulary can be extended;
▲ the differentiation of activities to meet individual/ group needs and abilities;
▲ the selection of appropriate historical source materials;
▲ the ways in which children's work can be assessed and used for planning future historical activities;
▲ the records of children's progress and attainment in history.

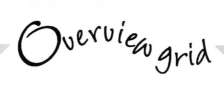

Learning objective	PoS/AO	Content	Type of activity	Page
Life in Tudor times				
To learn about Tudor monarchs and place them in chronological order.	1a; 4a. *Time and historical sequence (Level D)*	Arranging portraits in chronological sequence.	As whole class or as individuals studying key royal figures in Tudor period.	18
To develop knowledge and understanding of changes Henry VIII brought about to the church.	2a, b. *Change and continuity (Level D)*	Impact of radical change on the church.	Individual study of visual representation of change followed by class discussion.	19
To learn about some of the features of Henry VIII's lifestyle using documents.	2a; 4a. *Historical evidence (Level D)*	Analysis of Henry VIII's account book as evidence.	Individual reading. Discussion in class relating to transcribing Henry's account book.	21
To describe and identify possible reasons for the dissolution of the monasteries and to consider one of the consequences.	2b. *Cause and effect (Level D)*	Consequences and possible causes of Henry VIII's actions.	Individual and whole class activity related to sale of dissolved nunnery.	22
To find out about the persecution of Catholic priests in Elizabeth's reign using documents and pictures.	4a. *Historical evidence (Level D)*	Adventures of Father Gerard and priests' holes.	Whole class and individual empathy exercises related to hunted priests.	24
To identify and give reasons for different ways in which the past is represented and interpreted.	3a; 4a. *Historical evidence (Level D)*	Portraits of Elizabeth I.	Whole class and individual examination and comparative study of royal portraits and written descriptions.	25
To find out about the lives and values of wealthy people in Tudor times.	2a; 4a. *Historical evidence (Level D)*	Painted portraits of Tudor people in their social context.	Whole class and individual activity. Critical examination of portraits; making portraits using paint.	26
To learn about the importance of the Tudor court and what court life was like.	2a. *Historical evidence (Level D)*	Government under the Tudor monarchs especially Elizabeth I.	Whole class followed by individual study of evidence of royal patronage and other aspects.	27
To learn about law and order in Tudor times.	2a. *Societies of significance Level D*	Nature of crime and punishment.	Whole class discussion followed by paired and group role play.	28
To learn about Sir Francis Drake's achievements and to place them in the context of the 16th century.	2a, b. *People of significance Level D*	Drake's voyages.	Whole class study of geography of exploration. Individual investigation of Drake's life.	30
To learn about the Armada and develop children's understanding of invasion.	3a; 5b, c. *Events of significance Level C*	The Spanish Armada and its defeat.	Whole class followed by paired activity retelling the events.	31
To research Tudor pastimes and games from different sources and to record information.	2a; 5c. *Societies of significance Level C*	Study of Tudor games and pastimes.	Small group or paired investigation, playing and recording information.	33
To learn about Tudor schools and how children were educated.	2a. *Societies of significance Level C*	Tudor schooling.	Whole class discussion; individual making of hornbook followed by paired activities.	34

Learning objective	PoS/AO	Content	Type of activity	Page
To learn how timber-framed buildings were constructed in the Tudor period.	2a. *Historical evidence Level C*	Use of timber in building construction.	Whole class discussion; individual or paired model-making.	36
To find out about aspects of cultural life during Tudor times by studying the Globe Theatre and a story from a Shakespearean play.	2a; 4a. *Societies of significance Level D*	The Globe Theatre/ Shakespearean plays.	Whole class introduction followed by paired or group design of a programme.	37
Victorian Britain				
To learn about the development of the railway network and its effects.	2a, b. *Societies of significance Level D*	The coming of the railways.	Whole class introduction followed by individual investigation and whole class debate or role-play.	40
To understand the importance of steam power and Brunel's work on steamships.	2b; 5c. *People of significance Level D*	Brunel and three steamships; changes introduced over a 20-year period.	Whole class introduction followed by individual comparative study of steamships.	42
To learn about some of the religious practices in Victorian Britain and to consider some of the social aspects.	2a. *Societies of significance Level D*	Religion in Victorian times.	Whole class introduction followed by individual investigation.	44
To learn about the development of education with special reference to Ragged Schools.	2a. *Societies of significance Level D*	Beginnings of Victorian school education/Ragged Schools.	Whole class introduction followed by individual activity.	46
To find out about some aspects of Victorian family life using a census.	2a; 4a. *Historical evidence Level D*	Example of 1851 census.	Whole class introduction followed by paired investigation of a census.	48
To learn about some activities associated with Christmas in Victorian times.	2a, c. *Societies of significance Level C*	Victorian Christmas celebrations.	Whole class introduction; small group and individual activities. A class party as empathetic activity.	50
To learn about features of industrial life in the early Victorian period; exploitation of men, women and children.	2a; 4a; 5b. *Societies of significance Level D*	Industry and working conditions.	Whole class discussion followed by group investigation of statistical information.	52
To recognise some features of life in early Victorian towns and to describe and identify changes.	2a, b. *Change and continuity Level E*	Industrialisation – the changes it brought and its consequences.	Whole class discussion/ matching cause and effect.	54
To understand beliefs and attitudes towards the poor.	2a. *People of significance Level E*	The Victorian workhouse.	Whole class introduction and discussion followed by individual play writing.	56
To identify some buildings from Victorian times and to find out about their design and function.	2c. *Historical evidence Level C*	Victorian public buildings.	Individual or paired investigation.	57
Britain since 1930				
To learn about the main changes in farming methods during the twentieth century and to consider their effects.	2b, c. *Change and continuity Level C*	Changing farming methods.	Whole class discussion followed by individual comparative exercise.	60
To learn about the economic crisis of the 1930s and its effects on British industry.	1a; 2b. *Events of significance Level D*	The Depression and changes in industry.	Whole class introduction; group investigation. Class discussion to conclude.	62

Learning objective	PoS/AO	Content	Type of activity	Page
To place the development of the motor car within a chronological framework; to describe the impact of the car in Britain since 1930.	1a; 2b. *Time and historical sequence Level D*	Development of the motor car and changes in road traffic.	Whole class introduction; individual and group activity using statistical and historical data.	63
To find out about one member of HM Forces who took part in World War II using different sources, including documents, pictures and photographs.	4a; 5c. *Historical evidence Level D*	Evidence for one man's war and the links with the home front as well as the theatre of war in the East.	Investigation carried out in pairs or in small groups.	65
To learn about the evacuation of children to country areas and the effects on the children and their families.	2b; 3a. *Events of significance Level D*	Evacuation of children during World War II and its impact on individual lives.	Whole class introduction followed by empathetic activity as individuals or in pairs.	67
To learn about some of the effects of the war on Britain and what changes took place in the post-war period.	2a, b. *Change and continuity Level D*	Reconstruction of Britain after World War II.	Whole class discussion using primary sources followed by group or individual activity including interviewing and other forms of investigation.	68
To find out about the Coronation of Queen Elizabeth II using a variety of sources.	3a; 4a; 5b. *Historical evidence Level D*	Details of the Coronation and procession; the regalia used.	Whole class introduction followed by individual and small group activity using different sources, including an eyewitness account.	71
To place the development of the aeroplane within a chronological framework and to recognise some of the key changes that have taken place in air transport.	1a; 2b. *Time and historical sequence Level C*	Different kinds of aircraft developed over 8 decades.	Whole class introduction; paired investigation.	72
To learn about some of the features of shopping in the days before supermarkets.	2a, b. *Societies of significance Level C*	Shopping 40 or more years ago and similarities/differences with modern supermarkets.	Whole class introduction followed by role play including making the relevant 'props'.	75
To describe the development and impact of radio and television broadcasting.	1a; 2. *Events of significance Level C*	History of broadcasting and evidence for this.	Whole class introduction followed by individual work on timelines and model-making or poster-making.	78
To learn about the development of package holidays to the European continent.	2a; 4a. *Societies of significance Level D*	An account of a package tour by coach in the late 1950s.	Whole class discussion followed by paired investigation using an eyewitness account and an atlas.	80
To place the key events of space exploration within a chronological framework.	1a; 2c. *Events of significance; Time and historical sequence Level C*	The main steps in the development of space exploration and space travel.	Whole class discussion followed by work in pairs.	82
To learn why the European Community was established and the reasons for Britain deciding to join in 1973.	1a; 2b. *Events of significance Level C*	The development of the European Community.	Whole class discussion followed by individual or group activity.	84

Overview grid

Learning objective	PoS/AO	Content	Type of activity	Page
Local history				
To use local maps and information to identify and locate evidence of early settlements from prehistory to the fifth century AD.	1a, b; 2a; 5c. *Historical evidence; Making and using maps Level D*	Map making; storage and retrieval of data on archaeological sites.	Whole class introduction as well as small group investigation; presentation of findings.	89
To identify and locate evidence of settlements from early fifth century AD to Tudor times.	1a, b; 2a; 5c. *Historical evidence; Making and using maps Level D*	Map making; storage and retrieval of data on archaeological and historical sites.	Whole class introduction followed by small group investigation; presentation of findings.	91
To identify houses from different periods.	1a; 2a; 4a. *Historical evidence Level D*	Surveying housing in the local area; recognition of house styles/features in relation to date.	Field activity followed by paired work.	92
To study some features of old buildings and change in their use over four centuries.	1a; 2a, b; 4a. *Historical evidence Level D*	Study of a row of buildings in former dockland. Characteristic features and evidence/reasons for change of use.	Work in pairs.	95
To use documentary evidence to increase the children's knowledge of local sites.	2a; 5c. *Historical evidence Level C*	Account of an 18th century market in a busy port.	Whole class introduction followed by work in pairs. Presentation of their art work representation.	96
To look for clues about the past using maps from different periods and to describe some of the changes that have occurred within that time.	2c; 4a, b. *Historical evidence; Continuity and change Level D*	Comparative study of two maps. Maps as a source.	Work in pairs.	97
To use information in old street directories to investigate changes in a local area 1850–1900.	2b; 4a. *Historical evidence; Continuity and change Level D*	Comparative study of street directories. Use of directories as a source.	Work in pairs.	98
To use the information in a census to learn about some features of Victorian society.	4a, b. *Historical evidence Level D*	Using a Victorian census as an historical document.	Work in pairs.	100
To use the information in a tithe map to investigate changes in land usage in the nineteenth century.	4a, b. *Historical evidence; Continuity and change Level D*	Using a tithe map as an historical source.	Work in pairs.	101
To learn about the past using oral evidence.	2a; 4a; 5a. *Historical evidence Level D*	Preparing for/conducting interviews to gather information about the past.	Whole class activity.	103
To find out about how some Victorian and Edwardian artefacts might have been used locally.	2a; 4a, b. *Historical evidence Level D*	Studying and asking questions about artefacts. Considering how they might have been used in the local community.	Work in pairs or in groups of three.	104
To use visual evidence to investigate changes in the local area across different periods.	2c; 4a. *Historical evidence; Continuity and change Level D*	Study of old photographs including photographs of paintings or engravings of the area.	Work in pairs.	105

Entries given in italics relate to the Scottish 5–14 Guidelines on Environmental Studies (Social Subjects: Understanding people in the past).

HISTORY KS2:II

Life in Tudor times

Henry VII established the Tudor dynasty which ruled England and Wales from 1485–1603. He defeated his Yorkist opponent, Richard III at the Battle of Bosworth and brought peace following the disruption of the Wars of the Roses.

In 1509 he was succeeded by his son, Henry VIII, who married six times – Catherine of Aragon, Anne Boleyn, Jane Seymour, Anne of Cleves, Catherine Howard and Catherine Parr – and had three children, Mary, Elizabeth and Edward.

When the Pope, Clement VII, refused to grant Henry's divorce from his first wife Catherine of Aragon, Henry declared himself head of the Church of England. Parliament then passed the Dissolution of the Monasteries Bill in 1536. The break with Rome was consolidated during the reign of his son, Edward VI, with the issue of a new English Prayer Book and the simplification of church services. When Edward died in 1553, the Duke of Northumberland tried to maintain power by making his own daughter-in-law, Lady Jane Grey, queen. Support for this plan was not forthcoming and she was executed with her husband. Edward's elder sister, Mary, became queen.

Mary's determination to restore the Catholic faith led to the persecution of Protestants. This, together with her marriage to Philip of Spain made Mary very unpopular. She was succeeded by Elizabeth and England gradually returned to the Protestant religion. Mary Queen of Scots became the focus of attention for Catholic plotters and Elizabeth had her executed in 1587. Philip of Spain decided to invade England and restore Catholicism. His Armada was defeated in 1588. When Elizabeth died in 1603, she was succeeded by James VI of Scotland, the son of Mary Queen of Scots.

Timeline of the Tudors

1485	1497	1509	1534	1536-39	1547	1553
Battle of Bosworth. Henry Tudor becomes King Henry VII.	First voyage of John Cabot to Newfoundland.	Henry VIII becomes king.	Act of Supremacy made Henry VIII Head of the Church in England.	Dissolution of the monasteries.	Edward VI becomes king.	Mary I becomes queen.

A TUDOR FAMILY TREE

To learn about the Tudor monarchs and to place them in a chronological sequence within a family tree.

†† *Whole class or individual activity.*

🕑 *Whole class 20 minutes, then individual activity 40 minutes.*

Previous skills/knowledge needed

Some familiarity with family trees would be helpful. This activity can be used to assess children's knowledge of the Tudor monarchs after a period of study.

Key background information

Henry Tudor's victory at the Battle of Bosworth in 1485 signalled the end of the Wars of the Roses and the beginning of the Tudor dynasty. To strengthen his power Henry married the daughter of Edward IV, Elizabeth of York, thereby uniting the warring houses of Lancaster and York. The Tudor rose combined the white rose of the Yorkists with the red rose of the Lancastrians. Henry also made matrimonial alliances to secure peace with foreign countries and strengthen his position as king of England. Henry's eldest daughter Margaret married James IV of Scotland, and his eldest son Arthur married Catherine of Aragon, daughter of the king of Spain. Arthur died young, so Henry VII was succeeded by his second son who became Henry VIII. Henry VIII married his brother's widow, Catherine of Aragon. Catherine had several babies, but only a daughter, Mary, survived. Henry was desperate to have a son to succeed him. So he divorced Catherine and married Anne Boleyn who gave birth to a daughter,

Elizabeth. Anne Boleyn was executed and Henry then married Jane Seymour who produced a male heir, Edward. Jane Seymour died and Henry married a further three times. Anne of Cleves was his fourth wife (whom he also divorced), followed by Catherine Howard. After Catherine Howard was executed he married Catherine Parr who outlived him. Following Henry's death, his nine-year-old son Edward VI became king. Edward ruled with the help of advisers for six years. After his death he was succeeded by his elder sister, Mary who ruled for five years. She married Philip of Spain and was keen to make England a Catholic country again. When Mary died without children, her sister Elizabeth became queen. Elizabeth ruled for 45 years and firmly established the central power of the monarchy and the Protestant religion. She did not marry and had no children so the crown passed on to the Stuart family. James VI of Scotland became James I of England.

Preparation

Prepare one copy of photocopiable page 108 for each child.

Resources needed

Photocopiable page 108, pictures of different Tudor monarchs, pencils, crayons, felt-tipped pens, scissors, glue.

What to do

Use the background information to talk to the children about the

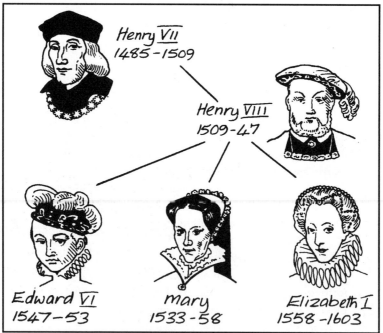

Henry VII 1485 – 1509

Henry VIII 1509 – 47

Edward VI 1547 – 53

Mary 1533 – 58

Elizabeth I 1558 – 1603

different Tudor monarchs. If possible refer to portraits of the monarchs from your resources as you talk about them. Begin by describing how Henry VII became king. Some children may have heard of Henry VIII. Ask them what they already know and be prepared to provide additional information or correct some of their existing knowledge. Talk about Henry's desire for a son and the children who succeeded him to the throne. Explain how the Tudor line died out following the death of Elizabeth. The new Stuart monarch, James I was

Life in Tudor times

1558	1564–1616	1577–80	1585	1587	1588	1603
Elizabeth I becomes Queen.	William Shakespeare.	Francis Drake circumnavigates the world.	Colony established by Walter Raleigh in Virginia.	Mary Queen of Scots is executed.	Defeat of the Spanish Armada.	Death of Elizabeth and accession of James I.

descended from Henry VII, whose daughter Margaret had married James IV of Scotland. Distribute photocopiable page 108 and ask the children to match the portraits of the monarchs at the bottom of the page to the correct space on the sheet. The portraits may be coloured before being cut out and glued to the correct place on the family tree.

Suggestion(s) for extension
Children can research further information to place on the family tree, for example, the spouses of the different monarchs. Some children might like to record the dates when different monarchs lived and reigned. The family tree could then be used as a source of information for finding out ages of different monarchs, how long they reigned etc.

Suggestion(s) for support
Some children might need help identifying the different monarchs and deciding where to place them on the family tree.

Assessment opportunities
This activity could be used at the end of a period of study to assess how much information the children have learned about the Tudor monarchs. If the activity is being used for assessment purposes, provide less detail from the background information and ask the children to complete the family tree, using knowledge which they already have about the period.

Opportunities for IT
Children could use a drawing package to create a family tree. The names of family members can be written into boxes which can then be positioned at the appropriate places on the screen. Connecting lines and other information can also be drawn in.

Display ideas
Children could create a larger family tree for display. Encourage the children to refer to portraits of the Tudor monarchs and use them to draw their own pictures of the monarchs for the family tree.

Reference to photocopiable sheet
Photocopiable page 108 assesses the children's knowledge of the Tudor dynasty – how the different monarchs were related and the order in which they reigned.

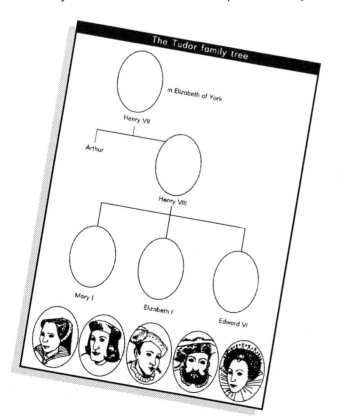

HENRY VIII AND THE REFORMATION

To develop knowledge and understanding of the changes brought about by Henry VIII in the Church.
Individual activity then class discussion.
30 minutes, then time for the class discussion.

Previous skills/knowledge needed
Any general information that children may have about the inside of a church.

Key background information
When Henry VIII came to the throne in 1509, England, like the rest of Europe, was a Catholic country, loyal to the Pope as head of the church. Henry was proud of his religious knowledge and the Pope had given Henry the title of 'Defender of the Faith' for writing a book criticising the

Protestant reformer Martin Luther. Henry was married to Catherine of Aragon for 17 years but, by 1527, Henry had grown tired of her and fallen in love with Anne Boleyn. He wanted to divorce Catherine and marry Anne, but he needed the agreement of the Pope. When the Pope refused, Thomas Cromwell, Henry's minister, advised the king that he should break away from Rome and become head of the Church in England. There were many members of Parliament who favoured the new ideas of Martin Luther and others who disliked the wealth and privilege of the established Church. Cromwell was able to push through Parliament a series of Acts which placed the Church under Henry's control and which led to the breaking of all links with Rome. Henry now became Supreme Head of the Church of England and was able to arrange his own divorce and marry Anne Boleyn. To enforce this change, everyone had to swear an oath of loyalty to the King as the new head of their church. Only a few people refused to do this. One of them, Sir Thomas More, was tried and executed. A number of monastic houses showed their fierce opposition and the monks were cruelly put to death.

The way was now clear for the traditional Catholic religion along with all its associated rituals and ornaments to be gradually swept away. During the years that followed churches were stripped of all their riches, their ornaments, priestly vestments, crucifixes and statues.

Preparation
Prepare one copy of photocopiable page 109 for each child. Collect pictures showing the inside of different Catholic and Protestant churches.

Resources needed
Photocopiable page 109, pictures showing the inside of churches which follow contrasting Catholic and Protestant traditions, writing materials.

What to do
Explain to the children the circumstances which led to the break between Henry VIII and Rome using as much of the above information as seems appropriate.

The aim of this lesson is for the children to appreciate the impact of these religious changes upon the appearance of churches. It may be helpful if some of these changes are discussed with the whole class before the children begin to make their own lists. Questions which will help to guide the children's responses could be asked: What are the things they notice about the church *before* the Reformation? Which of these items is no longer there in the second picture? What words would they use to describe the church *after* the Reformation?

Suggestion(s) for extension
Children could find out more about some of the features of the Catholic religion which were rarely seen in England after Henry's actions.

Suggestion(s) for support
Some children will need help to appreciate the main features of ritual associated with the Catholic Church. Make a list of items with drawings to help them: vestments of different kinds, candles, crucifixes, statues, incense burning in censers, sanctus bells, etc.

Assessment opportunities
Can the children identify some of the differences between religion before and after the Reformation? What might a service have been like before and after the Reformation?

Opportunities for IT

Children could either use dedicated timeline software such as ESM's *Time Traveller*, or create a vertical timeline using a word processor or desk top publishing package. Children should be discouraged from using the spacebar to position the text on the page. If they use a word processor they should be shown how to set tabs and create a hanging indent so that text 'wraps' at the correct points in the lines.

date type in the text and add a hanging indent so that when the text gets to the end of the line it automatically starts at the correct spot on the next line (as shown here).

If a desk top publishing package is used two vertical columns can be created with the dates in one and the accompanying text in the other.

Display ideas

Use a classroom wall for a display which shows the differences inside an English parish church before and after the Reformation. Use photocopiable page 109 as the basis. The wall can be divided into two halves and covered with white paper. The two scenes could then be roughed out using charcoal. The painting could be undertaken by groups of children in turn.

Reference to photocopiable sheet

The contrasting pictures on photocopiable page 109 will help the children to understand some of the changes that came about in English churches and church services following the Reformation.

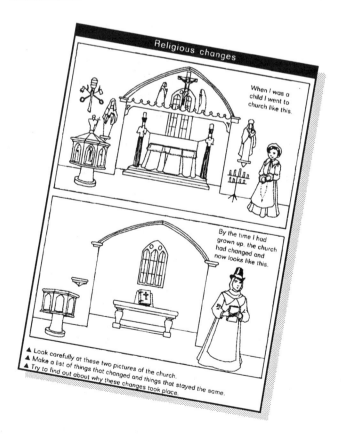

HENRY VIII AND HIS ° ACCOUNTS

To learn about some of the features of Henry VIII's lifestyle using documentary evidence.

†† *Individual work then class discussion.*

🕐 *45 minutes.*

Previous skills/knowledge needed

Any information the children already know about Henry VIII and his lifestyle.

Key background information

Among the records that survive from Henry VIII's reign are his account books which show the King's expenditure set out in columns, day by day. They record expenditure using the old money in pounds, shillings and pence. Written descriptions of the young Henry show that he enjoyed dressing extravagantly and his expense accounts confirm the King's taste for fine clothes and jewellery. They also contain a variety of other details of Henry's expenditure and the extracts on photocopiable page 110 provide additional information about life in Tudor times.

Preparation

Prepare one copy of photocopiable page 110 for each child.

Resources needed

Photocopiable page 110.

What to do

Explain to the class that they are going to look at some of the items that Henry VIII recorded in his account book. The children can work on this largely on their own but they may need some help to work out what the Roman numerals mean. They also may need some help with the old pre-decimal system of currency. They may wish to convert old money into new by using the rate of conversion which was used at the time of decimalisation: 1 shilling = 5 new pence.

Read this description of Henry's appearance to the children. It is given by the Venetian Ambassador in 1515: 'The king wore a cap of crimson velvet...with gold enamelled tags attached to it. His doublet was striped with white and with crimson. Closely fitting around his neck he wore a gold collar, from which there hung a round diamond the size of the largest walnut I have ever seen and from this hung a very round pearl. His mantle was purple velvet lined with white satin'.

What can be learned about Henry VIII's lifestyle using the evidence in these accounts? What evidence is there in his account books that Henry had expensive tastes? How valuable is a document of this kind for telling us about life in Tudor England?

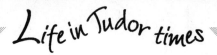
Suggestion(s) for extension

Children could make up some more accounts for the King, using information that they already know about Henry VIII. They can experiment with using Roman numerals and pounds, shillings and pence. They may need reminding that 12d = 1 shilling and that 20 shillings = 1 pound.

Suggestion(s) for support

Children may need help with Roman numerals and with pre-decimal money.

Assessment opportunities

What conclusions can the children draw about Henry's lifestyle from his accounts? Can they suggest other sources of information which could support their conclusions – for example, portraits of Henry or letters written about him at the time?

Display ideas

Children could produce some of Henry's accounts using a quill pen and paper made to look like parchment for the classroom display.

Reference to photocopiable sheet

Photocopiable page 110 provides a selection of items from Henry's account books for the year 1530. Children can work out equivalent values using Arabic numerals and decimal currency. They should note the enormous differences between Tudor monetary values and those of today. The accounts also provide additional information about Henry's lifestyle.

THE DISSOLUTION OF THE MONASTERIES

To describe and identify possible reasons for the dissolution of the monasteries and to consider one of the consequences of their dissolution.

†† Whole class then individuals or pairs.

🕑 About 60 minutes.

Previous skills/knowledge needed

Some awareness of monastic life will be needed. It will also be necessary for children to have some knowledge of Henry VIII's break with Rome.

Key background information

The suppression of the monasteries, nunneries and friaries throughout England and Wales between 1536–1540 took place at a time when enormous changes were happening in the Church of England. The power of the Pope had been renounced, and in 1534 Henry VIII acquired the title of Supreme Head of the Church. Many leading members of monastic houses criticised the break with Rome but most agreed to the changes. Those who refused were executed or fled abroad to Catholic countries.

In 1536, under the skilled guidance of Thomas Cromwell, an enquiry was conducted into the wealth of the religious houses and other parts of the Church. The results revealed that the Church possessed enormous wealth. Very soon afterwards, the sale of monasteries all over England and Wales was systematically carried out. In most cases the sites were purchased by wealthy individuals who built homes there. Those monasteries that refused to surrender voluntarily were severely dealt with. At Glastonbury, in Somerset, one of the greatest English abbeys, the monks were expelled and the buildings ransacked for hidden treasure. The elderly and sick inhabitants were imprisoned in the Tower of London, and the Abbot was sent to Wells for trial and was executed in 1539.

The central activity in this lesson plan is based on evidence of the sale of a nunnery at the time of the dissolution of the monasteries. Documents such as this survive for large numbers of monastic houses. The sell off suggests that the King, once released from obligations to the Roman Catholic Church, no longer saw the necessity to maintain monasteries and recognised an effective way of raising large sums of money for the Exchequer!

The report made by Henry's officials made the monasteries seem far worse than they really were. Some of the most critical reports are those included here. Many monasteries were causing no offence and committing no crimes. There has been much debate about whether or not the monasteries deserved the fate which befell them. The fact was that Henry needed the money.

Preparation

Prepare one copy of photocopiable page 111 for each child.

Resources needed

Photocopiable page 111.

What to do

Give each child a copy of photocopiable page 111. This contains two sets of information. Ask the children to read out the criticisms that were made by Henry VIII's officials when they surveyed the monasteries. Discuss with the class how this information might have influenced the King. Despite criticisms such as these, many monasteries were not guilty of any crimes. So why did Henry decide to close them down?

Refer to the detailed information on the right–hand side. This is a list of items from the actual sale of a nunnery. The prices obtained are shown in shillings and pence, and Roman numerals are frequently used for the numbers of items and for the prices obtained. The document also lists sums of money for the numbers of items and for the prices obtained. Point out to the children that there are a couple of examples of archaic spelling in the worksheet. Can they find them? (matress, barrel) Ask the children to consider what kinds of people would have attended the sale of monastic property. Invite them to choose up to ten items from different parts of the nunnery which are on the list and to say how they would use each object. Get the children to take it in turns to act as an auctioneer and the rest of the class could bid (using 'old' or decimal money) for objects they are keen to acquire.

Once the children have worked on the detail of selling monastic property, return to the earlier discussion: should they revise their view of Henry's reasons for closing the monasteries in the light of what they have learned? Did the King have an ulterior motive for closing down the monasteries? How was his decision linked to the break with Rome?

Suggestion(s) for extension

The children could work out what the actual sale of these items raised by calculating the totals given at the end of each item. This will involve them in working out Roman numerals and old shillings and pence.

Suggestion(s) for support

Several words in the lists of items for sale will be unfamiliar (a number are related to things used in the Catholic church

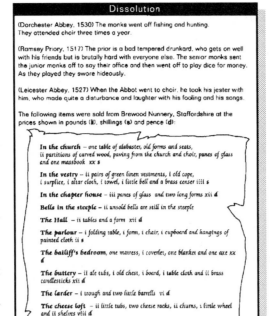

Dissolution

(Dorchester Abbey, 1530) The monks went off fishing and hunting. They attended choir three times a year.

(Ramsey Priory, 1517) The prior is a bad tempered drunkard, who gets on well with his friends but is brutally hard with everyone else. The senior monks sent the junior monks off to say their office and then went off to play dice for money. As they played they swore hideously.

(Leicester Abbey, 1527) When the Abbot went to choir, he took his jester with him, who made quite a disturbance and laughter with his fooling and his songs.

The following items were sold from Brewood Nunnery, Staffordshire at the prices shown in pounds (li), shillings (s) and pence (d):

In the church – one table of alabaster, old forms and seats, ii partitions of carved wood, paving from the church and choir, panes of glass and one massbook *xx s*

In the vestry – ii pairs of green linen vestments, i old cope, i surplice, i altar cloth, i towel, i little bell and a brass censer *iiii s*

In the chapter house – iii panes of glass and two long forms *xii d*

Bells in the steeple – ii unsold bells are still in the steeple

The Hall – ii tables and a form *xii d*

The parlour – i folding table, i form, i chair, i cupboard and hangings of painted cloth *ii s*

The bailiff's bedroom, one matress, i coverlet, one blanket and one axe *xx d*

The buttery – ii ale tubs, i old chest, i board, i table cloth and ii brass candlesticks *xii d*

The larder – i trough and two little barrells *vi d*

The cheese loft – ii little tubs, two cheese racks, ii churns, i little wheel and ii shelves *viii d*

Waggons – i wain and i dung cart *xvi d*

Hay – *x* loads of hay *xv s*

such as a censer for burning incense or vestments for the priest to wear). Children may need help with thinking about the uses they might make of specific objects.

Assessment opportunities

Use children's participation in the discussion to assess how much they have grasped about Henry's motives.

Display ideas

Children could make a display based on the plan of a real monastery and include pictures of all the items sold off when it was dissolved.

Reference to photocopiable sheet

This provides information to help the children understand more about monastic life in this period and how Henry raised money by selling off Church property.

HUNTED PRIESTS

To find out about the persecution of Catholic priests in Elizabeth's reign using documents and pictures.
†† *Whole class then individuals.*
🕐 *About 60 minutes.*

Previous skills/knowledge needed
The break with Rome and dissolution of the monasteries provides an appropriate background for this lesson.

Key background information
Once the Protestant regime of Elizabeth I was firmly established in England, many young English Catholic men went to Douai in France to be trained as Jesuits. Others were trained in Rome. These priests had the objective of keeping the Catholic religion alive in England especially after Elizabeth had been excommunicated and they were prepared to die for their faith. The attitude of the Government was to regard these priests as traitors especially when Catholics abroad, led by Spain, were trying to launch an invasion against England.

Once these priests had received their training, they returned home. We know that fourteen of them arrived in 1580. Some of them came by secret routes, landing in secluded places. They went to the houses of wealthy Catholic families who refused to accept the new Protestant religion (recusants). These people took great care not to be discovered sheltering priests as the penalties were very harsh. Priests would be passed off as friends of the family. However, sometimes wanted notices would be issued for known priests such as this notice for a Father Gerard:
'John Gerard the Jesuit is about thirty years old. Of a good stature, he is somewhat upright in his walk and in his appearance. He has a somewhat staring look. His hair is somewhat curly by nature and blackish and he does not have much hair on his beard. I think his nose is somewhat wide and turning up. His lips are thickish and are turned outwards, especially the upper lip.'

Preparation
Prepare one copy of photocopiable page 112 for each child. Collect pictures of priests' holes from this period. Prepare copies of other items as required for extension activities.

Resources needed
Photocopiable page 112 and pictures showing evidence of priests' holes, pens, felt-tipped pens, writing and drawing paper.

What to do
Explain the background to the story of Father Gerard using the information supplied above. Distribute photocopiable page 112 so that children can see how a priest's hole could be built into a large house and those hiding there could escape detection. Show the children any additional pictures of priests' holes as examples. Use some of the detail given above to help create an atmosphere of secrecy. What would the children do if they were being hunted? How would they hide in their own homes? Finally, read the extract from Father Gerard's story to the children. They can now continue with the story writing either from Father Gerard's point of view or from the point of view of those hunting him down. On this occasion Father Gerard's pursuers left empty handed despite stripping the plaster work in the house and making what they thought was a thorough search. However, he was captured in the next town and taken to the tower where he was tortured. But Father Gerard managed to escape by climbing along a rope stretched out across the moat!

Suggestion(s) for extension

The children could draw pictures to illustrate an episode from the Father Gerard story or they could draw pictures of Father Gerard based on the information given in the wanted notice.

Suggestion(s) for support

Some children may need help with getting started on their written assignment. They could be encouraged to extend the conversation which Father Gerard overheard while he was hiding, or be asked to imagine they were shut inside the priest's hole fearing every move outside. What thoughts would have gone through their heads? Would they be frightened? Hungry and thirsty?

Assessment opportunities

Children could be given pictures of priest's holes or the wanted notice given above and asked to describe what this evidence tells us about the persecution of the Catholics in Elizabethan England.

Display ideas

Children could make a priest's hole in the classroom (for example, by extending a cupboard area), sufficiently large for one child to crawl inside. The children's pictures of the story and of Father Gerard could add to the display.

Reference to photocopiable sheet

Photocopiable page 112 provides both visual and documentary evidence of the Father Gerard story to help the children understand more about the persecution of Catholics at this time.

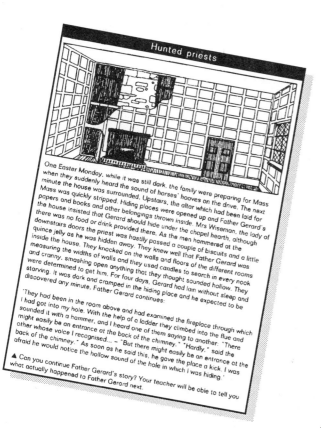

THE APPEARANCE OF ELIZABETH I

To identify and give reasons for different ways in which the past is represented and interpreted.

†† *Whole class then individuals.*

🕐 *30–40 minutes.*

Previous skills/knowledge needed

The ability to look at portraits and paintings closely to extract specific information.

Key background information

The written sources were produced by a French ambassador to England, André Hurault, and by an English courtier, Sir John Hayward. Both were written in the 1590s when the Queen was getting older.

Preparation

Prepare one copy of photocopiable page 113 for each child. Collect different portraits of Elizabeth I.

Resources needed

Photocopiable page 113, pictures of Elizabeth I in books, postcards and posters, drawing paper, pencils.

What to do

Distribute photocopiable page 113. This contains two descriptions of Queen Elizabeth written by people who met her. Ask the children to read the descriptions aloud and to comment on the differences between them. Can children suggest reasons why the accounts should be different? Distribute pictures of Queen Elizabeth around the class. What impression of the Queen do these paintings give? Do they differ from the written descriptions? Can children suggest reasons why?

The children should record their answers on the back of the photocopiable sheet before making their own portrait of Queen Elizabeth.

Suggestion(s) for extension

The children could write their own descriptions of Elizabeth I or another character from two different viewpoints.

Suggestion(s) for support

Help children to understand the unflattering aspects of the French ambassador's account. Then ask them if they can find anything which contradicts this either in the portraits or in the other written account.

Assessment opportunities

Check that the children understand how we can sometimes get conflicting descriptions of the same person or event.

Display ideas

Children can display their pictures of Queen Elizabeth I.

Reference to photocopiable sheet

Photocopiable page 113 includes two very different descriptions of Queen Elizabeth I. The children should notice the differences and try to account for them. This sort of evidence is generally a mixture of fact, opinion and judgement and it is important that the children sort out the accuracy of each description.

Elizabeth I

"On her head she wore a great red wig. As for her face it is and appears to be very aged. It is long and thin and her teeth are very yellow and unequal. Many of them are missing so that one cannot understand her easily when she speaks quickly."

A description by a French ambassador in 1597.

"She was a lady upon whom nature had given many advantages. She was of medium height and slim. Her hair was pale yellow, her forehead large and fair, her eyes lively and sweet but short sighted, her nose rising in the middle. Her whole face somewhat long but of admirable beauty."

A description by Sir John Hayward, an English knight in about 1590.

TUDOR PORTRAITS

To find out about the lives and values of wealthy people in Tudor times.

†† *Whole class introduction. Pairs or individuals for activity.*

🕒 *40 minutes.*

Previous skills/knowledge needed

This activity could build on earlier experience of looking at and drawing portraits.

Key background information

Tudor portraits are an excellent source of information about the important and wealthy people depicted, about their clothes, jewellery and general wealth. They also provide evidence of the growing prosperity of the period. Compare portraits of the simply dressed Henry VII with those of his granddaughter, Elizabeth I, in her sumptuous robes and jewels. The children could compare some of the different portraits of her and suggest why she never appears to grow older in any of them. Backgrounds can also provide information about different events, for example, the Armada portrait of Queen Elizabeth.

Sometimes whole families sat for portraits and children might use the painting of the Cobham family by Hans Eworth as a source of information about childhood in Tudor times. The memorial picture to Sir Henry Unton, painted in 1596, records his life from birth to his time as a diplomat and soldier and then his death and funeral. (National Portrait Gallery).

Preparation

Collect portraits of Tudor people from books, postcards and posters.

Resources needed

Portraits of Tudor people, pencils, paints, painting paper, magnifying glasses, sketching paper, coloured or gold paper.

What to do

Talk to the children about sources of information about our present Queen and royal family. How do we know what they look like? Children will probably suggest photographs, television, etc. Have they seen any painted portraits of the current royal family?

In Tudor times portraits were a means of showing how important a person was and how he or she wanted to be remembered by future generations. Show the children some examples of these portraits and discuss some of the detail. Then hand out the portraits of Tudor personalities and ask the children to talk about their initial impressions of the portraits.

Ask the children to work in pairs with a portrait which interests them. They might need magnifying glasses to make detailed observations. Ask the children to describe the person(s). What are they wearing? What is the expression on their face? What impression do they think the person is trying to convey? Ask the children to look at the background and accessories in the portrait. Do they give more information about the subject? Do they think the portrait is a good likeness or is the artist flattering the sitter? Why do they think the portrait was painted? Pairs of children can report back on their findings to a larger group. Alternatively, they could like to compare their impressions with children working with the same portrait.

Ask them to paint a copy of the Tudor portrait they have been studying. Discuss with the children how they will represent some of the details for example, the fine lacy ruffs.

Suggestion(s) for extension

Children could investigate more about the life of the person in their portrait. They can work with portraits of people painted at different times during the Tudor period. Encourage them to note the differences in the style and costume of people in their portraits. The portraits could be organised within a timeline to demonstrate the changing fashions.

Suggestion(s) for support

Children will approach this activity according to their different abilities and stages of maturity.

Draw children's attention to the details in the portraits they are working with.

Assessment opportunities

Can the children use the portraits as a source of information about the lives of wealthy and influential Tudor people? Are they able to make some suggestions about how the portrait could be interpreted and what messages the subject was trying to convey?

Opportunities for IT

Children could use a word processor to write a brief account of the portrait or of the artist which can be displayed alongside the picture. They will need to decide which information to include and how to present their writing so that it can be read from a distance. The children may be able to find information, or even other portraits, on a CD-ROM.

Display ideas

Frame the portraits with coloured or gold paper and arrange them to create a Tudor portrait gallery. Ask the children to compile a guide to the portrait gallery. Each child can write about the person they have painted and provide a brief life history.

THE TUDOR COURT

To learn about the importance of the Tudor court and what court life was like.

†† *Whole class introduction. Pairs and individuals for activity.*

⏲ *45 minutes.*

Previous knowledge/skills needed

This activity will draw on children's reading skills to interpret the list of gifts written in Elizabethan English.

Key background information

In the Tudor period, the court became the centre of power and government as well as a centre for culture and the arts. Henry VIII was able to keep his eye on potential troublemakers and reward loyal followers at his court. People flocked to Elizabeth's court to gain her favours and some of the honours which she could bestow such as pensions, monopolies, leases and titles. Amongst her favourites were the Earls of Leicester and Essex, Sir Walter Raleigh and Sir Christopher Hatton. Her political advisers were also important members of the court. The court did not remain in one place but moved constantly from palace to palace. In the summer, Elizabeth went on progresses to visit wealthy courtiers and landowners. These people were expected to feed and entertain the Queen and her entire court for several days with expensive pageants and masques, plays, music and dancing. Hosts were often left in debt after providing such royal entertainment.

Preparation

Prepare one copy of photocopiable page 114 for children to share in pairs.

Resources needed

Photocopiable page 114, pictures of Elizabeth and her courtiers, books and pictures illustrating life in Tudor times, pencils, crayons, felt-tipped pens, paper.

What to do

Talk to the children about the Tudor government and explain to them how the monarchs were personally involved in governing from their court. Use the background information above to discuss some of the people at Elizabeth's court; include politicians and administrators as well as courtiers who sought to entertain Elizabeth and gain her favours. Refer to pictures of Elizabeth and her courtiers and talk about how they amused themselves.

Distribute photocopiable page 114 and ask the children in pairs to read about the different gifts that were presented to the Queen. Can the children identify the most expensive gifts? Who bought the Queen these different gifts? Note the unusual/archaic spellings.

When the children have worked out what the presents were, ask them to draw pictures of some of the items on the list. They might need to refer to other sources of information to see what various articles looked like.

Suggestion(s) for extension

Encourage the children to research more details about life at the Tudor court. Children might like to find out more about Elizabeth and her progresses through the countryside. They could make a programme recording the different entertainments which were provided to amuse Elizabeth.

Suggestion(s) for support

Some children may need help reading photocopiable page 114. Pair slower readers with more able readers, or read through the page with them very carefully several times.

Assessment opportunities

Can children explain what happened at court? Why was the court important during Tudor times?

Opportunities for IT

Children could use an encyclopaedia CD-ROM to research information about the Tudor court. The children could also use software such as *Landmarks Elizabeth I* which enables them to examine how a Tudor manor house prepares for a visit from the queen.

A different approach would be for children to use multimedia authoring software to make an electronic presentation about the Tudor court. Different groups of children could research information about a particular aspect of court life; what was eaten, the games played, music and the progression around the countryside. Each group could then have three or four pages in which to present their information. This could include text, pictures and sounds.

The pictures could be taken from clip art or CD-ROM collections, scanned images from photographs or their own line drawings. Children could add their own voices, recorded using a microphone linked to the computer, or Tudor music which could be sampled from a CD-ROM or recorded using the microphone. The initial structure could be set up in

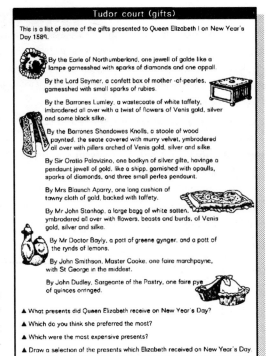

Tudor court (gifts)

This is a list of some of the gifts presented to Queen Elizabeth I on New Year's Day 1589.

By the Earle of Northumberland, one jewell of golde like a lampe garnesshed with sparks of diamonds and one oppall.

By the Lord Seymer, a confett box of mother-of-pearles, garnesshed with small sparks of rubies.

By the Barrones Lumley, a wastecoate of white taffety, imbrodered all over with a twist of flowers of Venis gold, silver and some black silke.

By the Barrones Shandowes Knolls, a stoole of wood paynted, the seate covered with murry velvet, ymbrodered all over with pillers arched of Venis gold, silver and silke.

By Sir Oratio Palavizino, one bodkyn of silver gilte, havinge a pendaunt jewell of gold, like a shipp, garnished with opaulls, sparks of diamonds, and three small perles pendaunt.

By Mrs Blaunch Aparry, one long cushion of tawny cloth of gold, backed with taffety.

By Mr John Stanhop, a large bagg of white satten, ymbrodered all over with flowers, beasts and burds, of Venis gold, silver and silke.

By Mr Doctor Bayly, a pott of greene gynger, and a pott of the rynds of lemons.

By John Smithson, Master Cooke, one faire marchpayne, with St George in the middest.

By John Dudley, Sargeante of the Pastry, one faire pye of quinces orringed.

▲ What presents did Queen Elizabeth receive on New Year's Day?
▲ Which do you think she preferred the most?
▲ Which were the most expensive presents?
▲ Draw a selection of the presents which Elizabeth received on New Year's Day.

advance with a front page with titles showing the different aspects of the Tudor court. By clicking on a title the user would be taken to a page showing the information on that subject which could be spread over several pages. This is a fairly ambitious project which will need support for children using the software for the first time.

Display ideas

Display the children's pictures of the New Year's presents with pictures of Elizabeth's court and portraits of some of her courtiers.

Reference to photocopiable sheet

Photocopiable page 114 will test the children's reading skills. They will have to use the information to make their drawings. The accuracy of their work will show how well they have read and understood the descriptions of the gifts.

LAW AND ORDER

To learn about law and order in Tudor times.
†† *Whole class then pairs and groups.*
🕐 *Introduction and pair activity 30 minutes. Group activity, two 40 minute sessions.*

Previous skills/knowledge needed

This activity will draw on children's ability to role-play as well as their knowledge of life in the Tudor period for example, food, clothing, social habits, etc.

Key background information

Law and order was a serious problem in Tudor England. There were many rogues, vagabonds and beggars, and legislation was passed throughout Tudor times to control their activities. In London, the local wards were responsible for law and order, and citizens were supposed to serve in rotation as watchmen. Cutpurses and pickpockets were widespread in the area around St Paul's.

Hookers would try to hook objects from rooms with open windows and shoplifters were everywhere. Punishments were severe for offenders who were caught. Cutpurses, coin-clippers and conny catchers (tricksters) could be hanged and lesser offenders would be whipped at the cart-tail, or put in the stocks or pillory.

Preparation
Prepare one copy of photocopiable page 115 for the children to share in pairs.

Resources needed
Photocopiable page 115, pictures and books about life in Tudor times.

What to do
Introduce the children to some of the problems of law and order during Tudor times. Distribute the photocopiable sheet and discuss the sorts of crimes which are recorded there. Refer to the background information for further detail. Organise the children in pairs and ask the children to talk about and describe different sorts of punishments. Do they think that they are suitable punishments? Do they think that they are cruel? Then organise the pairs of children into groups of four. Tell them they are going to retell the story of a crime and its detection in Tudor times. They will need to decide on the chief characters and a plot for the crime. Children will need to include how the plot was detected and the punishment of the criminals at the end. For example, a wealthy man might leave his purse near an open window. The hookers come by and steal the purse. The wealthy man interrogates his servant who describes the hooker. A search through the city follows before the hooker is finally identified.

When the children have worked on their plot, they could act it out for the rest of the class. They might choose to portray it as a courtroom scene where the crime is acted out before a magistrate who will then sentence the criminal if found guilty.

Suggestion(s) for extension
The children could write the story of the crime and its detection. Talk about the style of writing in the extracts on photocopiable page 115 and provide other examples of Tudor writing so that children can try and copy that style in their own stories.

Suggestion(s) for support
Some children will need support in reading and understanding some of the vocabulary in the extracts on photocopiable page 115. Read the extracts with the children, explaining some of the more difficult and unusual words.

Assessment opportunities
Can the children describe some of the features of law and order in Tudor times? For example, the sort of offences committed and the types of punishments.

Opportunities for IT
Children could use a word processor or desk top publishing package to create a class book about different aspects of law and order. This might include a selection of different punishments, with pictures taken from CD-ROMs, scanned from their own line drawings or created using an art or drawing package. Each pair of children could be given a single page on which they would need to present their information through pictures and text. They will need to create their text, select appropriate fonts and styles, format the text and pictures and to make the work interesting.

Display ideas
Show the variety of punishments meted out in Tudor times from different sources. The children may refer to these sources to draw pictures of their own villains. They could create a rogues gallery with the villains' offences as captions beneath each portrait.

Reference to photocopiable sheets
The children have to use the information in the photocopiable sheet to help them prepare and perform a short play about a crime in Tudor times.

Crime in Tudor times

Thomas Harman wrote about hookers in 1567. Hookers are thieves who '...vigilantly mark where or in what place they may attain to their prey, casting their eyes up to every window, well noting what they see there, whether apparel or linen, hanging near unto the said windows ... They customarily carry with them a staff of four or five feet long, in which, within one inch of the top thereof, is a little hole bored through, in which hole they put an iron hook, and... pluck unto them quickly anything that they may reach therewith.'

William Fleetwood was recorder of the City of London and he wrote about a school for cutpurses in 1585.
'There were hung up two devices, the one was a pocket, the other was a purse. The pocket had in it certain counters and was hung about with hawks' bells, and over the top did hang a little scaring bell; and he that could take a counter without any noise was allowed to be a Public Foister: and he that could take a piece of silver out of the purse without the noise of any of the bells, he was adjudged a Judicial Nipper.'

This picture shows the art of picking locks.

This picture shows a young man gambling with dice.

This picture is of John Selman who was a well known cut purse. He was arrested on Christmas Day, 1611 during a church service and executed a year later.

SIR FRANCIS DRAKE AND HIS VOYAGES OF EXPLORATION

To learn about Sir Francis Drake's achievements and to place them within the context of the sixteenth century.

†† *Whole class then individuals.*

🕐 *Introduction 30 minutes, individual activity 30 minutes.*

Previous skills/knowledge needed

This activity will draw on children's map reading and map making skills.

Key background information

Drake's voyages and attacks on Spanish shipping must be set against the need to find new trade outlets and attempts to end the Spanish trading monopoly with the New World. In particular, the West Indies offered an outlet for English cloth and slaves purchased in West Africa. Spanish merchants were forbidden to trade with foreigners who did not have a licence and whose goods had not been approved by the Spanish crown. In the 1560s John Hawkins tried to trade peacefully with the Spanish; he sold his first consignment of slaves in the West Indies and returned home with hides and sugar. Later voyages were attacked by the Spanish fleet so for the next thirty years English captains visited the West Indies as pirates and privateers, rather than as traders.

Drake's first voyage in 1571 was a reconnaissance but he did return with some booty. In 1573 he attacked a mule train near Panama laden with treasure and returned to England

with over £20,000. In 1577, Drake set off with five ships to search for a route to the East Indies through the south-west passage. Drake encountered terrible storms as he rounded Cape Horn. He then sailed up the coast of Chile and attacked Spanish treasure ships. Laden with treasure Drake sailed up to California and anchored near the later site of San Francisco. His ship, the *Golden Hind,* was overhauled and Drake left behind an inscription claiming the country for Queen Elizabeth. He crossed the Pacific, bought several tons of cloves from the Moluccas (or Spice Islands) and returned to England via the Cape of Good Hope, arriving in Plymouth on December 26th 1580. Queen Elizabeth gained financially from his voyage and knighted him the following year.

Preparation

Prepare one copy of photocopiable page 116 for each child. Collect illustrated information books about Francis Drake and Tudor ships and shipping.

Resources needed

Photocopiable page 116, books and pictures about Drake and Tudor ships and shipping, maps and atlases, pencils, crayons, felt-tipped pens.

What to do

Introduce the children to the extent of the Spanish Empire in the New World by looking at different maps. Locate some of the main areas of Spanish influence such as the West Indies, Bolivia, Mexico and Peru. People in these colonies needed many goods such as cloth, weapons, tools and hardware, books, paper, wine, oil and slaves. In return for these goods, animal hides, leather, sugar, gold and silver would be sent back to Europe. Talk to the children about Hawkins' attempts to trade with the West Indies and explain how he brought slaves from West Africa to sell in the West Indies.

Tell the children about Drake's voyages. Do the children think he was a pirate or was he justified in his attacks on Spanish shipping? Explain the reasons for Drake's voyage of circumnavigation and talk about the search for a south-west passage to reach the Spice Islands. Distribute photocopiable page 116 and ask the children to plot Drake's route on the map of the world. The children can devise their own key for the different symbols they use.

Suggestion(s) for extension

Children could research more information about Drake's circumnavigation. They could investigate what life was like at sea; the food, the ships and the type of navigation instruments that were used. Children could use this information in conjunction with photocopiable page 116 to write a log of Drake's voyage around the world. Children could also research other aspects of Drake's life and draw conclusions about his importance.

Suggestion(s) for support

Label some of the places before giving the map to the children so that they can plot Drake's voyage more easily.

Assessment opportunities

Can the children describe some of Drake's achievements and place them within the context of values and attitudes held at the time?

Opportunities for IT

Children could use a drawing or art package with a clip art map of the world. They could then plot on Drake's route, possibly adding other information such as dates, ports of call, storms or other notable events. An encyclopaedia CD-ROM could also be used to enable children to research other information about the voyage which could be included within their writing.

The children could also use a word processor to write a class diary of the voyage, with different groups writing about different parts of the voyage.

Display ideas

Display a large map to show the route of Drake's circumnavigation. Children might add some of their own drawings and paintings of Drake and his ships to the display.

Reference to photocopiable sheet

Photocopiable page 116 shows an outline map of the world. Dates of incidents occurring during Drake's circumnavigation are included to help children to plot his route.

▲ Draw the route which Sir Francis Drake took on his voyage of circumnavigation on this map of the world. Design your own key to record the information.

December 13th 1577 Drake leaves Plymouth.
June 18th 1588. Drake lands near Magellan Straits. One of his captains, Doughty tries to start a mutiny and Drake executes him.
August 20th 1588 Drake heads into the Magellan Straits.
September Drake's fleet emerges from the straits, but is scattered by gales.
October 7th 1588 Drake reaches the Chilean coast in the Golden Hind.
December 5th Drake captures 25,000 pesos of gold at Valparaiso.
March 1st 1579 Drake captures treasure ship Cacafuego with a load of Peruvian silver.

March 16th 1579 Drake reaches Nicaraguan coast.
April 16th 1579 Drake begins cruise up Californian coast.
June/July 1579 The Golden Hind overhauled and California claimed for Queen Elizabeth.
July/August 1579 Drake sets sail across the Pacific.
October 1579 Drake reaches the Moluccas and trades for cloves.
March 26th 1580 Drake sets off for Cape of Good Hope.
June/July 1580 Drake enters the Atlantic.
September 26th 1580 Golden Hind arrives back in Plymouth.

THE ARMADA

To learn about the Armada and develop children's understanding of an invasion.

†† *Whole class then pairs or individuals.*

🕐 *Introduction 25 minutes; two 60 minutes sessions.*

Previous skills/knowledge needed

Some background knowledge of the reasons for tensions between England and Spain during this period would be helpful.

Key background information

Tension between England and Spain had been growing for a number of years and for a variety of reasons. Philip of Spain was sending money to opponents of the English Crown in Ireland, and Elizabeth supported Protestant rebels in the Netherlands fighting against Philip. Philip had married Mary I and on her death had offered to marry his sister-in-law, Elizabeth, but she had declined. English sailors such as Drake and Hawkins were profiting from attacking Spanish ships in the colonies with the tacit approval of Elizabeth. The execution of Mary Queen of Scots in 1587 was seen as a further blow to the Catholic cause.

So Philip began to prepare a huge fleet of ships for a Catholic crusade. He intended to sail up the Channel and use Spanish soldiers based in the Netherlands to invade England.

However, Drake launched a surprise attack on Spanish ships in the harbour at Cadiz in April 1587 and burnt 24 ships and their supplies. The Armada was thus delayed but finally set off from Lisbon in May 1588. The Armada reached the English Channel in July and news of its arrival was sent up the coast by beacons lit on hilltops. The English ships were more manoeuvrable and harried the slower Spanish ships as they made their way up the Channel. The Armada anchored off Calais and the English sent in fire ships. The Armada scattered and the next day were attacked at Gravelines.

Many Spanish ships were badly damaged and the Armada sailed into the North Sea with the intention of sailing around Scotland and back to Spain. But the fleet was hit by storms and many ships were wrecked.

Preparation

Prepare one copy of photocopiable page 118 for each child and copies of photocopiable page 117 for children to share. Make small concertina books for children to write their Armada stories in.

Resources needed

Photocopiable pages 117 and 118, pictures, books and maps about the Armada, scissors, pencils, glue, children's writing books for the story of the Armada.

What to do

Talk to the children about their ideas of an invasion. What do they think it means? Can they think of any instances when countries have been invaded? Talk about Philip II's plans to invade England during the reign of Elizabeth. Use the background details given to provide the children with more details and refer to your resources if available. Distribute photocopiable page 117 for the children to share in pairs. Talk about the features on the map for example, the compass points, fleet of ships, places etc. Ask the children to trace the route of the Armada around the British Isles as you tell the story of the event.

Distribute photocopiable page 118 to each child. Talk about what is happening in the different pictures. Ask the children to draw other pictures in the empty spaces. Cut out the pictures and place them in the correct order to tell the story of the Armada. Ask the children to stick the pictures onto separate pages of their Armada books.

Use the pictures as a starting point for more writing about the Armada. The children could work in pairs; one child being a member of the Spanish fleet and the other child a member of the English fleet. Children could write a series of log entries to caption their pictures. This activity could provide opportunities for children to appreciate how the same event could be interpreted from different viewpoints.

Suggestion(s) for extension

Children could think about other people's experiences of the Armada. For example, the families of the sailors serving in the two navies. Children can investigate different sources of information about the Armada for example, eye-witness accounts, pictures and medals struck to commemorate the event, treasures found in the wrecks of Spanish ships. What sort of information do they provide?

Suggestion(s) for support

Some children may need help with the sequencing activity. Once the sequence has been checked, children can be supported in writing a sentence about each picture.

Assessment opportunities

Can the children explain some of the reasons why Philip II of Spain wanted to invade England? Can the children tell the story of the Armada in its correct sequence?

Opportunities for IT

Children could use a CD-ROM to search for information about the Spanish Armada. They could use a word processor to write a log of the events of the Armada. A desk top publishing package could be used to write an 'Armada Special' newspaper in which children write about different aspects of the Armada. An alternative to this would be to create a class magazine with different children working on each aspect; the English fleet, weather reports, life on board a Spanish or English ship, weapons used, a life history of Sir Francis Drake, etc. The whole could be published and bound as a class book.

Display ideas

Children could investigate pictures which were made to commemorate the Armada. Use these pictures as a resource to help the children to draw or paint their own Armada picture. The children could design medals to commemorate the event. Display the children's written work alongside their pictures.

Reference to photocopiable sheet

Photocopiable page 117 shows a map of the British Isles with the route of the Spanish fleet, drawn shortly after the time of the Armada. Photocopiable page 118 provides illustrations of the Armada, with spaces left for the children to draw their own pictures. The pictures on the page include lighting a beacon, the English fleet following the Spanish fleet in crescent formation up the Channel, fireships being sent into Calais, a Spanish wreck, the Spanish ships on fire, a storm at sea.

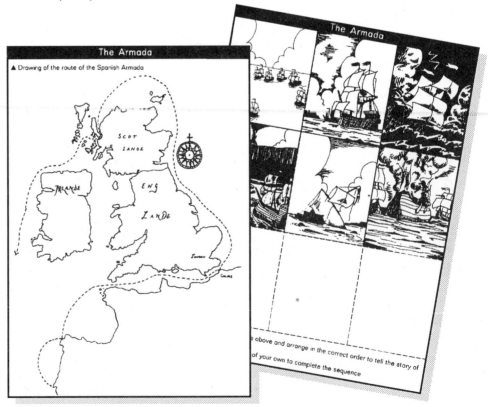

GAMES AND PASTIMES IN TUDOR TIMES

To research Tudor pastimes and games from different sources and to record the information in a book.

†† *Small groups or pairs.*

🕐 *Introduction 20 minutes then two 60 minute sessions.*

Previous skills/knowledge needed
This activity will require the children to use research skills to find out about games and pastimes from different sources of information.

Key background information
Before the Reformation there were over 90 holy-days (holidays), but these were reduced to 27 by Elizabeth's reign. On holy-days people spent their time drinking, playing or going to fairs. Some of the main holy-days were Shrove Tuesday, Mothering Sunday, Plough Monday and the twelve days of Christmas. On Shrove Tuesday country people held inter-village football matches. There were few rules and it was a very violent game. The football was made from a pig's bladder, blown up with air. Ball games also included stool ball, goff (a mixture of hockey and golf), ninepins, bowls and quoits. Other outdoor games included fencing, fighting with cudgels and archery. Children might play leap-frog, blindman's buff and hide- and-seek. Indoor games included card games and board games such as chess, backgammon and draughts. Music, singing and dancing were also popular pastimes.

Preparation
Prepare one copy of photocopiable page 119 for each pair or group of children. Collect illustrated information books about Tudor games and pastimes.

Resources needed
Photocopiable page 119, books and pictures about Tudor games and pastimes, cardboard for game base, ten counters, felt-tipped pens, crayons, pencils, paper.

What to do
Distribute photocopiable page 119 to pairs of children. Ask them to describe the activities in the picture. Which games are still played today? Ask the children how else they think Tudor people amused themselves? Tell the children that they are going to make a class or group book about Tudor pastimes. What sources of information will they use? Talk about ways in which they might conduct their research for example, listing outdoor games; ball games; indoor games; games played by the wealthy, boys' and girls' games. Provide the children with different sources of information from books and pictures. Ask them to note the source of information they use to find out about different pastimes. Discuss with the group what information they have found and what they are going to include in their book. Then ask them to draw and write about their selected games and pastimes.

Suggestion(s) for extension
The children might like to make their own Tudor board game of merelles or five men's morris. Ask the children to make a board using the following design.

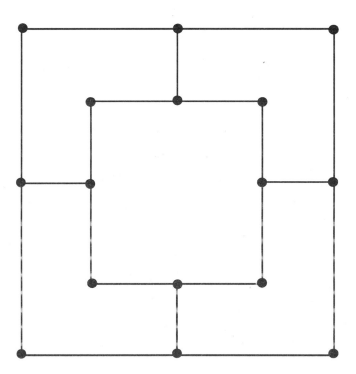

Both players have five counters and the object is to get five in a row. Players take turns to place counters on the dots trying to get a row of three. When all the counters have been placed they can be slid from one dot to another until one player gets a row. When a player has a row of three, the opponent's counters can be taken. The game continues until one player has only two counters left and so is unable to make any more rows.

Suggestion(s) for support
Some children will need help researching games and pastimes. Encourage them to use pictures as clues for different games that were played. Alternatively, restrict the activity to talking about photocopiable page 119 and describing those activities.

Assessment opportunities
Can the children recognise some similarities and differences between games played now and in Tudor England? Can they select and record relevant information from different sources?

Games

This picture shows a variety of games and activities which were popular in Tudor times.

▲ Which activities can you recognise? Are any of these activities still popular today?

Opportunities for IT

Children could use a word processor or desk top publishing package to write and present their book of Tudor games. Pictures could be included, either taken from CD-ROMs or clip art collections, scanned from the children's own line drawings, or created using an art or drawing package.

The children could also use a word processor to make up and present rules to Tudor games. They may need to look at some sets of rules to see how they are laid out. The activity could include some more sophisticated use of the word processor such as tabs to lay out the rules, bold and italics to highlight certain headings and words, numbering for the rules. Children should be shown how to use the formatting commands rather than use the spacebar to position text on the page.

Display ideas

Try to obtain a copy of Breughel's painting, *Children's Games* for display. Ask children to identify the different games they can see in the painting. Ask the children to draw and colour children playing different games basing their work on Breughel's painting. Cut out the figures of the children and arrange them to create a large collage.

Reference to photocopiable sheet

Photocopiable page 119 shows a picture of different games being played in the sixteenth century. The children should identify the games.

EDUCATION IN TUDOR TIMES

To learn about Tudor schools and how children were educated.

†† *Whole class then individual activity, followed by class and paired discussion.*

🕐 *Introduction 20 minutes then activity 80 minutes. Discussions 40 minutes.*

Previous skills/knowledge needed

Some knowledge of schooling in different historical periods would be useful.

Key background information

Schooling was not compulsory in Tudor times and whether children received an education depended on local circumstances. Girls generally stayed at home to learn housekeeping skills and needlework. Some wealthy girls received more education from private tutors or governesses. Queen Elizabeth was taught sewing, dancing and deportment, but also learned mathematics, geography, astronomy, French, Italian and Flemish. Many parishes had their own elementary schools often run by priests where the basics of reading and writing were taught. Children learned their alphabets and early reading skills from hornbooks, shaped like bats. Paper was very expensive and the writing on these books was protected by a thin layer of horn so that it did not wear away.

Most large towns had their own grammar schools. The quality and size of the schools varied. Parents generally had

to pay a termly fee, but if they were poor, their son might be able to pay his way by doing odd jobs around the school. Boys entered grammar schools at seven or eight, having first learned to read and write in English. Latin was the main subject and some children also learned Greek and Hebrew.

Divinity was important and boys were expected to know extracts from the Bible. Public speaking and logic were taught, with arithmetic, geometry and astronomy. Boys were expected to memorise many of their lessons. Punishment or the threat of punishment played an important part in school life.

Preparation
Prepare one copy of photocopiable page 120 for children to share in pairs. Collect pictures and information books about schooling and education in the Tudor period.

Resources needed
Photocopiable page 120, pictures of Tudor schools and schoolrooms, card to make hornbooks, tracing paper, gold card, brass paper fasteners, pencils, plain white paper. For extension activity, photocopiable page 121.

What to do
Can the children remember how they learned to read? Explain that not everyone could read and write in Tudor times. Books were expensive and children learned many of their lessons by heart. Distribute photocopiable page 120 and talk about the hornbook. Can the children read what is written on the book? Can they suggest why hornbooks were used?

Tell the children that they are going to make a hornbook. Copy the contents of the hornbook from photocopiable page 120 onto a plain sheet of paper. Stick the paper on to a piece of card in the shape of a hornbook. Cut out a piece of tracing paper to stick over the writing to represent the horn. Cut thin strips of gold card to hold the tracing paper in place around the edge of the card with brass paper fasteners.

Talk to the children about their current experiences at school. Ask them if they think children in the Tudor period would have had similar lessons. Use the background information to tell the children about parish schools and grammar schools in Tudor times. What similarities and

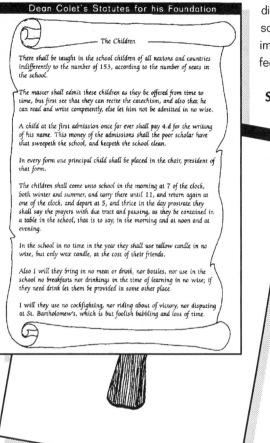

Dean Colet's Statutes for his Foundation

— The Children —

There shall be taught in the school children of all nations and countries indifferently to the number of 153, according to the number of seats in the school.

The master shall admit these children as they be offered from time to time, but first see that they can recite the catechism, and also that he can read and write competently, else let him not be admitted in no wise.

A child at the first admission once for ever shall pay 4.d for the writing of his name. This money of the admissions shall the poor scholar have that sweepeth the school, and keepeth the school clean.

In every form one principal child shall be placed in the chair, president of that form.

The children shall come unto school in the morning at 7 of the clock, both winter and summer, and tarry there until 11, and return again at one of the clock, and depart at 5, and thrice in the day prostrate they shall say the prayers with due tract and pausing, as they be contained in a table in the school, that is to say, in the morning and at noon and at evening.

In the school in no time in the year they shall use tallow candle in no wise, but only wax candle, at the cost of their friends.

Also I will they bring in no meat or drink, nor bottles, nor use in the school no breakfasts nor drinkings in the time of learning in no wise; if they need drink let them be provided in some other place.

I will they use no cockfighting, nor riding about of victory, nor disputing at St. Bartholomew's, which is but foolish babbling and loss of time.

differences are there with current schools? Children could report their impressions to the class during a feedback session.

Suggestion(s) for extension
Rules concerning the behaviour of children at St Paul's School, London (founded 1518) are printed on photocopiable page 121.

Children can read through the rules and compare them with their knowledge of school rules today.

Suggestion(s) for support
Some children may be unable to copy out all the contents of the hornbook. The card for the hornbook could be prepared for children in advance.

Assessment opportunities
Can the children recognise some of the differences between education in Tudor times and now? Can they think how learning to read and write may have affected people's everyday life at the time? For example, being able to sign documents, writing a letter, etc.

Opportunities for IT
Children could use a word processor or desk top publishing package to write and present a set of Tudor classroom rules.

Display ideas
Display the hornbooks alongside pictures of Tudor classrooms and schools. Children may like to make a large display of a classroom using the picture on photocopiable page 120 as a resource. Children can draw and paint figures engaged in different lessons which can be cut out and arranged within the classroom.

Reference to photocopiable sheets
Photocopiable page 120 shows a picture of an early seventeenth century hornbook which can be used as a model for the children's own book.

Photocopiable page 121 is a copy of Dean Colet's statutes for St Paul's School, 1518 which the children can use to compare with their knowledge of present day rules.

TUDOR BUILDINGS

To learn how timber-framed buildings were constructed in the Tudor period.
✝✝ *Whole class then individuals or pairs.*
🕐 *Introduction 25 minutes. Model making 90–120 minutes.*

Previous skills/knowledge needed

This activity will draw on children's construction skills, especially cutting and sticking.

Key background information

Many Tudor homes were built from oak frames. The buildings were made in sections. Oak trees were cut down, cut into lengths and transported to where the building was to be erected. The timbers were shaped and marked (usually with Roman numerals) so that the builders knew how they would fit together. Joints were cut and holes bored to hold the oak pegs which would keep the joints secure. Ropes and pulleys were used to haul the timbers into place. Spaces between the timbers were filled with bricks or wattle and daub. Wattle was made from thin hazel twigs intertwined together. It was plastered with daub, which was a mixture of lime, cow dung, chopped straw and water. Roofs were thatched or made from clay tiles. Windows were small as glass was expensive. When people sold their properties they often took their windows with them.

Many timber framed buildings still exist today: town houses, farmhouses, larger houses belonging to the nobility, guildhalls and market halls. Not all Tudor buildings had timber frames. Where there was a plentiful supply of local stone, buildings were made of stone.

Preparation

Prepare one copy of photocopiable page 122 for children to share in pairs. Collect pictures and illustrated information books showing a variety of Tudor buildings. Prepare a table with newspaper and necessary equipment for the model making.

Resources needed

Photocopiable sheet 122, books and pictures of Tudor buildings, card and reclaimed material, scissors, glue, sticky tape, pencils, paint, paint brushes.

What to do

Talk about buildings in Tudor times. Refer to books and pictures from your resources and distribute photocopiable page 122 for children to share. What sorts of buildings were constructed and what materials were they made from? Ask children to compare Tudor buildings with modern buildings. Talk about the buildings on the sheet and the people who might live in them. Ask the children in pairs to research how

Timber framed buildings in Tudor times

▲ Look at these different buildings. What materials are they made of? What were the buildings used for?

Moreton Hall

Grammar School

Guild Hall

Farmhouse

Suggestion(s) for support
This activity can be completed according to children's different abilities and stages of maturity.

Assessment opportunities
Can children explain how timber-framed buildings were made and why they were so popular in Tudor times? Can children compare Tudor building styles with buildings they have learned about from other periods?

Opportunities for IT
Children could use framework software like *My World 2* with the *Design a 3D Tudor Building* which enables children to print out a net and construct an accurate building.

Display ideas
Create a backcloth depicting a Tudor street scene and display the models in front of it. If children have made larger country houses, display the houses surrounded by parklands.

Reference to photocopiable sheet
Photocopiable page 122 shows some examples of timber-framed buildings: Moreton Hall, Cheshire, Stratford Grammar School, Leicester Guildhall and a reconstruction of a Tudor farmhouse at the Weald and Downland Open Air Museum. These examples will help the children with their research and also with the craft activity.

THE GLOBE THEATRE

To find out about aspects of cultural life during Tudor times by studying the Globe Theatre and a story from a Shakespearean play.

†† *Whole class then pairs or individuals.*
🕐 *Introduction 20 minutes. Model making 90–120 minutes.*

Previous skills/knowledge needed
This activity will draw on children's knowledge and experience of the theatre.

Key background information
Originally, many travelling actors performed plays in the open air, often in the courtyards of inns. Some theatres were built in London, including the Globe, which was built in 1599. It was a round building with the middle open to the sky. The stage was in the centre jutting out into the auditorium. Above the stage was a small balcony which was often used by actors in the plays. Spectators sat in the covered galleries around the edge or, if they were very wealthy, even on the stage. Poor people stood in front of the stage and were called the groundlings. There was no front curtain or scenery. A play averaged only five performances and young boys played

timber-framed buildings were constructed, or refer to the background information given to provide the children with the details.

In pairs, ask the children to build their own model of a timber-framed building. Select card or different shaped boxes from reclaimed materials to make the building. The timber frame can be painted on the boxes or card.

Alternatively, strips of black paper can be stuck on to represent the frame. The spaces between the timbers can be painted to represent wattle and daub or bricks. Tracing paper could be used to represent the small panes of glass in the window. Create a sloping roof with tiles or thatch and add chimney pots.

Suggestion(s) for extension
Ask children to research other Tudor buildings. They could investigate buildings made from other materials for example, stone-Hardwick Hall; or brick-Hampton Court.

all the women's parts. At the Globe, performances were acted from two o'clock in the afternoon until the evening. A flag was raised to show that a play was being performed. Many of Shakespeare's plays were acted at the Globe which was burned down in 1613.

Preparation

Prepare one copy of photocopiable page 123 for each child. Obtain a copy of Shakespeare's plays retold and simplified especially for children. Choose a play for the children to study.

Resources needed

Photocopiable page 123, Shakespeare's plays retold for children, writing materials and pens.

What to do

Talk to the children about the theatre. Ask them to describe a theatre and its different features. Talk to the children about Shakespeare and some of his plays. Read the story of the play you have chosen to the children and discuss the main points, different characters, etc.

Distribute photocopiable page 123 and explain that the children are going to design a programme for the play which is going to be performed at the Globe Theatre. Included in the programme will be a précis of the story, and pictures of some of the characters. How will they show the personalities of their chosen characters in their pictures?

Suggestion(s) for extension

Some children may like to write part of the story as a play in their own words. They could make simple costumes and masks and two or three of the best scripts could be performed.

Suggestion(s) for support

Some children may need to hear the story of the play read more than once. The names of the main characters could be written on the board for reference. A resumé of the plot and main theme(s) may be necessary.

Assessment opportunities

The quality and the accuracy of the different elements of the children's programmes will show how much they have understood the story of the play.

Display ideas

Display the theatre programmes and masks.

Reference to photocopiable sheet

Photocopiable page 123 provides an opportunity for the children to prepare their own Globe Theatre programme. They are required to write a précis of the story of the Shakespeare play that you have read to them. They then have to decorate their programmes and include pictures of some of the main characters.

Victorian Britain

Queen Victoria came to the throne in 1837 when she was only eighteen. In 1840 she married her cousin, Prince Albert. She had nine children, who through their marriages became connected to many of the royal families in Europe. Following the death of Albert from typhoid fever in 1861, Victoria retired from public life for many years and became very unpopular. Towards the end of the century, Victoria regained her popularity and there were great celebrations for her Diamond Jubilee in 1897 which provided opportunities for demonstrating the extent of British imperial power and influence in the world.

Victoria died in 1901, and her reign of 64 years saw tremendous changes in British ways of life. The railway network transformed systems of communication; the postal service developed and goods were transported more easily. Other forms of transport also developed, tram and bus services increased, the first cars were manufactured in the 1880s and cycling became a popular activity.

At the beginning of Victoria's reign most people lived in the country. By the turn of the century however, Britain's population was largely urban. People flocked to the towns from the country in search of work. In 1837 there were only five cities with a population of 100,000 but by 1891 there were twenty-three. Living conditions for workers were appalling in the crowded city slums; water supplies were often contaminated and there was a lack of adequate sanitation. Conditions did improve however, as legislation was passed to improve public health and hygiene, and the introduction of antiseptics and vaccinations helped to prevent and cure many diseases.

1836	1840	1842	1844	1848	1850
Victoria becomes Queen	Queen Victoria marries Prince Albert First national postal service introduced	Mines Act stops children under 10 working in the mines	Factory Act reduces children's working hours in factories to six and a half hours	First Christmas tree introduced	Most major cities linked by the railway network

THE RAILWAY REVOLUTION

To learn about the development of the railway network and some of the effects it had on everyday life.

†† *Whole class followed by individual activity then class discussion.*

⏰ *90 minutes.*

Previous skills/knowledge needed

Some knowledge of travel and transport in the pre-railway period, information about the development of steam power, knowledge of reading Ordnance Survey maps (interpreting symbols including understanding contour lines).

Key background information

It was not until 1788 when James Watt developed a steam powered engine that steam became the major source of energy that was to revolutionise both industry and transport. In 1804 Richard Trevithick developed the first steam locomotive based on Watt's design. But the 'railway age' really began in 1825 when George Stephenson built a railway to carry coal from Darlington to Stockton, about 32km (20 miles). His son, Robert, later developed a locomotive called the *Rocket* which reached 46kph (29 mph). The first railways carried coal, cotton and iron, but before long people were clamouring to use them too, so cross-country tracks were built linking main towns. Support for the railway network came from industrialists who were quick to see that the railways caused a huge increase in demand for coal and iron. The railways also offered mass employment, from the gangs of workmen (called navvies) who laid the tracks, to the drivers and other staff who ran the lines. But there was also fierce opposition from canal companies and stage-coach owners. Landowners and farmers also objected, but then demanded huge sums for the land the railways wanted. In the 1830s and 1840s many people regarded locomotives as 'iron monsters' and thought it both unnatural and dangerous for people to travel at such high speeds. Newspapers of this time printed articles and letters relating people's fears and complaints about the noise, pollution and severe damage to the countryside that the railways were causing. But railways became symbols of progress and by 1850 most major cities and towns were linked by the railway network.

Isambard Kingdom Brunel, one of the greatest engineers of the time, planned and constructed the Great Western Railway which ran from London to Bristol and then on to Plymouth, and through Wales to Milford Haven. Brunel designed the famous Box Tunnel between Bath and Chippenham, a distance of about 3km (2 miles) which took five years to complete. Brunel's railway involved the construction of dozens of bridges, large and small viaducts, cuttings and embankments which are still in use today.

The development of the railway network caused a number of far-reaching changes to everyday life in Britain. Cities, towns and country districts were linked as never before and expanded rapidly. New railway centres such as Swindon and Crewe developed. People could travel around the country more quickly and easily, and live outside crowded cities using the railway to travel to work. Iron, steel and coal as well as other goods, including fresh food, were transported more quickly bringing costs down. As the railway industry grew it became a source of revenue for the Government with locomotives, tracks and other goods being exported around the Empire to places like Canada, South Africa, India and Australia. By the end of the Victorian period many families travelled by train for seaside holidays, making resorts like Blackpool, Southend, Brighton and Scarborough extremely popular.

Preparation

Prepare one copy of photocopiable page 124 for each child, collect information books about the early railways and their construction, and maps showing the route of the Great Western Railway and other main routes.

Resources needed

Photocopiable page 124, information books about early railways, maps showing route of Great Western Railway and other main railway routes.

What to do

Briefly explain what travel was like in Britain before the railways, include information about the condition of roads and stage-coach travel. Then discuss the invention of the steam engine, the harnessing of steam power to create steam locomotives, for example Stephenson's *Rocket*, and

Victorian Britain

1851	1861	1870	1891	1900	1901
Great Exhibition at Crystal Palace opens	Prince Albert dies of typhoid	Education Act sets up local School Boards to provide schooling in every area	Education Act establishes free schooling for children 5–10 years	First underground electric railway opens in London	Queen Victoria dies and is succeeded by her son Edward VII

the use of iron track to transport coal. Introduce the plans of Isambard Kingdom Brunel to build a railway from London to Bath and Bristol, using the information above. Refer to a map showing some of the places through which the Paddington to Bristol railway line passes today: Slough, Reading, Didcot, Swindon, Chippenham and Bath. Discuss with the children why the Box Tunnel was built. Ask them to imagine that they were alive when the railway line was being planned. Distribute photocopiable page 124 so the children can work out the differences in travel time by stage-coach from one town to another and the same journey undertaken by train. Their findings and conclusions can then be discussed in class.

Divide the class into groups and explain that they are going to prepare a list of arguments either for or against building the railway, either in principle or along a particular route. The class could debate or use role-play to discuss the merits of the Great Western Railway. They should use any available reference books and include contemporary accounts and statistics to support their arguments.

Suggestion(s) for extension

Children could use large scale maps (1" OS sheet) and look in more detail at the route followed by Brunel, with a view to listing some of the problems that the railway engineer would have met. A similar exercise could be carried out using a map of the local area near the school. What obstacles would the builders have met with; what objections might there have been at the time? Some children might be interested in investigating the development of the London underground railway system and the electrification of trains.

Suggestion(s) for support

Some children may need help in developing their arguments for class discussion. Ask them to imagine that they live in a house which would have to be demolished if the railway is built. What arguments would they use to try and persuade people that this should not happen?

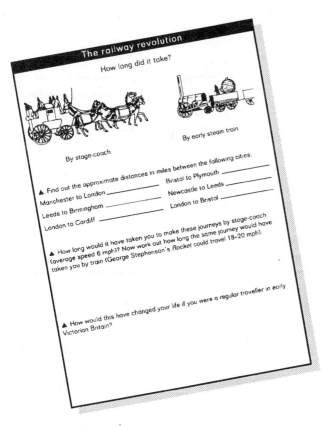

The railway revolution

How long did it take?

By stage-coach

By early steam train

▲ Find out the approximate distances in miles between the following cities:

Manchester to London _____
Bristol to Plymouth _____
Newcastle to Leeds _____
Leeds to Birmingham _____
London to Bristol _____
London to Cardiff _____

▲ How long would it have taken you to make these journeys by stage-coach (average speed 6 mph)? Now work out how long the same journey would have taken you by train (George Stephenson's *Rocket* could travel 18–20 mph).

▲ How would this have changed your life if you were a regular traveller in early Victorian Britain?

Assessment opportunities

How well have the children researched and presented their arguments either for or against the railways? Have they included all the main points, expressed their ideas clearly, used any statistics or eye-witness accounts to back up their arguments?

Opportunities for IT

Most LEAs have a licence for Ordnance Survey maps which allow them to be used in schools. The children could use computer-based Ordnance Survey maps of the school's own locality to plan a route for a railway, marking on the computer map the route of the line, stations and where cuttings, bridge or embankments might need to be made. Specialist software such as *Aegis* can be used for this work. Children could also use a word processor to plan their arguments for and against the railway which could be displayed alongside the map.

Display ideas

A large scale wall map could be made showing the route of the GWR or any local railway line. Drawings could be made to show some of the engineering work as the railway is built, together with some of the early steam locomotives.

Reference to photocopiable sheet

Children should use photocopiable page 124 to help them understand the differences between travelling by stage-coach and travelling by train in this period. This work will also help them to prepare arguments and express ideas and opinions either for or against the development of the railway network.

THE AGE OF THE STEAMSHIP

To understand the importance of steam power, the work of Isambard Kingdom Brunel and the development of steamships.

†† *Whole class then individuals.*

🕐 *60 minutes.*

Previous skills/knowledge needed

Some knowledge of steam power and the development of steam engines.

Key background information

The invention by James Watt in 1788 of a steam powered engine meant that ships had a new source of energy. Steam power was actually used in ships before steam locomotives and railways were invented.

As early as 1802 the *Charlotte Dundas* successfully pulled two barges down the Forth-Clyde Canal. But most of the early steamships also carried sails in order to save precious fuel (coal) and also as a safeguard if the engines broke down. In 1838 a trans-Atlantic race took place to find a ship that could make the crossing in the fastest time using only steam power. The race was won by the *Great Western* designed by Isambard Kingdom Brunel. The first steamships used paddlewheels but these were unreliable and easily damaged. In 1845 Brunel launched the *Great Britain* which was the first steamship to cross the Atlantic using a screw propeller as its driving force.

In 1857 Brunel built the *Great Eastern*. The hull of this steamship was made of iron and it could carry 4000 passengers. It was designed to make the return journey to Australia without refuelling. But it was a disaster. At its launch it got stuck because it was so heavy and it took two months before it was properly afloat. Then on its maiden voyage there was an explosion which killed five of the crew. Brunel died a few days later. By 1870 steamships were clearly replacing sailing ships and a new ship building industry developed. Steel also replaced iron in the construction of British steamships and because it was lighter this resulted in bigger, faster ships that could carry more cargo.

Preparation

Prepare one copy of photocopiable page 125 for each child, collect pictures of tall masted sailing ships in use before the age of steam. Find reference books about early steamships and Isambard Kingdom Brunel.

Resources needed

Photocopiable page 125, pictures of tall masted sailing ships from before the age of steam, reference books about Brunel and early steamships.

What to do

Children may be familiar with the story of James Watt and his development of the steam engine. Describe some of the early steamships with their paddlewheels and sails. Focus on the work of Isambard Kingdom Brunel and the steamships that he designed: the *Great Western*, the *Great Britain* and the *Great Eastern*. Concentrate on the story of the *Great Eastern*, Brunel's last and most ambitious ship. Tell the story of its manufacture and launch using the information above.

Distribute photocopiable page 125 and discuss the statistics with the children (some may need help with Imperial measurements). Then ask the children to write an account of the changes that Brunel made in the design of ships over a period of 20 years.

Suggestions(s) for extension

Children could find out more about the first steamships and how they took over from sailing ships.

Suggestion(s) for support

Some children may need help in understanding why steamships took over from sailing ships and how the first steamships worked. Use pictures and simple diagrams to support the explanation. The children could make drawings of both types of ship and write about the differences.

Assessment opportunities

Listen to the way in which children describe the changes that took place in the design of ships in this period. What reasons do they give for these changes? The children's

written accounts of the evolution of ships will provide summative evidence of their understanding.

Opportunities for IT

Children could use an encyclopaedia CD-ROM to research information about different Victorian ships and shipbuilders. Children might be able to save the pictures from the CD-ROM and import them into a word processor to add information about the ships. The children could use the information and work in pairs to write and present a class book about Victorian ships.

Display ideas

A display could be made based on a comparison of the three Brunel steamships or a large collage/painting based on the launch of the *Great Britain*.

Reference to photocopiable sheet

Photocopiable page 125 gives details of the three great steamships that Brunel designed. This information together with subsequent class discussions and the children's own research will provide essential knowledge about the enormous development in commercial shipping in Victoria's reign.

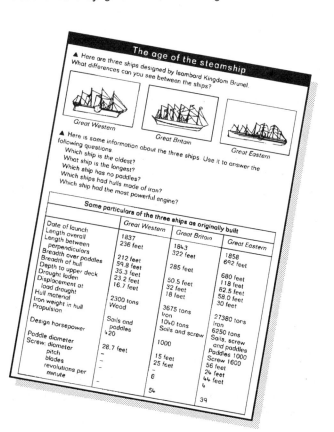

The age of the steamship

▲ Here are three ships designed by Isambard Kingdom Brunel. What differences can you see between the ships?

Great Western Great Britain Great Eastern

▲ Here is some information about the three ships. Use it to answer the following questions.
Which ship is the oldest?
What ship is the longest?
Which ship has no paddles?
Which ships had hulls made of iron?
Which ship had the most powerful engine?

Some particulars of the three ships as originally built			
	Great Western	Great Britain	Great Eastern
Date of launch	1837	1843	1858
Length overall	236 feet	322 feet	692 feet
Length between perpendiculars	212 feet	285 feet	680 feet
Breadth over paddles	59.8 feet		118 feet
Breadth of hull	35.3 feet	50.5 feet	82.5 feet
Depth to upper deck	23.2 feet	32 feet	58.0 feet
Draught laden	16.7 feet	18 feet	30 feet
Displacement at load draught	2300 tons	3675 tons	27380 tons
Hull material	Wood	Iron	Iron
Iron weight in hull		1040 tons	6250 tons
Propulsion	Sails and paddles	Sails and screw	Sails, screw and paddles
Design horsepower	420	1000	Paddles 1000 Screw 1600
Paddle diameter	28.7 feet		56 feet
Screw: diameter	–	15 feet	24 feet
pitch	–	25 feet	44 feet
blades	–	6	4
revolutions per minute	–	54	39

RELIGION, CHURCH AND CHAPEL

To learn about some of the religious practices in Victorian Britain and to consider some of the social aspects.

†† *Whole class then individuals.*

⏱ *45 minutes.*

Previous skills/knowledge needed

Some knowledge of the Church of England and religious practices in other periods.

Key background information

Religion played a very important part in Victorian society, although a religious census in 1851 showed that only a third of the population in England and Wales actually attended church or chapel on Sundays. This news provoked a reform movement in the churches with one group of Anglicans, called the Evangelicals, determined to convert unbelievers and help the poor and old in towns and cities. Evangelicals placed great emphasis on the maintenance of high moral standards and self-improvement. The movement inspired great altruism amongst many wealthy people including one of the great Victorian philanthropists, the Earl of Shaftesbury.

In Victorian Britain there was an expectation amongst wealthy and middle class families that Sunday would be kept as a solemn day, when all those who belonged to a religion attended church at least once a day. At home prayers were said both morning and evening and passages were read from the family Bible. Children were expected to remain particularly quiet and obedient on Sundays, with little or no time allowed for play.

The wealthy upper classes mostly belonged to the Church of England. Many middle class and working class families, particularly those living in the new industrial cities, attended non-conformist chapels such as those run by the Baptists, Methodists and Congregationalists. Their services had little ritual and the buildings both inside and out were plain and simple. Religious minorities included Roman Catholics and Jews. In Scotland the established Church was Presbyterian. The Victorians built many new churches and they copied the elaborate architectural styles of the mediaeval period. They also spent large sums of money in restoring over half the churches in Britain.

Tradition and prejudice ran very deep in Victorian society and there was constant antagonism between the nonconformist religions and the established Church of England. However, both groups ran their own schools in the absence of any government funded education. Some churches also ran Sunday Schools where poor children were taught the rudiments of reading and writing along with religious instruction. These children would otherwise have received no education at all.

Preparation

Prepare one copy of photocopiable page 126 for each child. Collect pictures and postcards of Victorian churches and chapels to show different architectural styles and contrasting interiors. Gather information and contemporary accounts of different church services and Sunday observances as practised by the different social classes.

Resources needed

Photocopiable page 126, pictures of Victorian churches and chapels, contemporary accounts of church services and Sunday observances, paper, writing materials.

What to do

The importance of religion in Victorian life should be described together with some of the differences in religious beliefs and practices between the Church of England as the established Church, and the nonconformists such as the Baptists and Methodists. Discuss how the different groups and classes spent Sundays.

Distribute photocopiable page 126 to the children. Then ask them to record as many things as they can about the Church of England and the nonconformists. The class could later be divided into two halves, one will investigate the Church of England while the second investigates the range and variety of nonconformist religions. A class discussion on their findings could follow.

Suggestion(s) for extension

Children could find out about particular places of worship in their local area that were built or restored in the Victorian period. Some children could investigate what a Victorian Sunday was like and compare a middle class family with a poor family living in a new industrial town.

Suggestion(s) for support

Children should be helped to recognise the characteristic architecture associated with nineteenth century dissent and the established church.

Assessment opportunities

Can the children identify the main differences between the Church of England and the nonconformist religions?

Opportunities for IT

Children could use a word processor to write labels and details of the different parts of churches and chapels for use in a large class display.

Display ideas

Children could make a large wall display of drawings and paintings of different Victorian churches. Some children could draw interior features such as carved pews or stained-glass windows. Examples of Victorian religious samplers could be included.

Reference to photocopiable sheet

Photocopiable sheet 126 will help the children to record the differences in religious practices between the churchs.

VICTORIAN EDUCATION AND RAGGED SCHOOLS

To learn about the development of education with special reference to Ragged Schools.

†† *Whole class introduction then individuals.*

🕐 *60 minutes.*

Previous skills/knowledge needed

Some knowledge of how different churches and chapels helped to provide education would be helpful.

Key background information

At the beginning of the nineteenth century most children who went to school attended establishments run by different churches or chapels. In 1834, Parliament made a grant of £20,000 to help fund these church schools. (This sum was half the amount given to Queen Victoria to spend on her stables!) The churches provided the rest of the money with the children expected to make a small contribution. But many children, especially those in large cities, were considered too unruly and too dirty to be acceptable by the church-run schools.

Little was done to establish a national system of public education before 1867. Rich families would employ a governess or private tutor who taught their children at home.

Older boys were sent away to public schools while girls stayed at home learning how to run the house or sewing and taking singing and piano lessons.

In the early Victorian period poor children in both town and country areas received very little education. Those who did attend school often only did so for about a year because they were expected to work to help support their families. However, some working children attended Sunday Schools organised by the churches and chapels. Here they were taught the basics of reading and writing along with religious instruction. Other poor children could attend a 'Dame' school, which was usually run by an elderly woman in a room in her house and sometimes a local tradesman would set up a day school to supplement his income. By 1844 there were 'Ragged Schools' in many large cities which catered for orphans and very poor working children who could attend in the evenings or at weekends. These schools were established by churches and charities and public figures like the Earl of Shaftesbury. They had huge classes which were held in places such as warehouses or even under railway arches. The children were taught simple, mechanical lessons by older children known as 'monitors' and there were very few books apart from The Bible.

By 1870 there was a marked increase in the number of schools being built and about half of all 6–10 year old children went to school. In 1880, an Act was passed making schooling for 5–10 year olds compulsory. Parents had to contribute at

least a penny a week for each child to attend school. Very few working class families could afford this nor could they afford to lose the money the children brought home in wages so truancy was rife.

School and lessons at this time were often very dull. Classes were very large, with up to 70–80 children, and discipline was very strict indeed. Lessons generally focused on reading, writing and simple arithmetic. The children wrote and did their sums using a slate pencil on a small slate board. Many lessons were taught by rote and had to be learned by heart. It was not until 1891 that elementary education became free for all children.

Preparation

Prepare one copy of photocopiable page 127 for each child. Collect pictures of Victorian classrooms and information books about education at this time. Find relevant passages in *Bleak House* and *Nicholas Nickleby* about schooling and education.

Resources needed

Photocopiable page 127, pictures and photographs of Victorian classrooms, reference books about the development of education, copies of *Bleak House* and *Nicholas Nickleby* by Charles Dickens.

What to do

Discuss with the children the general points of the development of education in Victorian Britain using the information given above. Place particular emphasis on the provision made for poor children and the development of Ragged Schools. Photocopiable page 127 relates the story of Mary Carpenter who was one of the pioneers of the Ragged School Movement. Distribute photocopiable page 127 and ask members of the class to read aloud the account of the Ragged School. The children could then imagine that they were attending Mary Carpenter's school for the first time and write about their experiences. What did they think of the other children who were there? What did they think about the teachers? What did they learn that day? How did they feel when they returned to the places where they spent the night? These accounts could then be read aloud and discussed in class.

Suggestion(s) for extension

Read to the children some relevant passages about Victorian education from *Bleak House* and *Nicholas Nickleby*. Ask the children to look again at the quotation from the Earl of Shaftesbury on photocopiable page 127. Lead a class discussion about the children who might have attended a Ragged School. What do these accounts add to what they have already learned about the need for schools and education in Victorian times? Children could find out more about other kinds of schools.

Suggestion(s) for support

Some children may need help with reading the text on photocopiable page 127. Difficult words or concepts should be highlighted and explained.

Assessment opportunities

Children's accounts about the Ragged School and contributions to class discussions will show how well they have understood what conditions were like for poor children in this period.

Opportunities for IT

Children could use a word processor to write a letter to their MP about the lack of education for the poor. They should be shown how to set out the letter using the appropriate formatting commands such as right justify for the address rather than positioning the text using the spacebar.

Display ideas

Children could draw an interior scene of a Ragged School with different groups contributing to the picture.

Reference to photocopiable sheet

Photocopiable page 127 provides information to help the children's understanding of conditions for poor children in this period. It should be used as the basis for their own imaginative accounts about Ragged Schools.

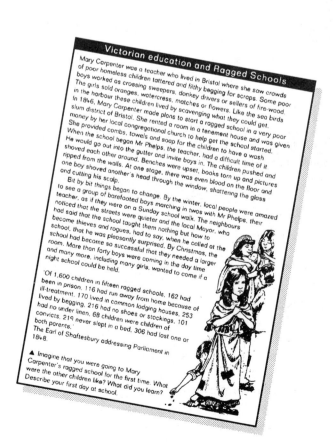

◆ A VICTORIAN CENSUS

To find out some aspects of Victorian family life using the census as a source of information.

†† *Whole class introduction then pairs.*

🕐 *Introduction 20 minutes; paired activity 45 minutes.*

Previous skills/knowledge needed

Families in Victorian Britain were much larger than they are today, the average family in 1870 had five or six children. Middle and upper class families would also have several servants who often lived in. So when a census was taken, all the children, any other relatives and all the servants had to be counted as members of the household. Governments have held censuses in Britain since 1801, the most recent one was taken in 1991. Today, each household is issued with a form comprising a list of questions about the people living in the house, their names, ages, jobs, etc. In Victorian times all this information was handwritten into record books.

Preparation

Prepare one copy of photocopiable page 128 for children to share in pairs. Collect pictures of different Victorian houses from poor tenements and back-to-back houses, to middle class and large expensive homes. Gather books showing how the different social classes dressed and how they furnished and decorated their houses.

Resources needed

Photocopiable page 128, pictures of different Victorian houses, books showing how different social classes dressed and how they furnished and decorated different rooms, writing materials, sheets of drawing paper A4 or A3 size (depending on the size of the display to be made), paper fasteners, crayons, felt-tipped pens.

What to do

Ask the children if they know how many people live in Great Britain. (In early 1995, 58,540,000 estimated.) Encourage them to make some guesses. Talk about ways of finding out the answer. Can the children make any suggestions? Tell the children about the census and how the data is collected today. Why would it be important for the government to have such information?

Explain to the children that they are going to look at a census which was taken in 1851 and use it to find out information about people who lived at the time. Distribute photocopiable page 128 and read through the census material with the children. Talk about the sort of information which the census provides. Ask the children to describe the members of the household at one particular address. Who lived there? What were their ages? What sort of occupations are listed in the census? Do these occupations still exist? Show children pictures of different types of Victorian houses and ask them to describe the sort of people who might live there, their ages, jobs etc.

Divide the class into pairs and tell them that they are going to describe the street on the census form. Each pair will need to select a house. Hand out the drawing paper and ask the children to fold it in half. On the top fold ask them to draw the outside of a Victorian house. Let the children use the pictures and books from your resources to help them include accurate details. Open the paper out and ask the children to then draw, on the bottom half, all the people who are members of their chosen house as recorded on the census form. Again encourage the children to refer to other sources of information to check that their characters are appropriately dressed and to include Victorian furnishings in the interior of their houses. When the houses are finished, they can be displayed in a row to represent a Victorian street. Paper fasteners could be used to fasten the front of the houses, which then could be undone to reveal the occupants inside.

Suggestion(s) for extension
Children may use the census information to write a story about the household that they have drawn. This activity could also be used as a starting point for children to work with the census material from their own locality. Census returns for a particular street could be analysed to show how the households changed over a period of time. These returns are available at local libraries; this information could be used to find out about the families that lived in a particular house that a member of the class lives in now.

Suggestion(s) for support
Children might need support in reading and extracting information from photocopiable page 128. Discuss one particular household with the children and explain what the census can reveal about the people who lived there.

Assessment opportunities
Can the children use the information from the census sheet to draw the correct number of people in the different houses in the street? Are the children able to describe the sort of information which can be obtained from a census?

Opportunities for IT
Children may like to create their own census. Discuss what information they would like to find out and how they might be able to obtain it. What ways could they use to record such information? This may need sensitive handling to take into account the different personal circumstances of children in your class. Alternatively children could use a commercial census database file such as *Census 1851* for use with the *Junior Pinpoint* software. This provides three different files that children can explore. Children could be shown how to find out about:

▲ people living in a particular house
▲ average number per house
▲ occupations of different sexes and ages

Children can also use the statistical facilities to find average occupancy, ages and multiple searches using to narrow down the data, for example:
▲ how many children between the ages of 5 and 12 were at school?

The children can also use the graphical facilities to display the results of their searches as bar, pie or line graphs.

Throughout this work children should discuss the implications of data held on computer, its accuracy, who has access to it and the use to which it might be put. Children could have a look at the 1981 census data to show the kind of information that is collected now.

Display ideas
Arrange the completed houses so that they are in the same order as the street recorded in the census form. Display the census return beside the street and ask the children to check whether their street provides an accurate representation of the facts.

Reference to photocopiable sheet
Children should use photocopiable page 128 to help them find out about Victorian family life.

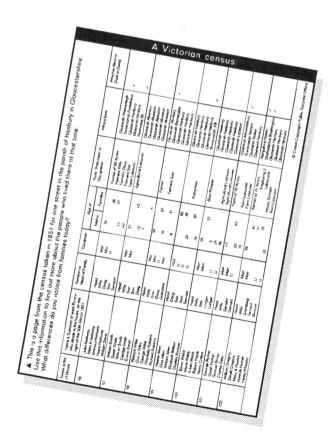

49

A VICTORIAN CHRISTMAS & ENTERTAINMENT AT HOME

To learn about some activities associated with Christmas in the Victorian period.

†† *Whole class, small groups and individuals.*

🕐 *It is suggested that one full afternoon is set aside for the children to 'stage' a Victorian Christmas party. There should be lesson time prior to this to plan and prepare the party.*

Previous skills/knowledge needed

The ideal time for this lesson plan would be near to the Christmas holiday. Most schools incorporate Christmas activities into the school programme during the last weeks of the autumn term including class parties and carol singing. If the Victorian study unit coincides with the autumn term, much could be made of the opportunity for linking some of the Victorian innovations to the Christmas festival. Some knowledge of Victorian family life among the different classes would be helpful.

Key background information

The children should be aware that in the Victorian period families had to make their own entertainment and there were no televisions, videos, CD players or radios. For poor families Christmas made little or no difference to their daily lives, as they had no money for any special food and certainly no money for presents.

At Christmas time middle class and wealthy families would decorate their houses with holly, ivy, mistletoe and Christmas roses, and large households would have a special Yule log to burn on Christmas Day. Other decorations might include a holly wreath for the front door and home-made paper decorations. Christmas trees were introduced from Germany in the 1840s by Victoria's husband, Prince Albert. The trees would be decorated with fruit and nuts, sweets and tiny home-made presents and lit by candles in metal holders. The first Christmas cards appeared in 1843. These were made for Sir Henry Cole to sell in his London art shop. They became very popular and in the Victorian period postmen even delivered on Christmas Day.

From about 1870 children would hang stockings for Father Christmas on Christmas Eve. Poor children might find an orange, a few sweets such as marzipan fruits or a home-made toy. Children's main presents were usually home-made but they might receive metal or wooden toy soldiers, a doll, a book or a ball. Only wealthy families could afford to buy toys as they were very expensive, these might include a Noah's ark, a dolls' house, a rocking horse or clockwork models.

Middle class and wealthy families would go to church on Christmas Day where they would sing carols and wish each other 'the compliments of the season'. Meanwhile, their servants would be busy preparing a special dinner, so there was no day off for them! Victorian families were large, often there were five or six children and at Christmas relatives and close friends would all be invited to the house for dinner and entertainment, so the household was even busier than usual. In the early Victorian period roast goose was very popular at Christmas time and this would be followed by a big, round plum pudding and sweet pastries. But by the 1880s roast turkey had become the most popular Christmas dinner. Many rich families would pull Christmas crackers after they had eaten. These were invented in 1846 by Thomas Smith and they usually contained sweets, paper hats and wise-sayings or proverbs. Everyone would then gather around the piano and sing carols and songs; often each member of the party would perform a song, recite a poem or tell a story. Sometimes games such as charades or forfeits would be played and a magic lantern show put on.

Preparation

Prepare one copy of photocopiable page 130 for each child. Find books with pictures of the Victorians at Christmas, examples of the sorts of toys children might receive and also some of the first Christmas cards. The words and music of popular Victorian Christmas carols should be available.

Resources needed

Christmas cards:
Photocopiable page 130, pictures of different Victorian Christmas cards, paper or thin card, felt-tipped pens, paints, crayons, glue, scissors.

Christmas decorations:
Paper chains: strips of coloured paper, scissors, glue or sticky tape.

Christmas tree: a small evergreen could be bought or a thin branch of a tree decorated instead. Branch, earth, pot, green paper (to cover 'tree'), fir cones, sweets, nuts, fruit, tiny toys, candles, candle holders.

Christmas templates: these can be hung on the tree or around the classroom. A bell, star, Christmas tree, candle, Christmas stocking, coloured paper or card, felt-tipped pens, crayons, paint, cotton or thin string.

Christmas games:
Charades: a list of two syllable words (varying in difficulty) for the children to act out.

Alphabet games: a large box, several sets of letters of the alphabet on separate pieces of paper.

The elements: a soft ball attached to a piece of string.

Christmas party:
A piano, examples of popular Victorian Christmas carols, sweets for winners and losers of games.

What to do

Talk to the children about Christmas in Victorian Britain using the drawings on the photocopiable sheet. Show the children pictures of what Christmas was like for the different social classes. Ask the children to describe some of the differences. Then show them pictures of some of the toys children might receive as presents. Discuss how different they are from those exchanged today.

Discuss the preparations for the Victorian Christmas party. Explain that they will be decorating the classroom and also making and/or decorating a Christmas tree using the photocopiable sheet as a guide. They will also be making and designing Christmas cards which would be facsimiles of Victorian cards. They will then hold a 'family' party.

The whole class can pretend to be members of a large Victorian family. Each will have to prepare a 'party piece' for presentation to the assembled company as would have been done in a Victorian family party.

Suggestions for entertainment given by groups of children, pairs or individuals might include: conjuring tricks, a ventriloquist, recitations of poetry, songs appropriate to the period, Christmas carols, simple plays.

The following are Victorian games to play with the children:

Charades Give one group of children a piece of paper with a two-syllable word written on it, for example, toadstool. This group should leave the room and work out how they will act out the word. They should first act an improvised scene in which the word 'toad' is included during the conversation. They then return to act a second scene in which the word 'stool' is used. Finally they act a scene in which the whole word 'toadstool' is used. The rest of the class have to guess what the word is.

Alphabet games Groups of four or five children could play this game together. Prepare a box containing a large number of letters of the alphabet on pieces of paper. They can be used in a number of ways for example, one person spells out a word then gives the letters to others to work out what the word was; the whole group can spell out a long word and then see how many other words they can make from the same letters; give each person a few letters drawn out of the box at random and let them see how many words they can make from them.

The elements The children and teacher sit in a circle. The teacher has a soft ball attached to a piece of string which she/he throws to each child in turn, as this is done the teacher shouts out one of the four elements: earth, air, fire and water. If it is earth, air or water the person receiving the ball must, before the count of ten, respond by naming something that lives in that environment (that is on land, in the air, or in the water). The rest of the class should do the counting. If the child fails they should pay a forfeit. However, if 'fire' is mentioned, the child must not say anything. Anyone who does so, pays a forfeit.

A spelling bee In the Victorian version, as for mental arithmetic or general knowledge quizzes, children stood in a long line. They are asked to spell words orally in turn. As they answer correctly they can move up a place. If they get their spelling wrong they move down a place. You will need to handle this with care giving appropriate words to pupils who are weak spellers.

Suggestion(s) for extension

Children could research some other popular Victorian Christmas traditions and games. They might also be interested to find out more about the toys that children received as presents.

Suggestion(s) for support

Children may need help with some of the practical

preparations for the party. They may also need help in preparing their 'party pieces'.

Assessment opportunities

Following their own research and preparations for their party, the children should be able to describe what a Victorian Christmas was like. What did the Victorians eat? What sorts of presents did they receive? How did they entertain themselves?

Opportunities for IT

Children could use a word processor to write and present the rules for some of the Victorian family games. They may need to be shown how to use specific formatting commands such as tabs and hanging indents to align the text without using the spacebar. Children could also experiment with different font styles to try and create a Victorian look to their work.

Children could use an art or drawing package to create their own Victorian Christmas card. Greetings could be added using the text facilities of the art package. They could also use a word processor to write their own message.

Display ideas

The Victorian Christmas tree, cards and decorations will form the basis of a Victorian Christmas display.

Reference to the photocopiable sheet

Children should use the photocopiable sheet as a guide to their Victorian Christmas.

A Victorian Christmas

CONDITIONS IN FACTORIES, MILLS AND MINES

To learn about some of the features of industrial life in the early Victorian period: the exploitation of men, women and working children.

†† *Whole class then groups.*

🕐 *45 minutes.*

Previous skills/knowledge needed

Some knowledge of early Victorian social history.

Key background information

In the first half of Victoria's reign more and more factories and mills were built in towns and cities, and coal mines expanded. A huge workforce was needed and whole families were employed, including very young children at an age when today we should expect them to be in full-time schooling.

Some textile mills employed children as young as four years of age because they could crawl into and under the machines to tie broken threads or to collect fluff to prevent them from jamming. In the early Victorian period some children worked up to sixteen hours a day, six days a week. They were frequently beaten for not working hard enough or for falling asleep at work and injuries were very common. It was not until 1874 that a Factory Act was passed making it illegal for a child under fourteen to work full-time.

Both women and children worked underground in coal mines. Children as young as five or six worked as 'trappers', opening the traps or doors in the tunnels. Other children were employed to push the loaded wagons, these children were called 'carters' or 'hurriers'. Reform was slow in coming and it was left to social philanthropists, like the Earl of Shaftesbury, to push legislation through Parliament to improve conditions in factories and coal mines. In 1842 he introduced a law to stop boys under ten and women and girls from working underground in coal mines. However, older children were still permitted to work up to twelve hours a day in the mines.

Men were employed as mechanics or did heavy work in iron and steel foundries, mines or factories. After 1850 ironworks and engineering factories expanded as demand from different new industries increased. Factories were incredibly noisy and dirty. They were also dark, hot and airless and often quite dangerous places. Before 1870 machinery had no proper safety guards and was rarely inspected. Most men were expected to work for twelve to fourteen hours a day, six days a week and many employers enforced strict rules of behaviour that all workers were expected to obey. There were fines for a variety of misdemeanours such as lateness or absence. In 1840, one Manchester factory also fined workers if they were found washing themselves, opening a window and even for whistling.

down the mines or in the iron factories.

Is it possible to work out the number of children in the school compared with the total population of the local community today? The groups should start by working out the total number of adults in their own homes compared with the number of children (not forgetting to include themselves). The groups can then add this information together to produce totals for the whole class. These figures could be collated on the chalkboard. The class should be reminded that their own households will only represent those which include children of school age and that there will be many households which have no children. Nevertheless the total figure will provide a useful starting point for discussion, and will prove a stark contrast to the number of children attending school in Welsh parishes in 1839.

Children could then be asked to put together a list of differences between life for children of their age today and conditions they might have had to face in the early Victorian period. Alternatively they could describe a day in their life as a child labourer in a factory or coal mine.

Suggestion(s) for extension
Children could research what life was like for children in towns and cities who scavenged for work on the streets or for children in country areas. These children did not benefit from the early reforming legislation.

Suggestion(s) for support
Children may need support in reading and understanding the figures on the photocopiable sheet. It may also be helpful to use counters to help some children to realise more graphically the contrast between those attending school today and the percentage at school in 1839.

Assessment opportunities
Listen to the children's descriptions of the conditions they might have experienced in the early Victorian period. Are they making effective use of the sources of information available to them?

Opportunities for IT
Children could use graphing software to display the results of the statistics on working children in 1839 and the present time. The information could also be put into a simple spreadsheet, either by the teacher in advance or by the children themselves. They could then use the spreadsheet to work out totals, averages, ranges and to plot graphs of the different figures. Children will need to be shown how to add formulas to make the calculations.

Display ideas
Using the reference material the children could make pictures of children at work in factories or mines. These drawings could illustrate their written descriptions.

Preparation
Prepare one copy of photocopiable page 130 for each child. Find information books with pictures of conditions in factories and mines for men, women and children. Find a copy of *The Water Babies* by Charles Kingsley and *The Old Curiosity Shop* by Charles Dickens which contain powerful descriptions of working conditions in the Victorian period.

Resources needed
Photocopiable page 130, books with contemporary pictures of working conditions in factories and mines, *The Water Babies* and *The Old Curiosity Shop*.

What to do
Introduce the topic by using the information above. Read to the children relevant passages from *The Water Babies* and *The Old Curiosity Shop*. Discuss what the children think of the descriptions. Then show them pictures of working conditions in factories and mines, pointing out the work that children were expected to do. Distribute photocopiable page 130 and read the text with the children, explaining any unknown or difficult terms such as Dame School or Elementary School, Divide children into groups and ask each group to look at the figures given for the number of children at school compared with the total population in each parish. What do these figures tell us? They suggest that a very high proportion of children never attended school but worked

Reference to photocopiable sheet

Photocopiable page 130 provides statistics for the children to use to discover information about school attendance and working children.

THE GROWTH OF TOWNS

To recognise some of the features of life in early Victorian towns and to describe and identify changes within the Victorian period.

†† *Whole class then individuals.*

🕐 *60 minutes.*

Previous skills/knowledge needed

Some knowledge of and reference to other social topics would be helpful, such as the growth of education, working conditions in industry and treatment of the poor.

Key background information

As a result of the Industrial Revolution towns in Britain grew rapidly. The first census in 1801 recorded that only about one-third of the population lived in towns. But by 1851 this had increased to half. As new industries developed so old towns expanded and new towns sprang up. There was a huge influx of people from country areas desperately seeking work and higher wages, and the towns were unable to cope with the additional population.

The new factories and mines employed thousands of workers and many employers built houses for them within walking distance of the factories. These houses were built very quickly, often very badly and used the cheapest materials. The rooms were very small, candles provided the only light, they were without proper toilets or drains, and water was collected from a communal pump. All rubbish was thrown out into the streets where it was left to rot. These workers' houses were also built very close together; back-to-back houses were a common sight in many industrial towns. This meant overcrowding on a colossal scale with many poor families being forced to live in one room. The houses were so close together that there was very little fresh air or light. With such desperate poverty and overcrowding and no proper police force, disease and crime in Victorian towns was serious and widespread.

In 1842 Edwin Chadwick released a report on health and conditions in towns entitled *Sanitary Condition of the Labouring Classes*. This report shocked many people into realising that poor housing, dirty water and lack of sanitation caused widespread disease. (In 1848 there was an outbreak of cholera which killed 62,000 people.) In the 1840s the average life expectancy of a worker living in Manchester was only 17 years; large graveyards were a feature of all industrial towns.

Living conditions were slow to improve. In 1848 a Public Health Act was passed which forced town councils to send carts to collect rubbish from the streets, but this was then usually dumped in the rivers that were used to provide drinking water. It was not until 1875 that another Act forced councils to supply clean drinking water in major towns and appoint Medical Officers of Health. By the 1880s more improvements had been made with reservoirs supplying purer water which was piped to houses for drinking and flushing toilets. Sewers were built and the streets were cleaned regularly. By the 1880s a town worker's life expectancy had increased to 30 years.

Preparation

Prepare one copy of photocopiable pages 131 and 132 for each child. Find books and pictures which show living conditions in some industrial towns. It would be useful to find statistics showing the population growth of a local city or town. These statistics will show how the population of Britain increased during the nineteenth century; the figures for the growth of particular industrialised towns and cities were even more spectacular.

Resources needed

Photocopiable pages 131 and 132, pictures and books showing urban conditions in the early Victorian period, local population statistics.

Victorian Britain

What to do

Show the children pictures of early Victorian cities and discuss some of the details. The conditions of the urban poor can be described using the information given above. Distribute photocopiable page 131 and read the description of Victorian Manchester with the children. Ask them to find out what the words in bold letters mean. The picture on this sheet together with the description will help the children to produce their own picture of life and conditions in an industrial city. Distribute photocopiable page 132. Read through the sheet with the children and explain that they have to match the bad conditions on the left of the sheet with the appropriate change or reform on the right.

Suggestion(s) for extension

The children could be asked to imagine that they are poor children living in an industrial city in the early Victorian period. They could write an account of what their home and their town are like to live in.

Suggestion(s) for support

Some children may need additional help with reading photocopiable page 131. They may also need support in completing the task on photocopiable page 132.

Assessment opportunities

The children's drawings, their written accounts and contributions to class discussion will show their knowledge and understanding of what conditions were like in industrial towns. Can the children say why the towns expanded so rapidly? Can the children give some specific details about housing conditions? Can they then describe some of the changes that brought improvements?

Opportunities for IT

Children could use graphing software to present statistical information on the growth of towns in their own area. Alternatively a spreadsheet could be set up to show the statistics for several towns so that children could compare the growth. Data might be found from the 1851 census onwards.

1	a	b	c	d	e
2	Date	Town 1	Town 2	Town 3	Town 4
3	1851				
4	1861				
5	1871				
6	1881				
7	1891				
8	1901				

A database could also be used with each record showing the population growth for, say, the 10 census periods for a single town.

Display ideas

Children could make a large picture to show the skyline of a Victorian industrial city. The picture can be captioned with some of the information that the class has discovered about conditions and changes during the Victorian period.

Reference to photocopiable sheet

Photocopiable pages 131 and 132 provide a contemporary account of industrial Manchester, together with a list of bad conditions and reforms that were made. Children will obtain a vivid picture of conditions in an industrial town in the early Victorian period.

THE WORKHOUSE

To understand beliefs and attitudes in Victorian times towards the poor.

♦♦ *Whole class then pairs.*

🕑 *60 minutes.*

Previous skills/knowledge needed

Some knowledge and reference to other aspects of Victorian society will be helpful.

Key background information

The new industries in Victorian Britain brought mass employment but it was essentially precarious. The invention of new machines throughout the period meant that many jobs done by people disappeared and there were also times when people lost work because of a fall in trade. There was no proper provision in the law to offer aid to the unemployed, sick, old or poor. So people who were destitute had two basic options, they starved or begged in the streets. The only existing legislation relating to the poor was the Elizabethan Poor Law of 1601 passed to help solve the problem of rural poverty. This Act was quite unable to deal with the needs of a growing industrial society in the early nineteenth century.

The drive for reform came chiefly from Edwin Chadwick. Following the findings of his Commission, Parliament passed a Poor Law Amendment Act in 1834. It forced parishes to group together into a 'union' to provide a workhouse at public expense. So if the poor were unable to support themselves or their families, they went to the workhouse to find help as a last resort.

At the workhouse the poor received food and shelter in exchange for work. This work was similar to that done by convicts – breaking stones, grinding bones for fertiliser (able-bodied men), or picking oakum, washing clothes (women,

children and old men). The diet was poor and consisted of gruel, dry bread or potatoes. Hunger was constant and in one workhouse the men fought to eat the scraps of old meat from the bones they were to crush. Husbands and wives were kept apart from each other and their children. They were not even allowed to talk if they ate at nearby tables. Meals were taken in total silence.

In order to discourage scroungers conditions in workhouses were designed to be as hard and unpleasant as possible. There was a terrible stigma attached to any workhouse relief and this prevented many poor people, who were genuinely desperate, from getting help and employment. Later in the period the poor received help from private groups and charities such as the Salvation Army, founded in 1878 by William Booth.

Preparation

Prepare one copy of photocopiable page 133 for each child. Find relevant passages from *Oliver Twist* by Charles Dickens about the poor and the workhouse, collect contemporary photographs and engravings of workhouses and some of the inmates.

Resources needed

Photocopiable page 133, a copy of *Oliver Twist*, pictures and photographs of workhouses and their inmates.

What to do

Tell the children about some of the conditions in workhouses using the information above. Read the passages from *Oliver Twist* and discuss the story with the children. Show them pictures of workhouses and some of the inmates. Distribute photocopiable page 133 and read the text. Then explain to the children they are going to work in pairs and write their own plays based on life in the workhouse. They should write dialogue which can be pieced together to make a more extended drama.

Suggestion(s) for extension

What can the children find out about union workhouses in the local area? The local county or district records office will be able to suggest what records survive and where they can be studied. There may be locally produced accounts of life in the local workhouses (for example, working conditions, rules, diet sheets, etc.) which could be consulted. Many former workhouses became hospitals caring for the elderly sick and are now the site of modern hospitals.

Suggestion(s) for support

Some children may need help with understanding the text on the photocopiable sheet and also in writing the dialogue for their plays. Explain some of the difficult words and repeat the main points of what conditions for the poor were like in Victorian Britain.

The workhouse

This is a description of a workhouse written by Friedrich Engels in 1844:

'The food is worse than that of the most ill-paid working man while employed and they work harder... The food of criminal prisoners is better, as a rule, so that the paupers frequently commit some offence for the purpose of getting into jail. For the workhouse is a jail too: he who does not finish the task gets nothing to eat; he who wishes to go out must ask permission, which is granted or not, according to his behaviour or the inspector's whim; tobacco is forbidden, also the receipt of gifts from relatives or friends outside the house; the paupers wear a house uniform... the men break stones... the women, children and aged men pick oakum.'

(These were jobs that were usually done by prisoners in jails. Oakum was ship's rope, stiff with tar which had to be broken down into small pieces for making ships' timbers watertight.)

▲ Imagine that you have just visited a workhouse and are very unhappy with the conditions that you have seen. Write a letter to the Board of Guardians who control the workhouse. Tell them some of the things that you saw and suggest what could be done to improve conditions.

Assessment opportunities

What can the children say about conditions for the poor in industrial cities? Can they describe what conditions were like in the workhouses?

Opportunities for IT

Children could write their plays about the workhouse using a word processor or desk top publishing package. If a word processor is used, children should be shown how to use the formatting commands to lay out their writing in the form of a dialogue without positioning text using the spacebar. You may also need to set up hanging indents to make sure that the spoken text wraps around in the correct plane.

For example:

| Interviewer | *Why are you in the workhouse?* |
| Man | *I fell ill and could not work, so I had no money to buy food for my family.* |

The same effect can be created with a desk top publishing package by setting out two frames and typing directly into them. This method is probably the easier for the children to use once the columns have been set up.

Interviewer		*Why are you in the workhouse?*
Man		*I fell ill and could not work, so I had no money to buy food for my family.*

Display ideas

A backdrop for the children's plays could be designed and painted to represent the interior of a Victorian workhouse.

Reference to photocopiable sheet

The information provided on the photocopiable sheet will help the children to obtain a picture of what conditions were like for the poor in workhouses.

ARCHITECTURAL STYLES AND PUBLIC BUILDINGS

To identify some of the buildings of Victorian Britain and to find out about their design and function.

†† *Individuals or pairs.*

🕐 *60 minutes.*

Previous skills/knowledge needed

Investigative skills, making friezes.

Key background information

Victorian Britain saw many great achievements in architectural design. In their attitude towards building the Victorians were reacting to what they thought was the dull, unimaginative architecture of the Georgian period. Many Victorian architects adopted an eclectic approach to design and dipped into different historical periods, recreating in their buildings what they considered to be the best elements. They were particularly influenced by Greek, Italian and Gothic architecture and also used many Renaissance symbols to decorate public buildings. A minority of Victorian architects sought to establish their own style of design with a sensible and imaginative use of new materials. But the majority pursued a diversity or blending of different styles.

Victorian architects did not allow themselves to be controlled by rules as to which style was most appropriate for which kinds of buildings. The results of this attitude can be seen today in many towns and cities where town halls resemble Greek temples and railway stations like St Pancras in London resemble elaborate churches. The latter years of Victoria's reign saw a massive increase in building with public offices, hospitals, banks, libraries and department stores becoming more and more ornate and highly decorated. The architects used the new materials from the ever expanding industries such as iron and glass, and built many imposing buildings to show off the new found wealth and prosperity of the period.

Preparation

Prepare one copy of photocopiable page 134 for each child or for the children to share in pairs. Collect books with pictures of different Victorian buildings from different towns and cities.

Resources needed

Photocopiable page 134, books with pictures of Victorian buildings, scissors, glue, sugar paper, black paper.

What to do

The children can work either as individuals or in pairs. Ask them to cut out each of the buildings on photocopiable page 134. These can then be mounted on coloured sugar paper and the buildings arranged in a row. The children could then find out more about these buildings, using the following checklist of questions:

▲ When was it built?
▲ Who was the architect?
▲ What was it used for?
▲ Has its use changed?
▲ Is there anything special about the way it was designed?
▲ Is there anything special about the way it was built?
▲ What else can you say about this building?

Suggestion(s) for extension

Children could look for examples of Victorian public and private buildings in their local area, or in the nearest town or city. What styles did the Victorians use? Did they copy Greek and Italian styles? What building materials did they use?

Suggestion(s) for support

Some children may need help with finding information about the buildings. They could be encouraged to record the dates when they were built and what they were intended to be used for.

Assessment opportunities

As a result of looking at pictures and their own

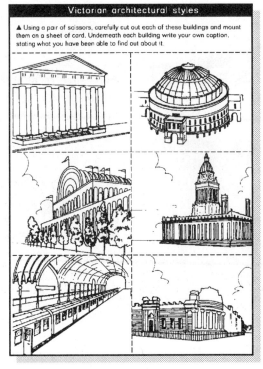

Victorian architectural styles

▲ Using a pair of scissors, carefully cut out each of these buildings and mount them on a sheet of card. Underneath each building write your own caption, stating what you have been able to find out about it.

research, children should recognise some characteristics of Victorian architecture. Can they recognise elements of Greek, Italian and Gothic styles in any buildings? What was new in Victorian architecture?

Opportunities for IT

Children could use a CD-ROM encyclopaedia to look for information about particular Victorian buildings. They might also find pictures on CD-ROM photo collections. Once they have found information they could work in pairs with a word processor or desk top publishing package to write and present their own class book of famous Victorian buildings. If there are enough examples in your local area the book could be based on these buildings; if not, it could be a wider collection.

Children could use the list of questions to act as a prompt for information to be recorded about each building. This could either be done as sentences or displayed under a series of headings. The latter would involve the use of tabs and indents to align the text.

Alternatively, children could create a database of famous Victorian buildings using the checklist of questions as the basis for the fieldnames in the database.

Display ideas

A large display of Victorian buildings could be made in the form of silhouettes cut from black paper against a skyline of blue with a sunset. Examples of local Victorian buildings could be added to the display and the children could caption their drawings with some of the information they have researched.

Reference to photocopiable sheet

Photocopiable page 134 provides pictures of some famous Victorian buildings which will help the children become familiar with some of the architecture of this period.

Britain since 1930

The development of a scheme of work based on this Study Unit should ideally make use of examples drawn from the local community. There will be many opportunities to make use of oral history. In addition, there is likely to be a vast amount of documentary material available which relates to events from recent decades. Apart from sources such as local newspapers, there will be the material available in many households either from those who lived through the period or from those who have inherited personal memorabilia, such as letters and photographs, from an older generation.

There will need to be a balance in the selection of political, economic, social and cultural material from the period. In the case of Britain since 1930, there have been massive changes in the heavy and manufacturing industries from the stagnation of the depression years, through the years of wartime production and post-war boom, to the dramatic contraction of the 1980s. In the later twentieth century, change in heavy industries such as coal, steel, shipbuilding and aircraft manufacture was matched by an emergence of new technologies.

The impact of the Second World War and the immediate post-war period of reconstruction must inevitably form a major part of this chapter and a principal aspect of this study will involve the impact of war upon the lives of individuals, both those who served in the armed forces and those who were left at home.

At the very least, children on completion of this chapter, should be aware of the dates of the 1939–45 World War and of the accession of Queen Elizabeth II in 1952.

MECHANISATION COMES TO FARMING

To learn about the main changes in farming methods during the twentieth century and to consider their effects.

†† *Whole class then individual activity.*

🕐 *60 minutes.*

Previous skills/knowledge needed

Some knowledge of changes in farming methods following the Agricultural Revolution would be useful.

Key background information

The Victorian period had seen a revolution in British agriculture. Traditional methods of farming, which were labour intensive, were radically altered by the new machines that industry provided, such as the steam traction engine and steam threshers. In addition, with the increase in cheap food imports, prices fell sharply. British farmers could not compete and so agricultural production went into a severe depression. This situation spelled disaster for many farm labourers who, desperate for work and higher wages, drifted towards the towns hoping to find new jobs. In 1851, a time of boom in British agriculture, there were 1.3 million farm workers in Britain. By 1901 there were only 0.7 million working on the land.

Although the invention of tractors had a major impact on the agricultural industry their introduction was a slow and gradual process. In the 1930s horses still outnumbered tractors on British farms, and many rural areas were without mains electricity. The effects of the world economic crisis that was hitting industry so severely at this time were passed onto agriculture and a similar depression ensued. Many farmers tried to sell their land without success and had no money to buy tractors to replace their horses.

The Second World War stimulated a demand for food at home as ships carrying imports were threatened and attacked by German U-boats. This meant that there were food shortages and people in Britain were asked to 'Dig for Victory' and grow food on every available piece of land. Some of the steep marginal land that needed to be ploughed and sown could not be worked by tractors, and so horses still had a vital role

to perform. As male farm workers were called up to join the Forces, so women were sent to replace them and the Women's Land Army was established to work on farms throughout the country.

After the war, mechanisation of farms began in earnest. The new Labour government guaranteed the prices that farmers would be paid for their produce, which enabled them to borrow money to buy new machinery. A team of horses could plough half an acre in one day but a tractor could plough 50 acres. Farmers were faced with sending their horses for slaughter and reducing their human workforce.

During the late 1940s and 1950s machines which had actually been around for many years were gradually introduced into British farms. For example, a milking machine that had first been invented in 1862 was not in general use in British dairy farms until the Second World War and post-war years. Combine harvesters which could perform a number of different farming tasks, were also introduced in many farms.

In 1973 Britain joined the European Union and one of the areas most fraught with controversy has been the Common Agricultural Policy (CAP). The EU was first created against the background of post-war food shortages, and agriculture was more inclined to creating an agreed policy on prices and markets. By the 1980s, there was concern to control the overproduction of food. The creation of butter and beef mountains and wine lakes had become a major cause for concern. Initiatives included a policy of 'set aside' whereby farmers were paid to take surplus arable land out of production. However, many areas of disagreement remain.

Mechanisation comes to farming

By 1850s   By 1950s   By 1990s

Milking

Ploughing

Harvesting Grain

▲ Look at the pictures carefully. Describe in your own words the developments that had taken place in agricultural methods by the 1950s.

▲ Make your own drawings in the boxes on the right of modern farming methods in the 1990s or write about some of the changes that have happened since the last century.

should then write a letter to a friend explaining some of the decisions that they have to face.

Distribute photocopiable page 135 and explain to the children that they are going to describe in their own words some of the changes that have taken place in farming since 1850.

Suggestion(s) for extension

Can children suggest reasons why it took a long time for mechanisation to happen? Ask them to imagine what it might have felt like to be a farm labourer on a farm where new machinery was being introduced. Some children may be interested to find out more about the Women's Land Army in the Second World War. How were they organised? How were they recruited? What experience did the women have of farming?

Preparation

Prepare one copy of photocopiable page 135 for each child. Collect illustrated information books and pictures about the development of farming and farming machinery in the twentieth century.

Resources needed

Photocopiable page 135, illustrated information books and pictures about farming methods and machinery in the twentieth century.

What to do

Talk to the children about life on a farm at the beginning of the twentieth century. At this time most farmers only had horse-drawn ploughs and carts and their own bare hands to help them with farm work. Ask the children to consider the processes involved in the following tasks: ploughing, planting different crops, harvesting, baling, milking and shearing sheep. Show the children examples in information books and pictures to illustrate the discussion. Talk about some of the traditional farming tools and methods – ploughing with a horse, broadcasting seed, using scythes to cut the crop and flails to thresh the grain. Investigate sources of information from local museums.

Introduce the invention of the petrol driven tractor and explain how it gradually replaced horses on the farm. How do the children think this would change the farmer's way of working? Ask the children to imagine that they are farmers in the post Second World War period when mechanisation accelerated. Government support will enable them to invest in new machinery. What machines will they buy? What differences will this make to the farm? Will so many horses be needed? Will so many people be needed? The children

Suggestion(s) for support

Some children may need help to see the connection between processes undertaken by hand or using horses and those undertaken mechanically.

Assessment opportunities

The children could be asked to list the reasons for mechanisation and the effects of these changes on agricultural production.

Opportunities for IT

Children can use a word processor to write their letter to a friend explaining the changes that they faced in farming. They should be shown how to set out the letter using the appropriate formatting commands rather than using the spacebar to position text.

Display ideas

The children could make a frieze showing horses being used on a farm in the 1930s, they could include a ploughing scene or a harvest scene, and also separate processes for reaping, threshing and baling.

They could also illustrate some of the developments they have learned about, for example, the use of petrol driven tractors instead of horse-drawn equipment, combine harvesters and milking machines.

Reference to photocopiable sheet

Photocopiable page 135 will help the children to understand some of the developments that have taken place in farming methods since 1850.

DEPRESSION AND CHANGE IN BRITISH INDUSTRY

To learn about the economic crisis of the 1930s and its effects on British industry and the workforce.

†† *Whole class then group research and class discussion.*

🕐 *90–120 minutes.*

Previous skills/knowledge needed

Research skills and some knowledge of industrial growth during in the Victorian period might be helpful.

Key background information

In the Victorian period there was massive industrial growth in Britain. Many new industries developed and traditional industries expanded. British goods were exported to every corner of the world as the growing British Empire provided more markets for exports. Britain became the world's richest trading nation; most of the articles that people used in their everyday lives were made in Britain.

In the decades following the First World War Britain's industrial power began to decline. By the beginning of the 1930s there was a serious slump in trade as many foreign countries could no longer afford to buy British goods. Britain's heavy and traditional manufacturing industries suffered most, and as a result, factories, mills and shipyards experienced a sharp fall in orders. This slump in industry also had serious effects on farming and agricultural production.

As the 1930s progressed, in Tyneside, Merseyside, Clydeside and Belfast shipbuilding ground to a virtual halt. Companies could no longer afford to pay employees' wages and thousands of workers were laid off. The textile industry also suffered. In Lancashire, where the Industrial Revolution had far reaching effects, many factories were still using old, outmoded machinery. As a result, British companies did not work as quickly or as efficiently as their foreign competitors and their products were more expensive. As far as the cotton industry was concerned, countries such as India (a traditional market for British textiles) were now producing their own cloth using new machinery. Employers in Britain were forced to employ workers on a part-time basis.

As many factories and mills began to close down, so the demand for coal was dramatically reduced. Many coal mines closed and miners lost their jobs. There was a similar impact on the iron and steel industries. This economic crisis, known as the Depression, was felt worldwide with countries such as the USA and Germany being more seriously affected than Britain. Nevertheless, huge areas of Britain suffered and in 1932 about three million people were unemployed. This led to much hardship and to protests. In 1936 a group of unemployed men from Jarrow in Tyneside marched to London in an attempt to bring their plight to the notice of the government. In spite of a lot of publicity and support from people around the country, the government virtually ignored their protest and the men went home again.

However, by the end of the 1930s the threat of war stimulated many depressed industries such as iron, steel and shipbuilding, and many new factories were established to make fighter aircraft and armaments. This meant more jobs and employment for thousands of people.

Preparation

Write the names of different industries on cards for each research group. Prepare headed sheets for each group to record the findings of their research. Collect pictures and information books about different British industries from the 1930s to the present day. Industries in the local area might provide additional material and statistics to assist the children's research. Also find books showing conditions for the unemployed in the Depression years.

Resources needed

Pictures and information books about different industries in the twentieth century, information from local industries, pictures and books about the Depression and conditions for the unemployed, research sheets, small pieces of card, pencils.

What to do

Discuss with the children some of the details of the economic depression and its effects on British industry using the information above. Explain how the effects were felt worldwide and how if one industry suffered a decline then this would also be felt by many others. Discuss the term 'slump' and then what it meant to be unemployed in the 1930s.

Divide the class into groups and give each one an industry to research for example, coal mining, shipbuilding, aircraft production, car manufacture, textile production, pottery and glass manufacture. Give each group a sheet of paper with the following headings, so that they can record their findings of what happened to their industry in the different decades of the twentieth century:

1 the 1930s – the Depression;

2 1939–45 – the war years;

3 1950s and 1960s – post-war and the increase in demand for consumer goods;

4 the present day – is the industry still there?

A class discussion should then follow in which each group presents their findings. What are the similarities and differences in the fortunes of each industry in the different periods? How did the industries change over the different periods? Discuss how customisation and advances in new technology have affected the industries and the workforce.

Suggestion(s) for extension

The children could find out more about the Jarrow Crusade and what life was like for the unemployed and their families. Alternatively, children could investigate what kinds of goods are manufactured in Britain today in place of the traditional industries. They could place particular emphasis on the new micro-electronic and computing industries.

Suggestion(s) for support

Children may need help with their research. Help them to devise a set of questions to answer about their industry to guide and structure their investigation. Alternatively, children could concentrate on one industry at the height of its success. This could then be used as a starting point for looking at the change that has taken place since.

Assessment opportunities

The results of the children's research together with their contributions to the subsequent class discussion will show how much they have learned and understood about the topic.

Opportunities for IT

The children could use a word processor to write and edit the results of their research into different industries. If they have access to a suitable CD-ROM they should be shown how to save text from the CD-ROM and import it into a word processor for further editing. The same approach can be taken with pictures. An alternative approach would be for children to use multi-media authoring software to create an electronic presentation on the changes in industry.

Display ideas

The class could present a display showing changes in local and/or national industries since 1930.

THE DEVELOPMENT AND IMPACT OF THE MOTOR CAR

To place the development of the motor car within a chronological framework; to describe the impact of the car in Britain since 1930.

✝✝ *Whole class then individual and group activity.*

🕘 *90 minutes.*

Previous skills/knowledge needed

Some knowledge of the history of other modes of transport.

Key background information

The first motor car with a petrol driven engine was produced in Germany in 1885 by Karl Benz. The development of the motor car progressed rapidly, but for many years only the very rich could afford to own them. By 1909, however, cars were being mass produced on an assembly line in the USA by Henry Ford. By 1930 over 15 million Model T Fords had been sold.

Britain's car industry began to develop in the 1920s. Thousands of Morris cars were made at the Cowley factory in Oxford, founded by William Morris. He began his career repairing bicycles and by the 1930s his cars had made him a millionaire. Morris had a rival, the Austin 7. This was developed in 1922 by Herbert Austin in Birmingham. The Austin 7 became extremely popular, it undercut the Morris on price and was cheaper to run. However, cars were still expensive and by 1939 only one family in ten owned a car.

During the war, petrol was severely rationed and there was no petrol allowance for family cars. In the 1950s small cheaper cars became more popular, culminating in 1959 with the production of the Mini Minor. These cars were hugely popular and represented a major breakthrough for Britain's export trade.

Here is a sequence of events and developments which can produce a framework for this topic:

1930	More than one million privately owned cars in Britain
	Road Traffic Act requires drivers to be physically fit to be allowed to drive and introduces compulsory third party motor insurance
1933	Traffic lights introduced
1934	Driving tests introduced for all new drivers
	Cats' eyes introduced to illuminate roads at night
	30mph speed limit introduced in urban areas
1935	Belisha Beacons introduced to mark crossing places for pedestrians
1939–45	Petrol rationing introduced during Second World War
1946	Two million vehicles on the roads
1951	Zebra crossings introduced
1958	First stretch of motorway opened (the Preston by-pass)
1959	Introduction of the Mini Minor
	First lengthy motorway (with three lanes, between London and Birmingham)
1965	Breathalyser introduced in an attempt to reduce drinking and driving
1968	Parking meters introduced
1978	6,831 people killed on Britain's roads; 82,51 injured

Number of private cars on the roads of Britain:

1930	1,056,000
1950	2,258,000
1960	5,526,000
1970	11,515,000
1980	16,821,000
1990	19,700,000
1993	23,000,000

Preparation

Prepare one copy of photocopiable page 136 for each child, collect photographs, pictures, advertisements and books about the history of motor cars since 1930. Some car companies may provide additional useful pictures and information.

Resources needed

Photocopiable page 136, pictures, advertisements and books about the history of motor cars since 1930.

What to do

Talk to the children about the development of the motor car focusing on some of the events and changes provided in the information above. Show the children some of the pictures, advertisements and books about cars and discuss some of the main points of design and how they compare with modern cars. Children whose parents own cars will be able to make some personal contributions to this discussion. Distribute photocopiable page 136 and explain that the children have to match the problems associated with the development of the motor car to their correct solutions.

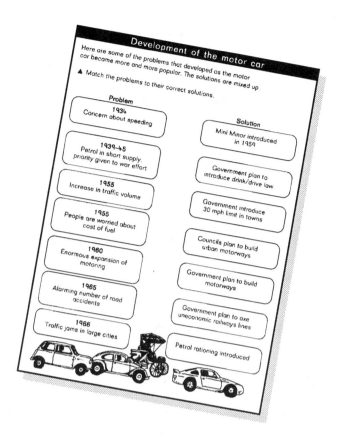

Development of the motor car

Here are some of the problems that developed as the motor car became more and more popular. The solutions are mixed up.

▲ Match the problems to their correct solutions.

Problem

1934
Concern about speeding

1939-45
Petrol in short supply, priority given to war effort

1955
Increase in traffic volume

1955
People are worried about cost of fuel

1960
Enormous expansion of motoring

1965
Alarming number of road accidents

1966
Traffic jams in large cities

Solution

Mini Minor introduced in 1959

Government plan to introduce drink/drive law

Government introduce 30 mph limit in towns

Councils plan to build urban motorways

Government plan to build motorways

Government plan to axe uneconomic railways lines

Petrol rationing introduced

processor or a drawing package. They could also collect other statistical information and use either a graphing package or spreadsheet to present their data and create graphs and charts to illustrate the work. Children could use CD-ROMs to search for information on different cars, manufacturers or data about the growth of transport.

Display ideas
Some children may like to draw pictures of favourite cars. Examples from the 1930s to the 1990s would show how car design has changed and provide a comprehensive display. Some children may like to prepare advertisements for cars that interest them. They could draw a picture of the car and then make up a sentence or slogan that describes it. They could also write some specific selling points.

Reference to photocopiable sheet
Photocopiable page 136 will help the children to understand the impact the development of the motor car had on Britain. It will also give the children the opportunity to examine some of the problems and attempted solutions in detail.

Ask the children to make their own timelines tracing the development of the motor car and motoring from 1930 to the present day. They should include the introduction of road safety measures, any statistics about the numbers of deaths and injuries year by year, and the numbers of cars and other vehicles on the roads. The children could then make bar charts to show the growth of road traffic against the numbers of deaths and injuries in road accidents.

Suggestion(s) for extension
Children could investigate how many cars are made in Britain today. How many are sold here and how many are exported? They could also find out how cars were made in Britain in the 1930s, 1950s and the present day, and the role of robots and other forms of new technology.

Suggestion(s) for support
Children may need help with the preparation of their timelines. They may also need guidance about how to present information in the form of bar charts. Show the children examples of simple bar charts and explain how they work.

Assessment opportunities
After the children have completed their timelines and bar charts ask them to discuss their findings and to explain some of the events in more detail if they can.

Opportunities for IT
Children could create their own transport timelines using specific software such as ESM's *Time Traveller*, a word

ONE MAN'S WAR

To find out about one member of His Majesty's Forces during the Second World War using different sources of information, including copies of original documents, pictures and photographs.

†† *Pairs or small groups.*

🕐 *90 minutes.*

Previous skills/knowledge needed
Some experience of doing investigations using primary sources. Any general knowledge about the Second World War, especially the war against Japan, would be helpful.

The focus of this is on the war time career of Leading Aircraftsman (LAC) Frank Jackson. The children should be given some background information about the events and conduct of the war, particularly about the war in the Pacific where LAC Jackson served.

Key background information
Leading Aircraftsman (LAC) Frank Jackson came from Bolton in Lancashire. He joined up in 1941 and served as an airman during the Second World War. He kept all the papers relating to his time in the services and it is possible from this information to work out what part he played during the war in the Pacific against the Japanese. From this documentary evidence it can be seen that Frank Jackson played an important part behind the scenes during the war. He was required to service RAF aircraft in India that were used in the campaigns against the Japanese in the Burmese jungle. At one point he was involved in laying an air-strip on the

Cocos Islands in the Indian Ocean. His belongings included several notebooks about how to repair aircraft (a diagram from one of them is included on photocopiable page 137), lists of the kit he was issued with, a photograph of himself with his young daughter, a vaccination certificate and evidence for retraining for civilian life in a laundry on his return.

Preparation

Prepare one copy of photocopiable pages 137 and 138 for the children to share in pairs or small groups. Collect information books and pictures about the Second World War, include pictures of aircraft that Frank Jackson was required to repair, together with maps showing the campaigns of the Allied forces in Burma.

Resources needed

Photocopiable pages 137 and 138, books and pictures about the Second World War (especially the war in the Pacific), pictures of British fighter aircraft of that date, maps of the Pacific region and India.

What to do

Talk to the children about the war, describing some of the events. Explain that by the end of 1941 the war had spread to the Pacific region where the Japanese were fighting to gain control of new territories. The children will need to see a map of this region in order to identify the area where Frank Jackson was based. Show them pictures of the aircraft that he had to repair (such as Spitfires, Hurricanes and Lancasters) and talk about conditions for the forces overseas. In Burma, for example, they had to cope with a poor diet and a very difficult climate and environment – extreme humidity, and plagues of mosquitoes. As a result many servicemen fell ill.

Distribute photocopiable pages 137 and 138 and talk to the children about the different documents it includes. Read the sheet with the children explaining any difficult vocabulary or concepts. Then ask the children to work in small groups and use each document to extract as much information as they can about Frank Jackson. They could cut up the sheet and stick each piece of evidence onto a separate piece of paper. Each group could make a list of all the things they have found out and then write a short biography. Alternatively, they could present their findings in the form of a poster with Frank Jackson's face in the centre and radiating arrows pointing to the different things they have discovered.

Suggestion(s) for extension

Discuss other things they would like to know but have been unable to discover from the evidence. Some children may like to draw pictures based on the items included on the photocopiable sheets for example, the aircraft Frank Jackson serviced, an ENSA entertainment, some items Mrs Jackson may have knitted, some items from Frank Jackson's kit, *The Mauretania* docking at Liverpool, Frank with his daughter.

Suggestion(s) for support

Some of the documents use official language; others are handwritten. Children may need help with reading and understanding these.

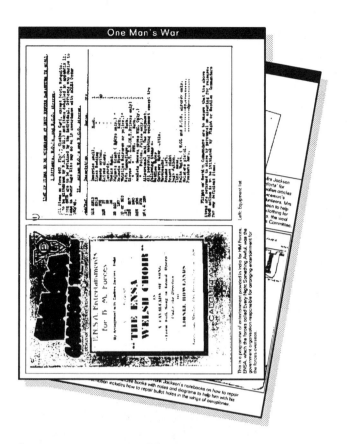

One Man's War

Assessment opportunities

The children could list the facts they have discovered based on the evidence; things which they think *might* be true; and finally, things which they cannot find out from evidence available. If they have written a short biography, this could be used to assess their précis skills and whether they have a general understanding and picture of the events.

Opportunities for IT

The children, or teacher, could use an encyclopaedia CD-ROM or photo-collection CD-ROM to look for other information on the Second World War. The children could then use a word processor to write a short bibliography about Frank Jackson from the material collated. The bibliography could be a part of a larger poster which incorporated pictures taken from CD-ROMs or scanned from books or other materials.

Display ideas

A general display entitled 'Frank Jackson's War' could be made. This would include the children's posters, written biographies and pictures they have made to illustrate some of the items from the photocopiable sheets.

Reference to photocopiable sheets

The copies of the personal documents on the photocopiable sheets will help the children to understand what the war was like for one man serving in the RAF. The children are required to use this primary source material to extract information and gain a picture of some of his war time experiences.

CITY CHILDREN EVACUATED

To learn about the evacuation of children to country areas and the effects on the children and their families.

†† *Individuals or pairs.*

🕐 *90 minutes.*

Previous skills/knowledge needed

Some experience of doing investigations using eye-witness accounts. Any general knowledge about Britain at the outbreak of the Second World War would be useful.

Key background information

The government had drawn up contingency plans for the evacuation of children from Britain's major cities to safer, country areas long before war was actually declared. In the months before war broke out, and as the threat of war became imminent, these plans were put into action. During the summer of 1939 over one and a half million children were evacuated from Britain's cities to stay with families in the country. This was because everyone expected that Germany would begin extensive bombing raids on British cities as soon as war was declared.

Most of the evacuees came from the poor districts of the cities and many of the children had never been away from their parents or home before, some had never been to the country. Some of the evacuees thought they were just going on a school day trip or a Sunday school outing, and parents had no idea where their children would be going or how long they would be separated. Despite assurances from the government that the children would be well treated many parents were desperately worried and distressed.

The families who were to look after these city children had little idea what to expect, and in many cases were shocked at their poverty and at their behaviour. Generally children did settle down and enjoyed being in the countryside with its open space and better lifestyle. However, there were others who were terribly hurt and bewildered by the experience and became dreadfully homesick.

By January 1940 the expected German bombing raids still had not happened and children started to return home. However, in September of the same year the Blitz began and Britain's biggest cities were subjected to constant serious attack. As a result, many children had to be evacuated to the country all over again.

Preparation

Collect illustrated information books and pictures of British children being evacuated to the country. It is essential to obtain a variety of eye-witness accounts, written by evacuated children, parents of evacuees and their host families.

Resources needed
Information books and pictures of evacuees, eye-witness accounts.

What to do
Talk to the children about the period just before the outbreak of war and the reasons why so many city children were evacuated to the country using the information above.

Discuss with the children what it must have been like to have been a) an evacuee, b) the parent of an evacuee and c) a member of a host family living in the country.

Read the different eye-witness accounts to the children. Explain that they have to imagine that they are either a), b) or c) and describe what they feel about what has happened to them. The children's accounts could take the form of a letter or a diary entry and their experiences could be compared.

Suggestion(s) for extension
The children could investigate the effects of the Blitz on the major cities. What safety precautions were taken? What did people do when there was an air raid? Further research could be undertaken to learn about doodlebugs and V2 rockets.

Suggestion(s) for support
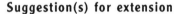
Some children may need hear the eye-witness accounts more than once. It might be helpful to make the choice of a), b) or c) for them. Explain some of the difficult words and concepts.

Assessment opportunities
The children's written accounts will reveal how much they have learned about this topic. When the accounts are complete they could be read aloud and discussed in the class.

Display ideas
The children could illustrate some elements of their written accounts, using the information books available for reference. For example, pictures of evacuees either leaving their homes or arriving in the countryside for the first time. They could create a poster showing the children boarding the trains, with their suitcases. This could then be mounted and the children's written accounts displayed alongside it.

POST-WAR RECONSTRUCTION

To learn about some of the effects of the war on Britain and what changes took place in the post-war period.
†† *Whole class or group work, then individual follow-up activity.*
🕐 *90 minutes.*

Previous skills/knowledge needed
Some knowledge of conditions in Britain before and during the Second World War would be useful. Reference should be made to the lesson plan, *Oral Evidence* on page 103, where oral history is suggested as part of a local study.

Key background information
One of the first important changes in Britain after the war was a change of government. Throughout the war years there had been an all-party coalition government led by Winston Churchill. However, following the general election of July 1945, the Labour Party swept to power in a landslide victory. The new Prime Minister was Clement Attlee who had been Deputy Prime Minister in the coalition. Churchill's defeat, so soon after leading Britain to victory in the war, astonished the world. But the result was seen as less of a personal rejection of Churchill than a clear and decisive wish for change.

The war had left Britain with a massive debt of £4,196 million; a quarter of the national wealth had been spent on the war effort. The chief task was to combat inflation and severe import restrictions were imposed. In the immediate post-war years there were shortages of nearly every commodity. Rationing continued and by 1948 it was more severe than it had been during the war. Many staple foods such as bread and potatoes were now rationed – a world food shortage was blamed. (In 1946 the Ministry of Food actually issued a recipe for squirrel pie!) People were also asked to economise on fuel by taking fewer baths and keeping the level of hot water down to 7cm when they took a bath.

The Labour Party's election slogan had been 'And Now Win the Peace' and once in power they embarked on a programme of radical social reforms. In 1942 the British economist William Beveridge published a lengthy report about poverty in Britain. He identified some main causes of suffering: disease, ignorance, want, squalor and idleness. Beveridge believed that it was the government's responsibility to help people 'from the cradle to the grave'. His report became the basis of some of Britain's most important post-war legislation.

Here are some of the major changes that took place in this period:

Housing: Many areas of Britain had suffered terrible bomb damage and about five million homes had either been damaged or destroyed. Local councils were given the go-ahead to develop large housing estates and a number of new towns developed – Telford, Harlow, Stevenage, Crawley, Cwmbran and East Kilbride. In some areas cheap emergency housing was provided. These homes were put up very quickly using prefabricated sections and were known as 'prefabs'.

Industry: The government nationalised or took control of key industries and public services including coal mines, road transport, railways, electricity and gas.

Health: In 1948 a National Health Service was introduced so that everyone could have free medical treatment from their doctor, dentist or hospital; free National Health glasses were also available. Payment for this 'free' service came from taxation and National Insurance contributions.

The British Empire: With such massive post-war debts to cope with, the responsibility of an empire had become a burden Britain could no longer afford. In 1947 India was granted independence and this was seen as the first step to Britain's abandonment of its empire in Asia and Africa.

Preparation

Collect contemporary photographs, journals, documents and video documentaries about post-war Britain. Invite grandparents, great-grandparents and any other volunteers to talk to the children about the end of the war and the conditions they experienced in the post-war period. Ask the visitors if they could bring any personal photographs, souvenirs and memorabilia to illustrate their talk. Prepare one copy of photocopiable page 139 for each child. This

Post-war reconstruction

Here is a list of questions that could be asked about life in Britain at the end of the war and the immediate post-war years, and then about life in Britain after 1950.

The end of the war and conditions in post-war Britain

What were you doing during the war?

Where were you living when the war ended?

How did you celebrate the end of the war?

Did you move house during the war or soon after the war ended?

What was rationing like and how did you manage?

Do you remember eating bananas for the first time after the war?

What do you remember about the general election of 1945?

What were the effects of the bitterly cold winter of 1947?

Please describe anything you can remember about it.

What were fashions like at this time? Did you use clothing coupons?

Can you remember having to pay for a visit to the doctor or dentist?

Did the introduction of the National Health Service make any difference to you?

If so, how?

After 1950

Did you have a radio? If so, what were your favourite programmes?

What were your favourite toys?

What can you remember about the Festival of Britain of 1951?

What books, newspapers, and comics did you read?

When did you first see television?

When did you get your first TV set?

Can you remember any early programmes on TV?

Did you see any events such as the Coronation on TV?

Did your family have a car by 1950? If not, when did they get one?

Do you remember getting your first washing machine?

How was washing done in your house before then?

---

accounts about post-war Britain. Distribute the photocopiable sheet and discuss the questions and possible answers they might expect to receive. The children may like to add some questions of their own to the sheet.

If several adults are available, the interviews could be undertaken as group work with one adult per large group. Alternatively, one or two adults could talk to the whole class before the questions are posed based on a pre-arranged schedule. Different children from each group or in the class should be allotted particular questions to ask. Other children should be assigned to take notes of specific questions while the talks and interviews are taking place. It may also be a good idea to have a tape recorder available for this part of the lesson so the children can replay the tape to check their notes and so that the interviews are available for future study.

Suggestion(s) for extension
The children may be interested to find out about conditions in their local area after the war. Was there a lot of bomb damage? Was there any post-war housing development? Were there any 'prefabs' in the area? What difference did the introduction of the National Health Service make to their family?

Suggestion(s) for support
Some children may need to listen to the tape recording of the interviews more than once before they write their accounts about post-war Britain. They may also need to look at the photographs and printed information again.

Assessment opportunities
Ask the children to describe some of the changes that took place in Britain after the war. What additional information did they discover from the interviews? Did they receive any unexpected replies to the questions?

Opportunities for IT
Children could write up their notes, taken during the interviews, using a word processor. If they start by typing in their notes they can use these as a basis for organising the information they have collected to create an account of life after the war. Children will need to know how to move text around using the 'cut and paste' or 'drag and drop' commands.

Display ideas
Put together a display based on the information the class has collected about changes in Britain after the war.

Reference to photocopiable sheet
The list of suggested questions on photocopiable page 139 is to help guide and structure the children's interviews. The questions are designed to provoke responses that the children can use in their own written work.

---

sheet contains a range of suggested questions for the children to ask. The precise questions chosen will depend upon the age(s) of the people invited. If possible give a copy of the children's questions to the visitors prior to the interviews. Have a tape recorder available to record the event. This lesson could be divided into the following:

1) topic to be introduced and discussed, and then interview questions prepared; 2) the adults talk to the children and are interviewed; 3) the children write their accounts based on the printed and oral information.

Resources needed
Photocopiable page 139, adults who remember the immediate post-war period, contemporary photographs, journals (e.g. *Picture Post*, old copies of *Radio Times*), documents (e.g. ration books), video documentaries about post-war Britain, video recorder, tape recorder, writing paper, pencils.

What to do
Discuss with the children some of the key developments that occurred at the end of the war using the information above, together with any contemporary photographs, journals, documents and video documentaries about the period.

If it has been possible to arrange for visitors to talk to the class, explain to the children that they are going to listen to some original historical evidence and then ask questions, with a view to using the information to write their own

THE CORONATION OF QUEEN ELIZABETH II 1953

To find out about the Coronation of Queen Elizabeth II using a variety of sources, and to examine the significance of the Coronation regalia.

†† *Whole class then individuals or small groups.*

🕐 *60 minutes.*

Previous skills/knowledge needed

Some knowledge of the concept of monarchy and of using eye-witness accounts will be useful.

Key background information

Princess Elizabeth was in Nairobi, Kenya on 6 February 1952 when she learned that her father King George VI had died. Although she immediately acceded to the throne her Coronation did not take place until over a year later on 2 June 1953. This was because there was so much to organise and plan. The streets of London were decorated and shop windows were full of special Coronation displays. The route of the procession from Buckingham Palace to Westminster Abbey was decorated with flowers. About 10,000 servicemen from the RAF, Army, Navy and Royal Marines marched in the procession. There were 2,000 bandsmen and 250 police horses. Overseas kings, queens, prime ministers and politicians all attended the service and took part in the procession.

Queen Elizabeth asked for the procession route to be extended so that more people, especially children, could see the event. The Queen rode in a golden state coach pulled by eight white horses. In Westminster Abbey after a long ceremony that has hardly changed for centuries, the Archbishop of Canterbury placed the crown on her head. There were 7,500 people in the Abbey, and about 25 million people watched on television in their homes or in public halls. Unfortunately, it was a cold, rainy day and many of the crowd were disappointed because the official coaches were closed up to protect the visiting dignitaries from the bad weather. But one visitor, Queen Salote of Tonga delighted the crowd by insisting on being driven in her coach with the top down so that the cheering crowds could see her clearly.

In many parts of the country there were street parties, band concerts and other celebrations taking place. In the evening most towns had more parties and firework displays.

Preparation

Prepare one copy of photocopiable page 140 for each child. Find a video that features 1953 with the Coronation and procession. There may be grandparents willing to talk about their memories of seeing the procession, watching the ceremony on television, going to street parties, etc. Collect original source materials, souvenir publications and artefacts such as a Coronation mug, programme of the day's events or newspaper reports. For the extension activity try to find photographs of the royal family in 1953 and photographs of the family today.

Resources needed

Photocopiable page 140, a video featuring the 1953 Coronation ceremony and procession, souvenirs, information books about the Coronation, photographs of the royal family in 1953 and photographs of the family today.

What to do

Watch the video of the year 1953 with the children. Ask them to pay particular attention to the Coronation service and the procession. What particularly impressed them about the day's events? Some of the children's grandparents may be willing to talk to the children about their recollections of the Coronation and how they celebrated that day. Distribute photocopiable page 140 and read the eye-witness account of the Coronation procession to the children, explaining any difficult words and concepts. Discuss the account with the children and then ask them to write their own imaginary eye-witness account of the

71

procession. Assign different children to be either a visiting foreign dignitary and to describe the service as well as their part in the procession, or to be someone in the crowd who was in London specially for the day. They should include details of the people they saw, what they heard, what they enjoyed most and what they did not enjoy. These accounts could be read out and discussed in the class and then compared with the video account. Discussion should focus on the similarities and differences between the accounts. All the people saw the same event and yet have interpreted it in a different way.

Talk to the children about the Coronation service itself. It has hardly changed for centuries. Why is this? Return to the photocopiable sheet and explain that it contains pictures of the Coronation regalia. Ask them to identify the different items and explain what they were used for or their significance in the ceremony. The children should work in pairs or small groups and use any information books available to complete their research.

Suggestion(s) for extension
Show the children photographs of the royal family as they were in 1953 and then as they are today. Discuss how they have changed. Having watched the video of the Coronation, ask the children to describe how different the TV coverage was from how events are reported today. If there was a Coronation today how would it be different?

Suggestion(s) for support
In order to write their eye-witness accounts some children may need to refer to information books and pictures to check their facts; they may also need to watch part of the video again as a reminder of the order of events. Children may need help in understanding the use and significance of some of the Coronation regalia.

Assessment opportunities
The content of the children's eye-witness accounts and subsequent contributions to the class discussion will indicate how much they have learned about this topic.

Display ideas
The children could make a large display of the state coach in which the Queen travelled on her Coronation day. They could also make their own pictures of some of the ceremonial regalia that was used in the service.

Reference to photocopiable sheet
The photocopiable sheet includes pictures of the Coronation regalia which the children have to match with their labels. The children have to select some items and, following their research, explain their significance. This activity will enable them to find out about some of the details of the Coronation ceremony that have not been changed for centuries.

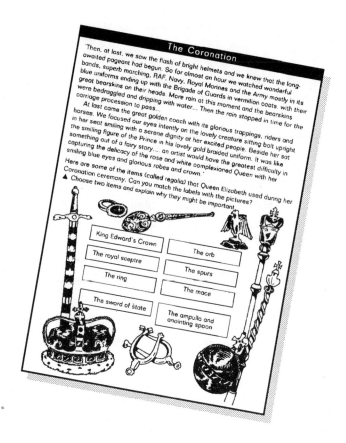

THE DEVELOPMENT OF AIRCRAFT

To place the development of the aeroplane within a chronological framework and to recognise some of the key changes that have taken place in air transport.
†† *Pairs.*
🕐 *90 minutes.*

Previous skills/knowledge needed
Some knowledge of the development of other forms of transport would be useful. Knowledge of timelines and how they are prepared.

Key background information
The main focus of this lesson is to chart the development of the aeroplane from the first powered flight by the Wright brothers to modern-day aircraft, and to include some of the most outstanding aeronautical achievements, particularly those relating to Britain. It is important that the children are helped to understand the links between each advance; how the various aircraft were modified and redesigned following each success or failure.

Here are the key developments, some of which are featured on photocopiable page 141:

1903 In America, two brothers, Orville and Wilbur Wright, develop a flying machine called the *Flyer*. The test flight lasts for 59 seconds. The craft only reaches a height of 3 metres and a distance of 260 metres. This successful experiment of a controlled powered flight is a momentous achievement that will completely revolutionise travel.

1909 Louis Blériot, a French aviator, makes the first flight across the English Channel in 37 minutes.

1914–18 Aircraft are used to drop bombs over enemy positions in the First World War. Pilots lean out of their aircraft and throw the bombs out by hand! At first they were not issued with parachutes as it was felt this might encourage cowardice.

1918 The Royal Air Force is formed. The force has more than 22,000 planes (in 1914 it only had about 270). Top speeds have increased from 90mph in 1914 to 140mph in 1918.

1919, June John Alcock and Arthur Whitten-Brown fly non-stop across the Atlantic from Newfoundland to Ireland in 16 hours 27 minutes. They are two RAF pilots who flew in a Vickers Vimy bomber. Their flight opens the way for the development of trans-Atlantic travel.

1919, August First regular international airline service begins. It operates between London and Paris and uses adapted biplane bombers from the war.

1924 The airline Imperial Airways is formed, operating a service from Britain to Canada, South Africa and later India (1926); mail is also taken on these flights. This improved communications between major countries of the British Empire.

1927 American pilot Charles Lindburgh makes the first solo non-stop flight across the Atlantic. His plane the *Spirit of St Louis* flies from New York to Paris in $33\frac{1}{2}$ hours.

1930 Amy Johnson became the first woman to fly solo from Britain to Australia. Her flight in a second-hand Gipsy Moth aeroplane takes $19\frac{1}{2}$ days.

1933 American pilot Wiley Post makes the first round-the-world solo flight. This flight in his plane called *Winnie Mae*, takes seven days, 18 hours and 49 minutes.

1941 First flight by a plane powered by a jet engine. The engine was designed by Sir Frank Whittle, a British aeronautical engineer.

1939–45 Bombers, fighter bombers and fighter planes play a vital part in the Second World War; these include bombers like the Lancaster and Wellington, fighter-bombers like the Mosquito and Typhoon and fighters like the Hurricane and Spitfire.

1944 The first British jet fighter, the *Gloster Meteor*, is used in battle.

1952 The first British jet airliner, the *Comet*, goes into service; there were some early problems with this aircraft and a modified version had to be designed. Meanwhile the initiative was lost to American aircraft manufacturers.

1969   *Concorde*, the world's first supersonic airliner makes its first flight. This was a joint British and French venture. The streamlined shape of the plane and its powerful engines enable the aircraft to travel faster than the speed of sound. The plane can carry up to 140 passengers who can now fly more quickly from London to New York.

1970   The first American 'jumbo jet' the Boeing 747, goes into service: it can carry 370 passengers.

Preparation

Prepare one copy of photocopiable page 141 for the children to share in pairs, collect a variety of books and pictures which describe the development of aircraft. There may be a parent or relative of one of the children who has collected or made model aircraft and who would be willing to talk to the children or lend models, etc.

Resources needed

Photocopiable page 141, picture books and posters, information books about the development of aircraft. Drawing paper and pencils, glue, scissors and paints.

What to do

Discuss with the children the main points of the development of aircraft; show them books and pictures of some of the key events and aircraft. Talk about some of the risks that the early pilots took and the dangers they had to face. It is important for the children to realise how quickly air travel developed – a fact that can be checked by looking at the top speeds and travel times of the various aircraft.

Photocopiable page 141 may be used as a starting point for the lesson or as a means of assessing what the children have learned. Each pair of children can be asked to identify a minimum of three different types of aircraft on the sheet from different dates. Some children may need clues to help them identify the planes from the resources available. If so, different categories could be suggested for example, one very early plane, one Second World War bomber or fighter, one jet fighter and one modern airliner.

The children could then be asked to draw and paint their aircraft to a specific size (for example, no larger than an A4 sheet of paper) and then mount it on card and cut it out. They should follow this up by writing down some of the ways in which each of the three planes is an improvement on earlier aircraft and add any further information that they know. The drawings produced by the children can then be part of a large wall display which shows the development of aircraft.

Suggestion(s) for extension

This study of flight could be extended to include much earlier attempts such as the Greek myth of Daedalus and Icarus, the ideas of Leonardo da Vinci and the Montgolfier Brothers' balloon. Alternatively, the history of flight by other sorts of aircraft could be explored, for example sea planes, helicopters and balloons (including the development of airships and Zeppelins). Some children may be interested in finding out more about some of the great early aviators and pilots such as the Wright brothers, the Red Baron and Wiley Post, and also what conditions and facilities were like for passengers on some of the early passenger airlines.

Suggestion(s) for support

Some children may need help with arranging the aircraft in chronological order. Concentrate on key features which will help the children to identify the major developments for example, the use of two pairs of wings in early aircraft (biplanes); the use of bicycle-type support wheels; aircraft powered by jet engines instead of propellers. Alternatively, help the children to identify several clearly recognisable aircraft which represent key developments in the history of aircraft manufacture.

Assessment opportunities

The children could be asked to arrange the pictures on photocopiable page 141 in chronological order to test their understanding of aircraft manufacture developments. They could be asked to use their completed timeline to describe the evolution of aircraft. This could be done either by producing a written account or by making an oral presentation to the rest of the class.

Opportunities for IT

Children could use a drawing package to make their pictures of aircraft. If this is too complicated they could create a silhouette 'spotters' guide where they draw just the outline from the side and below. This will involve the use of different shapes and fill commands to colour the aircraft black. It is important that children create closed shapes so that the colour does not 'leak' out and fill the whole drawing area. Alternatively, the children could either use dedicated timeline software such as Soft Teach Educational's *Timelines*, or create a vertical timeline using a word processor or desk top publishing package. Smaller versions of the silhouette outlines of the aircraft, scaled down using the drawing software, could be incorporated into the timeline.

Display ideas

Some children could try making a mobile of the different kinds of aircraft with the earliest aircraft at the top and later developments below. Alternatively, they could produce a large poster of the timeline based on photocopiable page 141 for the classroom wall. This could incorporate examples of other aircraft that the children have investigated. All the children's work on this topic, including their paintings of aircraft, could make up a large classroom display.

Reference to photocopiable sheet

Photocopiable page 141 can be given to the children with or without dates. The sheet can be used either to begin the topic or as a means of assessing what the children have learned. Children should be asked to place the aircraft in chronological order and to describe the main points of how flight has developed since the time of the Wright Brothers.

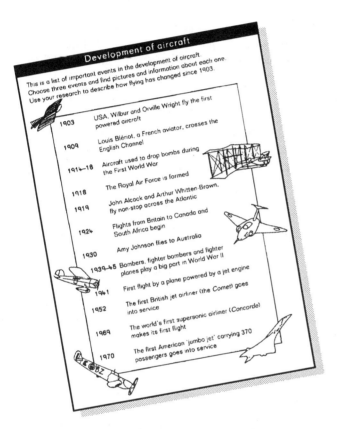

CHANGES IN HOW WE DO OUR SHOPPING

To learn about some of the features of shopping in the days before supermarkets and to compare them with shopping today.

†† *Whole class then group activity, followed by class discussion.*

🕐 *60 minutes.*

Previous skills/knowledge needed

Some knowledge of how food was sold in traditional grocer's shops in the 1950s and some experience of role-play would be useful.

Key background information

The first supermarkets opened in the late 1950s and were fiercely opposed by traditional retail shop owners who felt the competition was unfair and that they might go out of business. Their fears were completely justified because the arrival of the supermarket meant the end of trading for many small, local food shops. They could not provide the variety of items for sale that were available in supermarkets and, more importantly, they could not compete with the cheaper prices that supermarkets were able to offer.

Traditional grocery stores were present in all towns throughout the first half of the twentieth century. Some of these were locally owned, others were chain stores owned by national firms such as Home and Colonial, International Stores, Sainsburys and Liptons. The Co-operative Wholesale Society also followed this system before they, like Sainsburys, went over to the supermarket system. Central to the retail trade in traditional stores was the idea that customers did not serve themselves, but were waited on by assistants. There was a separation of food into sections, so

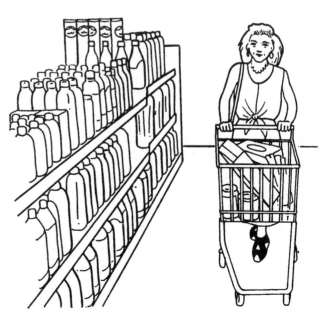

the individual shopper had to queue at a number of counters in the same shop where assistants would serve the required items. The shoppers would receive a record of what they had purchased and finally pay for all their purchases at a cash desk.

In the 1940s and 1950s packaging was on a much smaller scale than in supermarkets today. Dry goods such as brown sugar and dried fruit might be wrapped in sugar paper or sold in paper bags, while greasy items would be wrapped in greaseproof paper. Far fewer goods were sold prepacked. Cooked meats, bacon and cheese would always be cut using special slicing or cutting equipment and then weighed, wrapped and handed to the customer.

Preparation

Prepare one copy of photocopiable page 142 for the children to share in groups of five or six. Find pictures of some old style grocery stores, alternatively there may be local people who could help to reconstruct how the system was organised. Collect illustrated information books about early food stores and traditional ways of shopping. Collect pictures of early food packaging, selecting items and brands that are still sold in supermarkets today. Prepare facsimiles of pre-decimal notes and coins for use in the role-play. Prepare a simple chart which explains the relative values of the old money together with the Imperial system of weights and measures.

Resources needed

Photocopiable page 142, information books and photographs about traditional food stores, pictures showing early packaging of some food items, facsimile copies of pre-decimal notes and coins, sugar paper, felt-tipped pens, small recycled cardboard boxes, glue, scissors.

What to do

The majority of children today will be familiar with the weekly shopping expedition to a large supermarket such as Tesco, Asda, Safeways, Kwik-Save and Sainsbury's. We take for granted the self-service supermarket, in which customers are expected to select the items they wish to buy from the shelves and load up their baskets or trolleys, ready for payment at a checkout. Describe to the children what shopping in a traditional food store was like using the information above. Show pictures and photographs of some of these stores and discuss some of the details. Then ask the children to point out some of the differences between the traditional stores and supermarkets today. Are there any similarities?

Show the children pictures of some early food packaging. (A useful source of information is the Robert Opie Collection at the Museum of Advertising and Packaging, Gloucester.) Do the children recognise the brands? How has the packaging changed? Divide the children into groups of four

and tell them that they should cover two cardboard boxes with sugar paper and then draw a copy of the packaging on the outside of each box. These packets will be used in the next activity.

Explain to the children that they are now going to role-play the old style grocery shopping of 40 years ago and earlier. Divide the class into groups. Each group of five or six could be divided into shop assistants and customers. (Both groups will need to have some 'money' for this activity.) The customers will need to make out shopping lists of items they want to buy to feed a family of four. The shop assistants will need to list all items they would expect to sell. They should then consider how they will divide the groceries into logical categories for each counter for example, all the fats and dairy products (lard, butter, cheese and bacon) together. Children will need to think about dried goods which would often have been sold wholesale by the gross (hence the term grocer), such as sugar, flour, porridge oats, semolina, rice, dried fruits, tea and coffee. Many of these goods would have been weighed out for the customer according to their requirements. Fresh fruit and vegetables would have been sold by a greengrocer in a separate shop. Similarly, bread was sold in bakers' shops until the coming of packaged sliced bread in the 1950s. Can the children suggest some commodities that would not be available for purchase then?

Distribute photocopiable page 142 and explain to the children that it includes a number of items that were sold in a 1950s grocer's shop. Talk to the children about the different items and point out that they have been priced according to the old monetary system of pounds, shillings and pence at 1950s prices. The children should use the information on the sheet to make comparisons with how the items are sold in present day shops and supermarkets. They should look at weights, prices and packaging. Do they recognise any of the brands?

Suggestion(s) for extension

The commodities on sale should be priced using the old system of pounds, shilling and pence and weighed using pounds and ounces. This could form a useful mathematical exercise of comparing old and present day prices and weights. Some children could look at the commodities in terms of where they came from in the former British Empire. They could begin with a map of the Empire and identify likely food imports from each country. Some children may be interested in looking at how packaging has changed over the decades for specific food items. What are the main differences?

Suggestion(s) for support

Some children may need help with the pre-decimal notes and coins and the imperial weights and measures. Refer the children to the chart and explain the names and values of the money and the different weights. Children may also need help in grouping the different food items in the 'shops'. These children should refer to the available reference material and their knowledge of how food is grouped in modern supermarkets.

Assessment opportunities

The children could be asked to identify the main differences between supermarket shopping today and the traditional grocery store. Ask them to say why they think that supermarkets have been so successful.

Opportunities for IT

The children could create a spreadsheet in the form of a shopping list which automatically works out the costs of a number of items, and even converts the answers into decimal currency. The spreadsheet might use the following pattern:

Children should also have an opportunity to discuss the use of technology in the modern supermarket, the use of bar-codes, stock control and the latest introduction of shopping cards where the supermarket can monitor what different customers purchase each week. Children could use some actual till receipts and try to decide what sort of people or families bought the goods shown. They might also discuss the idea of data protection.

Display ideas

Make a display of a traditional grocer's shop window or shop interior. Use the children's packets to fill the 'shelves'.

Reference to photocopiable sheet

The photocopiable sheet contains a number of items that would have been on sale in a grocer's shop in the 1950s. The information about the items will help the children to understand how shopping has changed over the recent decades. They will also learn about how goods were weighted and sold, and differences in prices.

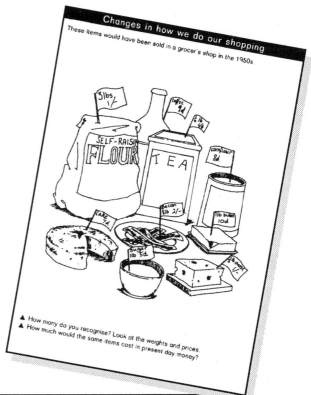

	1	2	3	4	Total
a	Item	sugar	butter	potatoes	
b	Cost	2d	3.5d	.5d	
c	Number	1	2	10	
d	Total	b2 × c2	b3 × c3	b4 × c4	sum (d2, d4)
e	decimal money	d2/2.4	d3/2.4	d4/2.4	sum (e2, e4)

BROADCASTING IN SOUND AND VISION

To describe the development and the impact of radio and television broadcasting.

†† *Whole class then individuals.*

🕐 *90 minutes.*

Previous skills/knowledge needed

Research skills, some knowledge of home entertainment in earlier periods would be helpful.

Key background information:

The first radio was invented by an Italian physicist called Guglielmo Marconi. He successfully transmitted radio signals across the Atlantic in 1901. His invention completely revolutionised communication and transformed home entertainment. Radio stations first started broadcasting in the 1920s but the signals were so weak that listeners had to wear large headphones containing loudspeakers in order to hear the broadcasts. The BBC was formed in 1922 and the first news bulletin was broadcast in November of that year. The programme was an extremely formal affair, the newsreaders actually wore full evening dress to read the news!

In the 1930s and 1940s radios, or wireless sets, worked off large batteries that had to be recharged when they ran down. This was because until the 1940s not every house was supplied with mains electricity. These radios sometimes had a separate loudspeaker which was usually shaped like a horn. By 1939 most households owned a radio but there were only two stations and both were controlled by the BBC. The radio became a vital source of information and entertainment for families during the Second World War. Everyone in Britain would try and listen to the latest news reports. Hitler even used the radio to try and undermine British morale by broadcasting programmes of pro-Nazi propaganda and bogus accounts of German successes in battles. The radio also provided much needed entertainment with a variety of music, drama, adventure serials and comedy shows. Children would listen to *Children's Hour*, a programme of stories, poems and songs for young children.

The 1920s also saw the first experiments with television. In 1924 John Logie Baird, a Scottish engineer, demonstrated the first television image, the flickering shape of a Maltese Cross. In 1926 he demonstrated moving objects on television. After a lengthy struggle, Baird persuaded the BBC to set up the first television 'service' using their transmitters. His first broadcast was in September 1929. Progress was swift and by 1936 the BBC broadcast the first high definition television programme. They had a very small audience as there were only about one hundred television sets in the

country at this time. Very few people could afford one as they cost about the same as a small car. These first televisions had tiny screens (about 15cm wide), but they were set within huge cabinets because they had so many large parts compared with sets today.

Television broadcasts were suspended during the war years but since then broadcasting has developed rapidly. Television became so popular in the 1960s that other forms of public entertainment suffered a sharp decline. The cinema was seriously threatened by television and many closed down, changing over to other uses such as Bingo halls. Theatres were also affected, and many people stopped listening to the radio in preference to seeing, as well as hearing, their programmes.

Preparation

Collect pictures of some of the first radio and television sets together with some of the first advertisements so children can learn about their various special selling points. Find books about the first radio and television broadcasts including the experiments of Marconi and Baird. Old copies of the *Radio Times* and information about popular radio and television programmes and personalities of the period would also be useful.

Resources needed

Pictures of the first radio and TV sets, advertisements of the first radios and televisions, information books about early radio and TV broadcasting, old copies of the *Radio Times*, information about popular radio and TV programmes of the period, cardboard boxes of different sizes, pencils, paint, scissors, glue.

What to do

Discuss the early attempts to broadcast radio and television programmes and the achievements of Marconi and Baird using the information above. Talk to the children about the role of the radio during the war and the sorts of programmes that were popular. Show the children pictures and advertisements of the first radio and television sets, and copies of early editions of the *Radio Times*, if available. Ask the children to compare these early sets with the sets we can buy today. How have they changed? Talk about some of the first television programmes. How do they compare with favourite programmes today? Then discuss the impact of television on other forms of entertainment. Why did television become so popular?

Using the information provided above and any available pictures, television magazines and books ask the children to prepare a timeline showing the main events in the development of radio and television broadcasting up to the present day. They should include examples of popular programmes if possible.

The children could then work in groups and using

cardboard boxes make simple models of the first radio and television sets. Some children could also make posters to advertise some of the early popular radio and television programmes.

Suggestion(s) for extension

Some children may be interested to find out more about some of the first children's television programmes. Who were the stars? Why were these programmes popular? Other children may like to prepare a radio script for a news bulletin that would be broadcast during the war. They should remember the formal presentation style of these broadcasts and also the need to include some 'lighter' news stories as well as reports about the war itself.

Suggestion(s) for support

Some children may need help with sorting information to prepare their timelines. A list of the most important dates in the development of broadcasting could be prepared for them to help guide and structure their research. The children may also need help with the research and writing of their news bulletins. Explain the formal style and some of the language that would be used in these early reports. Provide the children

with a short list of news items that they could adapt and include in their reports.

Assessment opportunities

The results of the children's timelines will show how much they have learned and understood about this topic. Have the children included all the main events in their lists?

Opportunities for IT

The children could either use dedicated timeline software such as ESM's *Time Traveller*, or create a vertical timeline using a word processor, desktop publishing or drawing package. A larger class timeline could be created using different styles of television sets as a frame for writing about each aspect of the timeline. The written part could be displayed on the screen of the television set. The children could also use CD-ROMs to search for other information about television and the history of broadcasting pictures.

Display ideas

The children's timelines, models and posters could make a classroom display about the development of radio and TV broadcasting.

PACKAGE HOLIDAYS TO EUROPE

To learn about the development of package holidays to the European Continent.

†† *Whole class then pairs.*

🕐 *90 minutes.*

Previous skills/knowledge needed

Map reading skills.

Key background information

In the 1930s taking a holiday was a luxury that few families could afford. Those that could afford to would mostly go to a British seaside resort for a week or go on day trips to the coast or into the country. (The Youth Hostel Association was founded in 1930 and the first Butlins holiday camp opened in 1936 in Skegness, Lincolnshire.) Travel abroad was extremely expensive so it was mainly the rich and famous

who could afford to go. After the war Britain's economy improved and this, together with the development of faster and safer passenger planes, brought a gradual change and more people began to travel overseas.

In 1957 some British people started to go to Spain on holiday and thanks to a favourable exchange rate were not only able to buy cheap food and wine but were also able to buy land and holiday homes in places like the Costa Brava. This period also saw the development of the package holiday. This is the idea of buying an all-in holiday where the price includes both fares and accommodation. In the 1950s people were able to buy a 'package' which included travel by coach to the Continent plus all meals and accommodation. At the time most of the Continent was beginning to recover from the turmoil and destruction of the war and many people from Britain were able to go abroad for the first time in their lives. People like Mr and Mrs Woods who are featured in this lesson had not travelled to the Continent before because of the war and the cost involved. But the relative cheapness of the package tour in which everything was organised for them at an inclusive price made this possible.

Preparation

Prepare one copy of photocopiable page 143 for the children to share in pairs. The cost of Mr and Mrs Woods' holiday tour was 40 guineas. (The children will need to be told that 1 guinea is the equivalent of £1 1shilling and then helped to work out the total cost of the trip in old money). Find atlases which show clearly the main places in the Woods' itinerary. Collect a variety of present day travel brochures which feature package holidays, including coach tours.

Resources needed

Photocopiable page 143, atlases of Europe, travel brochures, tracing paper, drawing paper, felt-tipped pens, pencils.

What to do

Discuss with the children what holidays were like in the 1930s and subsequent decades, placing particular emphasis on the changes in the 1950s and the development of package holidays and tours. Stress how novel it was in the 1950s for people to go abroad on holiday, and explain that Europe started to become a popular holiday destination as it recovered from the Second World War and as people began to feel better off.

Distribute photocopiable page 143 and explain to the children that it is a copy of part of the diary that Mr Woods kept throughout his holiday. It names all the places his wife and he visited and what they experienced at each one. Arrange for the children to have access to a map showing France and Spain. Read through the photocopiable sheet with the children and explain any difficult vocabulary. Tell the children that they have to trace an outline of France and Spain and then transfer their tracing on to drawing paper. Then, using the information on the photocopiable page and an atlas, they should draw in the route taken by the Woods' coach and include the principal places mentioned in Mr Woods' diary.

With the help of the photocopiable sheet, ask the children to find out all the things that Mr and Mrs Woods found particularly interesting and enjoyable on their tour. What did they dislike or find disappointing? The children could make two columns on a sheet of paper and list both categories.

Suggestion(s) for extension
Ask the children to look at the present day travel brochures. What are the main differences between Mr and Mrs Woods' holiday and those offered in the brochures? What type of holidays are there in present day travel brochures that were not available in the 1950s? Ask the children to find out what other sorts of holidays became popular in the 1950s and 1960s. (More and more people had their own cars, camping in Europe became more popular and there was an increased number in passenger flights available to a greater variety of destinations.)

Suggestion(s) for support
Some children may need help in finding the places on a map of Europe that the Woods visited. Go through the photocopiable sheet and make a list of the main places and the countries that the children have to locate. This could also act as a check list for other children to use. Others may need help in identifying the positive and negative aspects which Mr and Mrs Woods encountered on their tour. They may also need help with some of the vocabulary on the photocopiable sheet.

Assessment opportunities
Ask the children how they think travel and holidays have changed over the past four decades. Can they describe some of the main differences between Mr and Mrs Woods' tour and the equivalent holiday today?

Opportunities for IT
Children could use a word processor or desktop publishing package to create their own holiday brochures, either for the 1950s or the current time. They could use pictures taken from CD-ROMs or scanned from their own holiday photographs or postcards. The children could be introduced to a range of formatting commands to lay out the page in an interesting way. Alternatively, children could use a clipart map of Europe in a drawing package and identify the most popular holiday destinations of the 1950 and 1990s. Information about each destination could be laid out in boxes and then arranged around the map with lines linking the boxes to the correct positions on the map.

Display ideas
The children could make a large map and record on it, either by using simple drawings, symbols or brief written notes, some of the things that happened at various places on the holiday. This could be contrasted with the range and variety of tours on offer today: fast travel by jet, the Chunnel, opportunities to visit more distant places such as America or the Far East, activity holidays, etc.

Reference to photocopiable sheet
The children have to use the photocopiable sheet to extract information to complete their maps showing the route of the Woods' tour. They also have to select and list what the Woods liked and disliked about the places they visited.

EXPLORING SPACE

To place the key events of space exploration within a chronological framework.

†† *Pairs.*

🕐 *60 minutes or more, depending upon how the topic is developed.*

Previous skills/knowledge needed

Research skills and work on timelines.

Key background information

Many ancient peoples took a great interest in space and believed their gods lived among the stars. Stonehenge, built about 3,500 years ago, is thought to have been a centre where detailed observations of the sun, moon and stars were made. The ancient Greeks began scientific astronomy and made accurate observations of the moon, planets and stars. They used their observations to conclude that the earth was round. Aristarchus of Miletus actually proposed that the earth moved round the sun. This was confirmed in the seventeenth century when the great Italian scientist Galileo, using the newly invented telescope, confirmed that the earth as well as the other planets revolved around the sun.

The development of the radio telescope made it possible for scientists to probe deeper into space. These telescopes pick up a variety of different radio waves and computers turn their signals into pictures and maps. As astronomers and scientists became increasingly aware of the severe limitations of their earth based telescopes, so orbiting satellites were developed as observatories.

Scientists know a great deal about the moon because it is nearest to Earth but also as a result of the Russian and American space projects. In the 1950s and 1960s a space 'race' developed between the two countries and space exploration became inextricably tied to political prestige. Later this rivalry became closely linked to military strategy. The Russian and American space shuttle vehicles were mainly designed to put spy satellites into orbit and service them.

The following timeline includes the major events in the exploration of space:

1955   Radio telescope completed at Jodrell Bank.

1957   Russians launch an artificial satellite, *Sputnik 2*, carrying a dog (Laika) into space.

1958   USA launches an artificial satellite, *Explorer 1*.

1959   Russia launches *Luna 3*, it reaches the moon, circles it and takes photographs of the far side.

1961   Russian, Yuri Gagarin becomes first man to make a space flight around the Earth, it takes 108 minutes.

1963   Russian, Valentina Tereshkova becomes first woman in space, she completes 48 revolutions of the Earth.

1965   USA, *Mariner 4* reaches Mars, takes close up photographs showing surface craters, atmosphere (mostly carbon dioxide).

1969   Americans Neil Armstrong and Edwin Aldrin aboard *Apollo 11* became first men to land on and walk on the moon.

1974   USA, *Mariner 10* reaches Mercury and sends back photographs.

1976   Russian, *Venera 9* reaches Venus, transmits photographs of conditions, surface temperature recorded at 485°C.

1979   USA, *Voyager 1* flies near Jupiter and relays information about atmosphere and rings.

1979   USA, *Pioneer 11* flies near Saturn photographing and measuring.

1980   USA, first of new series of nine *Intelsat 5* satellites launched. Largest communications satellite to date, capable of relaying 12,000 telephone calls and two colour TV programmes.

1981   USA launches *Columbia* shuttle, first re-usable spacecraft.

1986	USA, *Voyager* probe flies to Uranus and sends photographs showing a featureless surface.
1990	USA, the Hubble telescope, weighing 11 tonnes, is launched into orbit as the world's largest space telescope.
1991	First British astronaut in space, Helen Sharman, joins US mission.
1994-5	Russian, Dr. Valeriy Poliakov spends 437 days in space, most of it in the space station, *Mir*.
1995	USA, space probe descends to surface of Jupiter.

Preparation

Prepare one copy of photocopiable page 144 for the children to share in pairs. Collect books about space exploration, pictures of early telescopes and radio telescopes together with examples of the information they produce. Find relevant passages in *War of the Worlds* by H. G. Wells. Collect pictures and information about key spacecraft, pictures of weather and communications satellites, cosmonauts, astronauts, photographs of the Earth from space and different planets taken from space.

Resources needed

Photocopiable page 144, information books about space exploration, photographs and pictures of early telescopes, radio telescopes and examples of the information they produce, pictures and photographs of some key spacecraft, pictures of some satellites in space (weather, communications), cosmonauts/astronauts, photographs of the earth and different planets taken from space, a copy of *War of the Worlds* by H. G. Wells, scissors, paper, pencils, felt-tipped pens, glue, recycled cardboard.

What to do

Talk to the children about space exploration using the information above. Then read to the children some relevant passages from *War of the Worlds* by H. G. Wells. Discuss some of the fictional ideas that bear some similarity to actual events and developments in space exploration. In the 1950s, a popular comic *The Eagle* serialised the adventures of Dan Dare who visited Venus and other planets. Television and radio also serialised space adventures. The children may also like to talk about some features of their favourite science fiction television programmes or films.

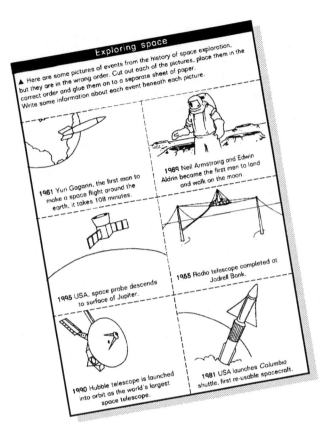

Exploring space

▲ Here are some pictures of events from the history of space exploration, but they are in the wrong order. Cut out each of the pictures, place them in the correct order and glue them on to a separate sheet of paper. Write some information about each event beneath each picture.

1961 Yuri Gagarin, the first man to make a space flight around the earth, it takes 108 minutes.

1969 Neil Armstrong and Edwin Aldrin became the first men to land and walk on the moon.

1995 USA, space probe descends to surface of Jupiter.

1955 Radio telescope completed at Jodrell Bank.

1990 Hubble telescope is launched into orbit as the world's largest space telescope.

1981 USA launches Columbia shuttle, first re-usable spacecraft.

Show the children some pictures and illustrated books about space exploration including those events that appear on photocopiable page 144. It is important to stress that since the 1950s our knowledge of space has increased by leaps and bounds. Distribute the photocopiable sheet and explain to the children that they are going to cut up the pictures and place them in chronological order. They should glue the pictures onto paper and then write some extra information beneath each one. Some children may need to refer to the pictures and books about this topic.

Suggestion(s) for extension

Children could investigate some of the information that has been relayed to us from space and also some of the benefits of space exploration. Examples include the growth of micro-electronics stimulated by the use of more compact computers in spacecraft; satellites orbiting the Earth relay pictures of the weather, including vital monitoring of weather systems such as hurricanes; communications satellites relay telephone calls and television programmes; other satellites study and observe the Earth and take photographs and measurements and relay the information back. Some children may be interested in researching some of the planets in our solar system and the information we have learned about them as a result of recent space exploration.

Suggestion(s) for support

Some children may need help with arranging the events on photocopiable page 144 in chronological order. They could paste their pictures on to a sheet marked with equal spaces to represent each decade since 1950.

Assessment opportunities

Children could discuss in general some of the key events included in their timelines. They could then talk in more detail about one or two events that have particularly impressed or interested them.

Opportunities for IT

The children could use encyclopaedias, or dedicated Space CD-ROM to research information. If the school has access to the Internet they could look for information from the NASA pages, where there are up-to-date pictures from space and details of current space missions. The children could either use dedicated timeline software such as ESM's *Time Traveller* software, or create a timeline using a word processor, desktop publishing or drawing package. They could also create a multi-media presentation about space using authoring software. Different groups of children could research specific aspects of space exploration and present their information using text, pictures and sounds.

Display ideas

Children could illustrate their timelines with pictures of some of the spacecraft or planets that they have included. They may also like to prepare large pictures of some of the planets in our solar system and models of some of the spacecraft that feature in their timelines.

Reference to photocopiable sheet

The photocopiable sheet will help the children to place some of the events in the history of space exploration in the correct chronological order.

BRITAIN AND THE EUROPEAN COMMUNITY

To learn why the European Community was established and the reasons for Britain deciding to join in 1973.

†† *Whole class then individual or group activity.*

🕐 *90 minutes.*

Previous skills/knowledge needed

Some knowledge of events in Europe at the end of the Second World War, map reading skills, research skills.

Key background information

At the end of the Second World War Europe was bankrupt and in chaos. The USA was left as the universal creditor nation, in a position of unparalleled economic dominance. Many Europeans feared the military strength of Russia on the one hand and disliked having to rely on the USA on the other. European leaders were therefore determined that

Europe should become a united force and never again be torn apart by war.

A Frenchman called Jean Monnet formed an 'Action Committee for the creation of the United States of Europe', but he was opposed by Britain. At this time Britain felt a strong loyalty and allegiance to the countries of the British Empire. Although many of these countries had become independent and others were seeking their freedom, Britain had received massive support from them throughout the war. Now that the war was over, Britain could not abandon these countries and join the European Group.

In 1952, six European counties decided to go it alone: France, Italy, West Germany, Belgium, Luxembourg and the Netherlands. First they created the European Coal and Steel Community, and then, by the Treaty of Rome in 1957, established the European Economic Community, or Common Market, which enabled the member countries to trade freely with each other. Britain was invited to join both these organisations but declined. But by the 1960s, Britain realised that a better future lay with Europe and not with the Commonwealth countries. Britain applied to join the EEC in 1961 and again in 1967 but was turned down on both occasions. This was because the French President General de Gaulle was bitterly opposed to Britain's membership. He felt that Britain was too closely tied to the USA to be a genuinely committed part of any European Community.

Britain finally joined the EEC in 1973 (de Gaulle had died in 1970), along with Ireland and Denmark. Since then other countries have joined and still more have applied to do so. British voters, in addition to voting for MPs to represent them in Parliament, now also elect MEPs to represent them in the European Parliament in Strasbourg. Meanwhile, there are plans since the Treaty of Maastricht in 1991 for the EU to move even closer to the original idea of a United States of Europe, whereby member countries retain many national traditions and powers but share many other aspects of government.

The 1991 Maastricht Treaty represents the single, most important development in the history of the EU. It set out in detail a timetable for economic and monetary union to be introduced by the end of the century. This included a common currency (the Euro) as well as social legislation. It also provided for common foreign and defence policies. Britain has opted out of some of these developments.

The biggest challenge facing the EU is its proposed enlargement from 15 to possibly as many as 27 countries. Many changes to a system originally created for six members will be necessary, if the EU is to function effectively in the early twenty-first century. Former communist countries of Eastern and Central Europe that have returned to democratic government, such as the Czech Republic and Poland, are among those that hope to join in the near future.

Preparation

Prepare one copy of photocopiable page 145 for each child. Find a recent map showing the countries of Europe as they are today. Contact the office of your local MEP who may

provide some additional information about the EU and the European Parliament. Collect information books about the establishment and organisation of the EU, the member countries and their flags.

Resources needed
Photocopiable page 145, a recent map of Europe, information books about the EU and the member countries, pictures of the flags of the member countries, plain paper, scissors, felt-tipped pens or coloured pencils.

What to do
Discuss with the children the reasons for the creation of the EU using the information above. Explain that the present EU is a voluntary association. Discuss with the children Britain's initial reluctance to join and then the reasons for joining in 1973. Show the children a map of Europe and point out the six original member countries and name them. Then point out the other members by name.

Distribute photocopiable page 145 and explain that the children are going to colour code all the current EU countries on the map according to the year they joined. The children could then draw and colour the flags and write the country name beneath each one together with the year they joined the EU.

The children may find it easier to write a number for each country on the map and write a numbered key to the countries' names. The children will need to refer to reference books and other material to research and check the country names, flags and joining dates.

Suggestion(s) for extension
Find out which other countries are currently applying to join the European Union. How will the map need to be redrawn then? What future changes are planned and being currently debated (notably the introduction of a common currency)?

Suggestion(s) for support
Children may need some help with locating the countries of the EU on the map. They could be given a map with the outlines of the member countries marked on and given a key to the map with a numbered list of the names. The children then write the numbers on their maps.

They could also record some information about each EU country alongside their map for example, the capital and populations of each. They will need to refer to maps and information books to complete this activity.

Assessment opportunities
Children should be asked to explain the reasons for the formation of the EU. Can they explain why Britain was slow in becoming a member? Why did Britain finally decide to join? What are the aims of the EU? How is it likely to develop in the future?

Opportunities for IT
The children could make a visual presentation of the EU using a map of Europe imported into a drawing package. The different countries can be coloured and labelled, and interesting information added around the edge of the map.

Alternatively, they could use multi-media authoring software allowing different groups of children to research different information about each of the countries in the EU. This might include details about the flag, population, capital city, date of entry, main industries, famous people, etc. Children could even add sound effects such as the country's national anthem sampled from an appropriate audio CD-ROM.

Display ideas
Children could work on a large map showing all the EU countries for display. They could choose symbols for example, famous buildings, national costume, particular foods, etc. to represent each country pictorially on their map. They could also gather facts and figures about each of the countries. Introduce one or two key phrases written in the different languages of the EU countries.

Reference to photocopiable sheet
Work on the photocopiable sheet will help the children to become familiar with maps of Europe and the names and flags of the members of the EU.

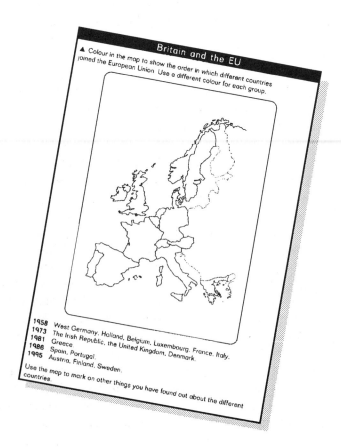

Britain and the EU

▲ Colour in the map to show the order in which different countries joined the European Union. Use a different colour for each group.

1958 West Germany, Holland, Belgium, Luxembourg, France, Italy.
1973 The Irish Republic, the United Kingdom, Denmark.
1981 Greece.
1986 Spain, Portugal.
1995 Austria, Finland, Sweden.

Use the map to mark on other things you have found out about the different countries.

Local history

The three aspects of local history which appear in this Study Unit are:

a) one aspect taken over a long period of time;

b) one aspect taken over a short period, or the local community's involvement in a particular event in history;

c) one aspect that illustrates developments taught in the Study Units.

Opportunities for studying aspects of local history will be readily accessible if schools are located in areas which have a long history as represented in the local housing, the existence of an ancient church, public houses and other old buildings. Most English villages have an Anglo-Saxon origin and thus have a history which spans more than a thousand years. Other schools built in the early years of this century or in the Victorian period will themselves provide evidence of the past (the physical structure as well as log books and attendance registers). The local community will also be able to supply an abundance of relevant documentation, the most obvious being street directories and census data. However, many schools will be situated in localities where the involvement with past events may be less obvious at first. For example, an enormous number of schools have been built to serve housing estates which developed in the post-war years. The intention of this chapter is to provide a framework which can be used by teachers to 'unpack' the history of their local area, using the kind of source material available in most parts of Britain.

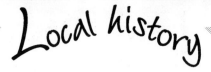
An aspect of the local community over a long period of time

A method of demonstrating this could be the organising of a pageant which would have the virtue of linking together different periods of time (including those which feature in the previous Study Units), and of involving more than one class. A further benefit would be to link with the local community in ways which would promote an interest in the history of the area: this activity would emphasise Key Elements: Chronology 1a/b and Historical enquiry 4a/b using artefacts, pictures, photographs, music, buildings and ancient sites as appropriate.

This activity could involve the whole school with each class being assigned a different period to investigate. The pageant could be as long as desired, stretching from prehistoric times to the twentieth century. Sources of information may appear to be very thin, especially for the earliest periods, but a few clues together with relevant secondary sources will enable an authentic reconstruction to be made and this will provide a framework for play writing, re-creation of appropriate artefacts, costumes, etc.

An alternative to the idea of a pageant is a series of wall paintings and collages which could be made and displayed in the school in the form of a timeline. Included in this display could be a series of maps and/or models of the local area which is an effective way of showing change and continuity over a period of time.

Each of the lesson plans and photocopiable sheets in this chapter will help teachers to explore one period in the development of their local area, suggesting some possible themes to develop within that period and providing sources of information to use.

With the exception of the first two lesson plans the emphasis is upon more recent local history. The source material for these periods is generally accessible in public libraries and record offices and is mostly straightforward to read. With the aid of street directories, census material and Ordnance Survey maps which show historical sites, the children will begin to appreciate the massive changes that have taken place within their local area. Though some may complain that they have no castle or ancient battle site near their school, every school is situated in a place which had an earlier history of its own and it is the intention of these lesson plans to help teachers to access this past.

An aspect of the local community during a short period of time or the local community's involvement in a particular event

One way of approaching this aspect of local history would be to choose a local area that is known to have undergone enormous changes over a specific period of time for example, over two decades. The area of study could either be close to the school or be a district of the nearest local town or city. Study should focus on those changes that have had the most far-reaching effects on the local community which the children could investigate. For example, the construction of motorways or major road systems which has involved the demolition of property and dislocation of established communities, or the development of modern housing estates. The children could use a variety of sources in this study such as street directories, which show how the population has changed year by year and provides evidence of changes to the shops and other commercial enterprises in the district. Ordnance Survey maps could be studied and local residents interviewed to provide first-hand accounts of change.

The second approach would be to investigate the history of a particular long-established local festival. This could form the focus for an historical project which traces the origin of the festival and the changes that have taken place over recent years. The local museum and local newspaper will be able to provide photographs and detailed information about the history and development of the event.

An aspect of the local community that illustrates developments taught in the Study Units

A local study which is linked to Study Unit 1, could involve the compilation of a data base (including computerised information put together by the class), for the area around the school during the period from the prehistoric Iron Age to the Norman Conquest. A variety of sources of information could be investigated such as the Ordnance Survey Map of Roman Britain which records the grid references for Romano-British sites. Local museums will also have maps and records to help identify local historic sites.

If this period is studied in the Local History Study Unit, care should be taken to identify a geographical area that is large enough to provide a sufficient quantity of information for the children to investigate. A school that is located within the area covered by Danelaw would be well situated for the study of settlement patterns represented by the Viking settlers as well as by the Romans and Anglo-Saxons.

A visit to a stately home could provide the focus for a local study linked with the Tudor or Victorian periods. Such a choice should provide archival as well as physical evidence for study. The Victorian period will offer an abundance of archival material for local study in addition to surviving buildings from the period.

Many of the lesson plans in this chapter show in detail how different kinds of source material can be used in the classroom. Industrial sites, as well as housing from the nineteenth century will often be available for study in conjunction with maps, street directories and census returns. Houses and shops can be studied for the changes that have taken place in occupancy or use over the decades since the Victorian times and up to the present day.

The development of a particular area may be traced from the Domesday Book right up to the present day; the opportunities for this type of study are manifold.

PREHISTORIC AND ROMAN SITES

To use local maps and information to identify and locate evidence of early settlements from the prehistoric period to the early fifth century AD.

✝✝ *Small groups then class discussion.*

🕐 *60 minutes then short time for class discussion.*

Previous skills/knowledge needed

Map reading skills including knowledge of map symbols and keys. Some knowledge of the type of settlements made by prehistoric peoples and the Romans would be useful.

Key background information

Evidence of early settlement in the area where the school is situated may be found in a variety of places. Here are some possible ways of finding out about the location of prehistoric and Roman sites. Obtain copies of Ordnance Survey 2cm to 1km sheets (formerly the 1 inch to the mile series, now referred to as the *Landranger* series). The Ordnance Survey Map of Iron Age Britain and the Ordnance Survey Map of Roman Britain both show the distribution of early settlements. Some museums have displays showing this information and in some areas local publications such as guidebooks may include distribution maps and descriptions of prehistoric and Roman settlements.

The local museum may also be able to provide access to a card index giving information about local sites (including recorded ancient monuments and chance finds). It is important to choose a fairly wide geographical area around the location of the school so that the children have plenty of scope for the activities suggested below.

Preparation

Prepare one copy of photocopiable page 146 for the children to share in groups of four or five. Identify the area that the investigation will cover. Choose a suitable scale of map which should be large enough to make a wall display of the finished product. An outline of the chosen area should first be made on tracing paper, together with some major features including the location of the school and, for example, present day large towns or villages, some physical features such as major rivers, coastline (where appropriate), and significant areas of high or low ground.

Resources needed

Photocopiable page 146, maps of the local area showing the location of prehistoric and Roman sites, reference material about the early local history of the area, a large sheet of tracing paper, pencils, felt-tipped pens.

What to do

Explain to the children that they are going to investigate the area around their school in the hope of finding evidence of prehistoric and Roman settlements. Some discussion might be needed about the sort of evidence that may be discovered. Some children could undertake the tracing of the large outline map of the area to be investigated (see Preparation above). Divide the class into small groups of four or five. Each group should be given sources of information such as guidebooks or museum hand-outs relating to the local area which contain the names and details of places where there are prehistoric and Roman sites. Children should be asked to list the sites they have found under the following headings: place, type of monument or find, period, approximate date, additional information. If there is a lot of information available, some children could concentrate on prehistoric and others on Roman settlements. It may be possible, depending upon resources, to allocate particular geographical areas or sections of the settlement to different groups. Sometimes there might be an abundance of one category rather than another.

Having tabulated the information they have gathered, each group should be in a position to pool their findings. There should now be a short class discussion when the children are asked to name examples of sites that they have found. This will help to clarify that everyone is working correctly and to enable any further guidance to be given about how the information might be recorded on the map. Distribute copies of photocopiable page 146 to each group. Allocate particular categories of monument or find to each group and ask them to make symbols which can be used on the map and also to make the key. Then, using the large map, ask the children to locate the sites for which they are responsible. Using the key, the children can then mark the positions of their particular categories on the map. This final stage may need to be delayed until all the information has been gathered.

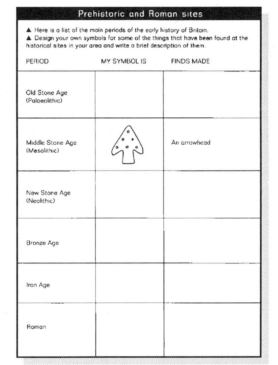

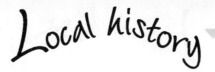

Suggestion(s) for extension

The children could find out more details about some of the archaeological sites they have found and supplementary information about these sites could be added to the map. If the children have discovered a lot of information they could make drawings of what they think the original settlement may have looked like and also make drawings of some of the artefacts that have been found.

Suggestion(s) for support

Some children may need help with finding sites on a modern map and in locating them on the large map. They may also need help with map symbols and keys. Make a list of some of the specific historical terms and map symbols that the children are likely to encounter in their research. Write a simple explanation beside each one to act as a reminder.

Assessment opportunities

There will be opportunities for the children to show how well they can read maps and also understand the importance of map symbols and the key. The final map could be given simplified eastings (A to T) and northings (1 to 20) and the children could record their sites using these co-ordinates.

Opportunities for IT

The children could use a commercial database of place names, such as the *Anglia Placenames* file which helps children to identify the origins and meanings of different Roman place names. Having used this, the children could create their own local database of placenames taken from the map being used.

The children could, in groups, research aspects of the local area identified on the map and make a presentation using a word processor or desk top publishing package. These could be published together as a class book of interesting places.

Display ideas

The classroom display will be centred around the children's map showing the location of ancient settlements in their local area. Children's written work or drawings relating to their discoveries could be added to the display.

Reference to photocopiable sheet

The children should use the photocopiable sheet to record their own symbols to represent the sites they have identified in the local area.

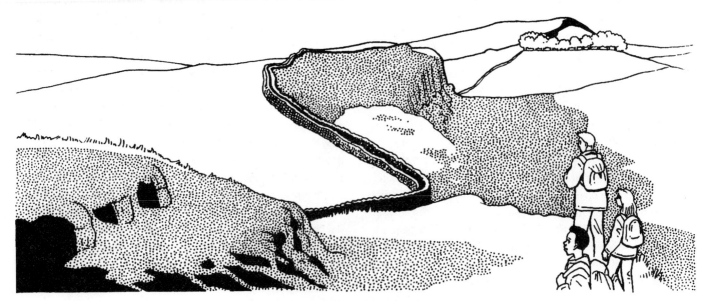

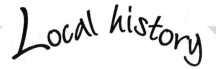
ANGLO-SAXON, VIKING, NORMAN, MEDIAEVAL AND TUDOR SITES

To identify and locate evidence of settlements between the early fifth century AD and c.1600.

†† *Small groups then class discussion.*

⏱ *60 minutes then short time for class discussion.*

Previous skills/knowledge needed

Map reading skills including knowledge of map symbols and keys. Some knowledge of the type of settlements made in Anglo-Saxon, Viking, Norman, Mediaeval and Tudor times would be helpful.

Key background information

Evidence of settlement during these periods in the area in where the school is situated may be found in a variety of places. Here are some possible ways of finding out about the location of these sites. Obtain copies of Ordnance Survey 2cm to 1km sheets (formerly the 1 inch to the mile series, now referred to as the *Landranger* series). The Ordnance Survey Map of Dark Age Britain and the Ordnance Survey Map of Monastic Britain both show the distribution of settlements covering much of this period. Some museums have displays showing this information for the earlier part of the period. In many areas local publications such as guidebooks will include distribution maps and descriptions of settlements.

The local museum may also be able to provide access to a card index giving information about local sites (including recorded ancient monuments and chance finds). It is important to choose a fairly wide geographical area around the location of the school so that the children have plenty of scope for the activities suggested below.

Preparation

Prepare one copy of photocopiable page 147 for the children to share in groups of four or five. Identify the area that the investigation will cover. Choose a suitable scale of map which should be large enough to make a wall display of the finished product. An outline of the chosen area should first be made on tracing paper, together with some major features including the location of the school and, for example, present day large towns or villages, some physical features such as rivers, coastline (where appropriate), and significant areas of high or low ground.

Resources needed

Photocopiable page 147, maps of the local area showing the location of Anglo-Saxon, Viking, Norman, Mediaeval and Tudor sites, reference material about the early local history of the area, a large sheet of tracing paper, paper, pencils, felt-tipped pens.

What to do

Explain to the children that they are going to investigate the area around their school in the hope of finding evidence of historical settlements. Some discussion may be needed about the sort of evidence that may be discovered. Some children could undertake the tracing of the large outline map (see Preparation above). Divide the class into small groups of four or five. Each group should be given information such as guide books or museum hand-outs relating to the local area which contain the names and details of places where there are Saxon, Viking, Norman, Mediaeval and Tudor sites. (The chronological study could be extended to include Stuart, Georgian and Victorian periods.) Children should be asked to list the sites they have found under the following headings: place, type of monument or find, period, approximate date, additional information. If there is a lot of information available for the children to work on, some children could concentrate on one phase (for example, the Anglo-Saxon period) and others on later settlements. It may be possible, depending upon resources, to allocate particular geographical sections to different groups. Sometimes there might be an abundance of one category rather than another.

Having tabulated the information they have gathered, each group should be in a position to pool their findings. There should now be a short class discussion when the children are asked to name examples of sites that they have found. This will help to clarify that everyone is working correctly and to enable any further guidance to be given about how the information might be recorded on the map.

Distribute copies of photocopiable page 147 to each group. Allocate particular categories of monument or find to each group and ask them to make symbols which can be used on the map and also to make the key. Symbols for any categories which are not covered could be designed by the children. Then, get

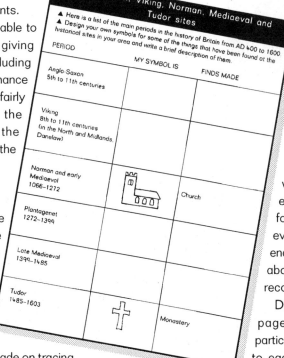

Anglo-Saxon, Viking, Norman, Mediaeval and Tudor sites

▲ Here is a list of the main periods in the history of Britain from AD 400 to 1600.
▲ Design your own symbols for some of the things that have been found at the historical sites in your area and write a brief description of them.

PERIOD	MY SYMBOL IS	FINDS MADE
Anglo-Saxon 5th to 11th centuries		
Viking 8th to 11th centuries (in the North and Midlands, Danelaw)		
Norman and early Mediaeval 1066–1272		Church
Plantagenet 1272–1399		
Late Mediaeval 1399–1485		
Tudor 1485–1603		Monastery

the children to locate the sites for which they are responsible. Using the key, the children can mark their finds on the map. This final stage may need to be delayed until all the information has been gathered together.

Suggestion(s) for extension

The children could find out more details about some of the sites they have identified and supplementary information about these sites could be added to the map. If the children have discovered a lot of information they could make drawings of what they think the original settlement may have looked like and also make drawings of some of the artefacts that have been found.

Suggestion(s) for support

Some children may need help with finding sites on a modern map and in locating them on the large map. They may also need help with map symbols and keys. Make a list of some of the specific historical terms and map symbols that the children are likely to encounter in their research. Write a simple explanation beside each one to act as a reminder or check list.

Assessment opportunities

There will be opportunities for the children to show how well they can read maps. The final map could be given simplified eastings (A to T) and northings (1 to 20) and the children could have the opportunity to record their sites on the map using these co-ordinates.

Display ideas

The classroom display will be centred around the children's map showing the location of Anglo-Saxon, Viking, Norman, Mediaeval and Tudor sites in their local area. Children's written work or drawing relating to their discoveries could be added to the display.

Reference to photocopiable sheet

The children should use the photocopiable sheet to record their own designs to represent the sites they have identified in the local area.

DESIGN FEATURES OF LOCAL HOUSING

To identify houses from different historical periods.
†† *Field work and in the classroom working in pairs.*
🕐 *60 minutes plus to walk round the local area.*

Previous skills/knowledge needed

Map reading skills, and some knowledge of using old street directories would be useful.

Key background information

The activities in this lesson are centred on the identification and classification of different house styles according to age. It may be necessary to use additional sources of information such as old street directories and maps when attempting to assign a date to houses in your area. The following points should be borne in mind when preparing for this lesson:

1 The categories given below are approximate only and there will be some variation according to the part of Britain in which your school is located. (London often set the trend and there was a delay before the new styles reached other parts of the country.)

2 The front of a building might be much more recent than the interior or even the rear side. It may be worth taking a look around the back, if this is possible.

3 Dates on buildings may indicate when a building was renovated rather than when it was actually built.

4 The list below gives a few key features of house design associated with different historical periods, but again this should not be taken too literally. Builders have often imitated styles that are out of period (for example, mock Tudor semi-detached housing in inter-war Britain and neo-Georgian styles on some modern housing estates).

Key features of house design in different historical periods:

▲ Mediaeval pre-1500 – usually timber-framed and plastered.

▲ Tudor/Stuart 16/17th century – half-timbering continues, gables, mullioned windows, lattice windows, anti-drip mouldings.

▲ Georgian c.1700 to c.1840 – casement windows with small rectangular panes; classical features (for example Greek style pediments and mouldings). Also keystone ornamentation over windows and mansard and (later) low pitched roofs.

▲ Victorian – terraced artisan houses straight on to the street.

▲ Late Victorian/Edwardian – large semi-detached and detached houses with bay windows and larger window panes.

▲ 20th century – semi-detached houses with garage space (different styles inter- and post-war).

▲ 20th century – detached villas and bungalows.

▲ Late 1940s – pre-fabricated building with single storey and flat roofs.

▲ 1960s – detached and semi-detached houses with large picture windows.

▲ 1960s and 1970s – high rise and low rise flats using industrialised building techniques (concrete and large windows).

Preparation

Prepare one copy of photocopiable page 148 for the children to share in pairs. Copies of old maps and street directories of the area to be studied should be available. Collect pictures of houses from different historical periods which highlight some of the characteristic design features. The children will need writing materials to record their findings.

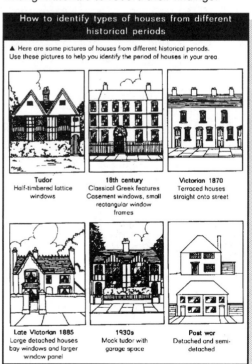

Resources needed

Photocopiable page 148, old local maps and street directories, pictures of houses from different historical periods showing main design features, clipboards, paper, pencils, felt-tipped pens, scissors.

What to do

Choose a group of houses in the local area for the children to study. Ideally this should include examples of houses drawn from different periods. However, this may not be possible in some areas where there are a lot of modern housing estates. In this case identify the sequence in which the houses were built, drawing on local maps and information from local residents from this research. The exercise can be supplemented by extending the children's knowledge to other earlier styles of building that they might find in other places.

When preparing to study an area which has examples of buildings from different periods, it will be helpful to have access to old maps and street directories in order to establish the approximate dates of the houses that the children will study. It should be stressed that there will be considerable variation in styles from area to area and that every locality will have its own particular building traditions and variations in design. Show the children pictures of some of the features they may see on the local houses and help the children identify the different historical periods concerned.

Use the diagram below to make a simplified map for the children to use.

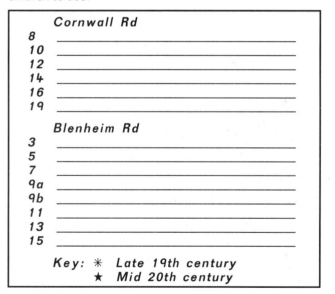

Distribute photocopiable page 148 and a clipboard to each pair of children and talk about the area and the houses they are going to study using the information above, as appropriate. Visit the local area and ask the children to write in the numbers of all the properties that they see on to their map. Using the information on the photocopiable sheet, they can then attempt to date the houses that they see. Each pair should choose two contrasting types of house and make a sketch, for enlargement later. On returning to school, the children could colour code the houses on their map according to date as shown in the diagram above.

The children can then make enlarged drawings of the particular houses that they have sketched. These can be coloured and mounted on card, and then labelled according to age, noting any particular points of interest, for display purposes. Pictures highlighting specific design features of housing from different periods will give extra support.

Suggestion(s) for extension

Some children could investigate particular features of older houses including Mediaeval, Tudor and Georgian buildings which are less likely to be in the immediate vicinity of most primary schools.

Suggestion(s) for support

Some children may be able to recognise the difference between two types of house, but will need help in seeing how one is older than the other. Show the children pictures of houses from different periods and point out some of the features which provide clues about when the houses were originally built. For example the sizes of windows; recent houses have bigger windows.

Assessment opportunities

The children could arrange a series of pictures of buildings from different periods in sequence to form a timeline.

Opportunities for IT

The children could use Ordnance Survey maps available from the LEA in digital format and load them into software such as *Aegis*. This will enable them to print out large scale versions of the maps showing individual houses or buildings. The map can be edited to show a single sheet. The children can then use this map as the basis for their fieldwork, shading different properties according to the dates they were built. An alternative activity would be to use a database set up for a record for each house. This could show a number of different features about the house. The actual filenames could be decided by the children in relation to the area being studied:

number	32
type	terraced
date	1870
construction	brick
roof	slate
chimneys	4
windows	sash
garage	no

Once the database has been created children can enter the information collected in the survey. They will then be in a position to question the data. Starting questions might include such things as: How many houses were built before 1900? How many houses are terraced? What percentage of houses have slate roofs? What is the most common roofing material?

Display ideas

A display of pictures of house styles from different periods could be arranged together with the individual drawings of houses produced by children; a frieze of houses could be made with a street background and with a corresponding key.

Reference to photocopiable sheet

The photocopiable sheet covers a range of typical house styles which may be found in the area near to your school. The children should use the information on the sheet to help them date some of the houses in their area.

LOOKING AT OLD BUILDINGS

To study some of the features of old buildings and any change in their use over the last four centuries.
†† *Pairs.*
🕑 *45 minutes.*

Previous skills/knowledge needed
Some knowledge of building styles in different historical periods would be useful.

Key background information
The pictures on photocopiable page 149 are of a street in Bristol in which the buildings have been constructed over the last 400 years. The examples show clearly some of the significant features of buildings that were erected in each of the last four centuries.

The original street was laid out in the mid-seventeenth century, following the draining of marshland. Today there remain some of the original seventeenth century gabled and half-timbered houses, an early eighteenth century town house, nineteenth century warehousing now converted to offices and twentieth century offices which have been purpose-built. This street is in the heart of the former city docks area which was closed in 1970. Consequently, some of the buildings once connected with the port of Bristol (notably warehouses), have now been converted to other purposes. This street mainly consists of office accommodation now, but also has a number of places for leisure and entertainment such as pubs and restaurants.

Preparation
Prepare one copy of photocopiable page 149 for the children to share in pairs.

Resources needed
Photocopiable page 149, and coloured pencils or crayons.

What to do
Distribute photocopiable page 149 to each pair. Explain to the children that old buildings sometimes survive in their neighbourhood and that it is possible to work out their approximate age and sometimes also, what they were originally used for.

Explain that the pictures on the sheet represent a street in present day Bristol. All of the buildings include features that are typical of the century in which they were built. Using the information supplied on the sheet and any other information to help them to date buildings, the children can work out to which century each building belongs and then colour code the diagrams on their sheet accordingly.

Suggestion(s) for extension
The children could suggest what changes have occurred to some of the buildings on the photocopiable sheet since they were first built for example, a warehouse converted to offices.

A similar investigation could be made of a street in the children's local area. How has the usage of these buildings changed?

Suggestion(s) for support
Some children may need help in recognising the significant design features which help to identify a building with one century rather than another. Show the children pictures of buildings from different periods and point out some of the design features which provide clues about the age of the building.

Assessment opportunities
The children could be given different styles of building dating from the sixteenth to the twentieth century and asked to classify them according to age.

Display ideas
A large version of the picture on photocopiable page 149 could be made as a collage, with each member of the class being assigned one of the buildings to design.

The children could also make a simple visual timeline in which a version of the street is displayed for each century for example:

1. showing only the sixteenth-century buildings;
2. showing only the seventeenth- and eighteenth-century buildings etc.

Reference to photocopiable sheet
The photocopiable sheet could be used as a starting point for identifying old buildings in your local area and for a study of how the buildings have been converted for a different use.

HOW TO INVESTIGATE A LOCAL MARKET

To use documentary evidence to increase the children's knowledge of local sites.

†† *Whole class then pairs.*

⏱ *60 minutes.*

Previous skills/knowledge needed

This lesson builds on the children's experience of using first-hand accounts of historical events.

Key background information

The methods of study of a local market in Bristol can be applied to a market in your local area or county town (see also Suggestion(s) for extension, below). The account on photocopiable page 150 is describing a typical market day in eighteenth century Bristol. The account relates to the markets held in Welsh Back, a part of the Bristol dockland which at one time was the place where trows (shallow-bottomed sailing boats which used to ply up and down the tidal rivers Severn and Avon) off-loaded their cargoes. The description gives a vivid account of the boats which came from the west and from the north bringing goods from Wales (hence the name Welsh Back), from the further reaches of the Severn Valley and from North Devon and as far away as Cornwall.

Preparation

Prepare one copy of photocopiable page 150 for the children to share in pairs. Collect pictures of some of the items from the account and illustrated information books about eighteenth-century costume. Collect pictures and information about a market in your local area or county town.

Resources needed

Photocopiable page 150, pictures of some of the items included in the account, picture books showing eighteenth century costume, pictures and information about a local market.

What to do

Photocopiable page 150 contains a contemporary historian's account of a market day in a local area. This can be used to help the children imagine what life was like over two hundred years ago. The children should think about the noise, bustle, and smells, etc. What was being sold? What sort of people went to the market? Which buildings would have been there in the eighteenth century at the time when the markets were held? Distribute the photocopiable sheet and read the account of market day to the class. Ask the children to choose one or more of the items of merchandise described, and then to make a drawing of a market stall selling those items. These drawings can be included in a large collage of market day on Welsh Back.

Suggestion(s) for extension

Work on this lesson could be continued to include a study of a market in your local area or county town. The local museum will be a good source of information. Choose a historical period when the market was flourishing or when it was first established. What items or produce did it use to sell? How has the market changed? Have any features stayed the same?

Suggestion(s) for support

Those children who have difficulty with drawing may need to consult picture books to help them with some of the commodities and activities described as well as some elements of historical costume for their figures.

Assessment opportunities

The children could be shown pictures of a market day in a different eighteenth century town or from a period that they have studied. They should then describe what the market was like using the information they have learned in this lesson.

Display ideas

The children could make a collage of market day in the King Street/Welsh Back area of Bristol or of their local area. A model of a market stall could be made by the children, with the drawings of items for sale and the people in the market being mounted on card to create a realistic scene.

Reference to photocopiable sheet

The photocopiable sheet provides a contemporary account of a market day in the eighteenth century in a particular area of Bristol. It should be used to help the children to discover what a market was like in this period, the different items that were sold, and the different sorts of people who were there selling and buying.

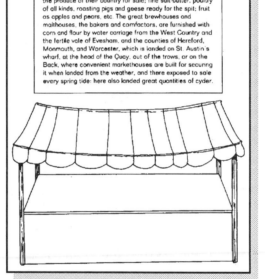

Market Day

▲ Read this description of a market in Bristol 200 years ago. Choose one or two items that are being sold and make a drawing of them on the market stall.

An eighteenth century view of Bristol
A market is also held on Back every other Wednesday where the Welsh boats, arriving at spring tides, discharge the produce of their country for sale; fine salt-butter, poultry of all kinds, roasting pigs and geese ready for the spit; fruit as apples and pears, etc. The great brewhouses and malthouses, the bakers and cornfactors, are furnished with corn and flour by water carriage from the West Country and the fertile vale of Evesham, and the counties of Hereford, Monmouth, and Worcester, which is landed on St. Austin's wharf, at the head of the Quay, out of the trows, or on the Back, where convenient markethouses are built for securing it when landed from the weather, and there exposed to sale every spring tide: here also landed great quantities of cyder.

HISTORICAL CLUES FROM MAPS

To look for clues about the past using maps from different periods and to describe some of the changes that have occurred within that time.

†† *Pairs.*

🕐 *60 minutes.*

Previous skills/knowledge needed

Map reading skills.

Key background information

The map shown on photocopiable page 151 links with the corresponding map on photocopiable sheet 152. Both maps are for use with this lesson plan. There will be a number of opportunities for looking at major changes, notably in the process of urbanisation, that have taken place during the past century or so. But there will also be many features that have remained the same. Examples should be taken from the area in which the school is situated. Typically these might show that an entirely rural community has been submerged within the modern conurbation as the fields are sold off for housing and as country lanes become modern highways. But look for the continuity in the shapes of field boundaries which have become 'fossilised' in the layout of the modern town. How far do the lines of modern streets follow the patterns of the old fields? How far are the roads on the same

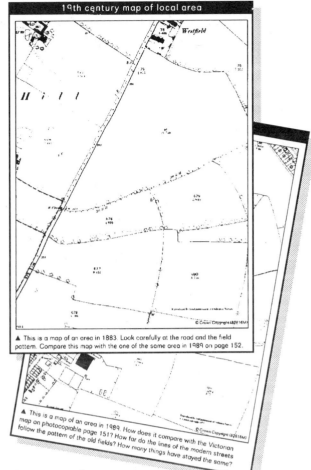

19th century map of local area

▲ This is a map of an area in 1883. Look carefully at the road and the field pattern. Compare this map with the one of the same area in 1989 on page 152.

▲ This is a map of an area in 1989. How does it compare with the Victorian map on photocopiable page 151? How far do the lines of the modern streets follow the pattern of the old fields? How many things have stayed the same?

alignment as former country lanes and trackways? It will be helpful to link the study of historical and modern maps to a walk around the local area looking at such things as old boundaries. Are these the original field boundaries from c.1000 years ago?

Preparation

Prepare one copy of photocopiable pages 151 (on paper) and 152 (on acetate, if possible) for the children to share in pairs. Obtain modern OS maps and copies of historical maps of the local area around your school.

Resources needed

Photocopiable pages 151 and 152, OS maps of the local area, copies of local historical maps, writing paper, pencils.

What to do

Distribute one copy of photocopiable page 152 to each pair of children. Explain that the map shows the area more or less as it is today, but that there have been a number of changes over the years. Ask the children to look for clues that might tell them about this area in the past. They should look at names, any evidence of old buildings and historic sites. When they have done this for ten minutes or so, brainstorm their ideas as to what might once have stood in the place of the modern housing. Now introduce

HISTORY KS2:II

Display ideas

A large pair of maps or table top models, based on the local area could be prepared for display. The children's written work and drawings could also be included.

Reference to photocopiable sheets

The photocopiable sheets will help the children to see the changes that have taken place in an area over a 100 year period. They should take particular note of original field boundaries and current road and street patterns. This activity could be continued in a study of the local area.

USING STREET DIRECTORIES

To use information in old street directories to investigate changes in a local area from 1850–1900.

†† *Pairs.*

🕐 *30 minutes.*

Previous skills/knowledge needed

Previous work using old maps and census material about the same locality would be useful.

Key background information

Street directories first became popular in the mid-Victorian period as the post, telegraph and railway systems developed. Many of these directories for large towns still survive along with some from the seventeenth and eighteenth centuries. These were compiled to meet the needs of expanding businesses. Copies of street directories will normally be held in public reference libraries. They were produced for large towns but normally include the surrounding villages.

Points to be remembered when using street directories are:

1. the needs of a nineteenth-century user are not the same as the needs of a twentieth-century local historian;
2. the information they contain about residence is very incomplete and should be compared with a census return for a similar period;
3. the most useful street directories are those which also list occupations.

Preparation

Prepare one copy of photocopiable page 153 for the children to share in pairs. Prepare photocopied pages from local directories of the area near your school if possible.

Resources needed

Photocopiable page 153, photocopied pages from Victorian local street directories, pens.

photocopiable page 151 and ask the children to compare the two maps. They should then divide a sheet of paper into two columns and write a heading one side, things that have changed and on the other, things that are the same. When everyone has had the opportunity to complete this activity, discuss with the children which things on the present day map can be explained by what they have found on the older map.

Suggestion(s) for extension

Show the children a pair of maps of the area in which the school is situated. What can the children learn by doing the same exercise using these maps? If possible, provide an opportunity for linking this comparative exercise with first-hand observation.

Suggestion(s) for support

Some children may have difficulty in making comparisons between the modern map and the older map. They should concentrate on those parts of the map where the contrast is most dramatic (for example, the Roman road), and where there are one or more features for comparison.

Assessment opportunities

The children could be asked to make a pair of drawings to show how life has changed in one place over 100 years, based on what they have learned from the photocopiable sheets or their work on local maps.

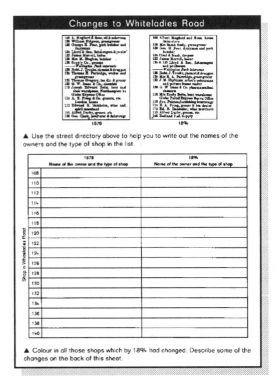

Changes to Whiteladies Road

▲ Use the street directory above to help you to write out the names of the owners and the type of shop in the list.

	1878 Name of the owner and the type of shop	1894 Name of the owner and the type of shop
108		
110		
112		
114		
116		
118		
120		
122		
124		
126		
128		
130		
132		
134		
136		
138		
140		

Shops Whiteladies Road

▲ Colour in all those shops which by 1894 had changed. Describe some of the changes on the back of this sheet.

What to do

Talk to the children about the early street directories, the sort of information they included and how they worked. Distribute photocopiable page 153 and explain that the children should work in pairs to complete the form. They can then record the changes that have taken place over a sixteen-year period. The children should then try and list some of the conclusions that can be drawn from their findings.

Suggestion(s) for extension

Distribute the photocopied pages taken from local street directories. Discuss the area that they cover. Some children may be familiar with some of the streets. What changes can they identify? If there are shops in the area the children should study the changes that have taken place over longer periods, including modern times.

Suggestion(s) for support

Some children will need help in seeing the connection between the same shops at different dates and the changes that have taken place. Choose one or two examples of the same shop as recorded in the two directories. What has changed?

Assessment opportunities

Ask the children to talk about their findings and to explain some of the changes that have taken place within earlier times as well as those relating to today.

Opportunities for IT

The children could use a program such as *Touch Explorer Plus* which works with a concept keyboard and which enables a diagrammatic representation of a street to be shown at different periods of time. Each year of the directory is a separate 'layer' which enables children to see what changes have taken place for a particular building. An alternative approach could use a database where each record is one particular building or site. The record would contain data on the use of the building over the period of time being studied:

Number	42
1910	being built
1911	chemist
1912	chemist
1913	chemist
1914	grocer

Searches on a particular year would show the use of each building at that time. These could be printed out and displayed together to show the changes over time. Searching for different uses might also allow children to track, say, the decline in grocers' shops and to give reasons for this.

Display ideas

The children could make pictures of the different shops to show what they have learned from the directories. Their pictures could take the form of symbols which represent the types of shops for example, a piece of meat for a butcher's, a loaf of bread for a baker's, etc.

Reference to photocopiable sheet

The photocopiable sheet provides information about the same row of shops as recorded in two street directories published sixteen years apart. By studying this material the children will be able to discover how some shops have changed and how others have stayed the same.

USING A VICTORIAN POPULATION CENSUS

To use the information in a census to learn about some features of Victorian society.

†† *Pairs.*

🕐 *60 minutes.*

Previous skills/knowledge needed

Some knowledge of street directories or old maps of the area represented by the census returns. Reference should be made to page 48 where a census is used as a starting point for looking at the Victorian family and social structure.

Key background information

The first census returns were compiled in 1801 but they were simple and did not contain a great deal of information. The most interesting material dates from 1851, since when a census has been carried out at ten yearly intervals. (Population totals, parish by parish, can be found in the *Victoria County History* if your school is situated in England.) These figures could be used to plot a simple graph to show the population changes that

took place in the nineteenth century; between 1801 and 1901. It would also be interesting to compare the rapid growth in towns with the decline in some rural communities as industrialisation developed.

In some areas of Britain it should be possible to obtain print-outs from microfiche or photocopies of census material from the local county reference library. The city or county library and/or City or County Record Office will advise how material for your area can be obtained. The handwriting of the census enumerators is variable in clarity however, so the information should be transcribed in a similar way to the example shown on photocopiable page 154.

Preparation

Prepare one copy of photocopiable page 154 for the children to share in pairs. Obtain census material for the area in which the school is situated and transcribe it so that it can be read easily.

Resources needed

Photocopiable page 154, examples of census material for the local area near to the school, paper, graph paper, pencils.

What to do

Explain to the children what a census is and why they are taken. Discuss the sorts of questions they contain and the information they provide once the forms have been collected and analysed. Distribute photocopiable page 154 to the class. Ask for the children's reaction to this document which was compiled more than 100 years ago. Ask them what sort of information they would like to find out using this document. Write the children's questions on the board, alternatively cards can be written out and used as prompts. Finally, the children can contribute to a discussion using their findings. If material is available for the school area, then the activity can be extended to incorporate that material.

The following questions could be addressed in relation to the local census material:

Jobs Make a list of all the jobs that people did. How many people were there in each category? How many of these jobs are still done today?

Ages How many people are there (male and female) in each of the age ranges 0–20, 21–40, 41–60, 61–80, 81+? A bar chart could be made to show the findings and possibly compared with statistics from a modern day census.

Children How many children are

Assessment opportunities

Ask the children to list the major differences between families in Victorian times and today. What have they learned about some of the people who lived in Etloe Road?

Opportunities for IT

The children could be introduced to census data on a computer using one of the commercial files such as the *1851 Census* files from Longman. Once they have experience in using this they can set up their own database using logical census returns. They should begin by discussing the sort of questions that they want to answer and which information from the returns will enable them to do this. Children could work in pairs to research and collate the data for a small number of houses, entering the data on a data collection sheet agreed in advance. Once they have done this they can take it in turns to type the data into the computer. As the process takes some time it is important to start this activity well in advance of wanting to use the class database.

Display ideas

The children could make bar graphs and drawings of Victorian children to illustrate the popularity of names then and now.

Reference to photocopiable sheet

The photocopiable sheet can be used as a starting point for looking at census material and its potential for local history investigations.

under 14 years? How many are employed/listed as scholars? What are the names of girls and boys? How do they compare with children's names in the class/school? Which were/are the most popular names?

Place of birth Where were people born? What percentage were born outside the immediate area? Children could make a diagram to show how far people's original birthplaces were from the local area. The children could compare census returns for the same area over a ten or twenty year period.

Suggestion(s) for extension

More able children will be able to try transcribing the census enumerator's writing for themselves. Some children may like to concentrate on two or three houses and, using the information in the census write about some of the people who lived there and draw imaginary pictures of them.

Suggestion(s) for support

Some children may need to concentrate on one or two categories of information only. They may also need a list of prepared questions to help them structure and direct their research.

TITHE APPORTIONMENT MAPS

To use the information in a tithe apportionment map to investigate changes in land usage in the nineteenth century.

†† *Pairs.*

🕒 *60 minutes.*

Previous skills/knowledge needed

This activity could be linked with previous work using old maps and census material about the same locality.

Key background information

A tithe map and its associated schedule of apportionments is a specialised document mainly produced in the late 1830s and 1840s for a specific purpose. An Act of Parliament passed in 1836 enabled tithes (traditionally one tenth of a farmer's produce paid in kind by the laity to the established church) to be changed to money payments. Commissioners went from parish to parish apportioning rents to be paid in money to each landowner according to the state of cultivation

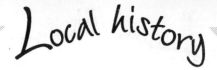

at the time of the survey. The commissioners completed their work in 1851. Although they were produced for a very specific purpose, a tithe map is a rich source of information about any parish.

The map is usually drawn on a large scale and each plot of land is numbered. The schedule provides a key to the map, listing landowners, occupiers, size of fields, how the land was used and the tithe charge payable. A surviving copy of the tithe map and schedule should be available for about seventy-nine percent of the parishes in England and Wales. They can be found in the City or County Record Office. It is not permissible to photograph or to photocopy these documents, but it will normally be possible to make a tracing of the map and to make a transcript of the details of a schedule. Although the work involved will take some time to complete, a copy of the mid-nineteenth century tithe map for the parish in which the school is situated will be a rich source of information about the area, at a time which precedes the Ordnance Survey and most street directories. The extract from a tithe map shown on photocopiable page 155 is based upon the transcription of a section of a map from the 1840s and the associated entries in the schedule.

Preparation
Prepare one copy of photocopiable pages 155 and 156 for the children to share in pairs. It may be useful to have copies of the earliest Ordnance Survey map for the area available for reference. Collect illustrated information books about Victorian costume, farming methods and farm tools.

Resources needed
Photocopiable pages 155 and 156, examples of other tithe maps (or information derived from the tithe map), an early Ordnance Survey map of the area, information books about Victorian costume, farming and farm tools, pens, coloured pencils, felt-tipped pens.

What to do
Talk to the children about the tithe map and explain what it was and why it was first produced using the information above. Distribute photocopiable pages 155 and 156 and tell the children that they have to write on each field and plot of land on photocopiable page 155 the name of the occupier and, where appropriate, the name of the field from the

information on photocopiable page 156. They could refer to pictures of Victorian costume and make drawings to represent the different occupiers and/or go on to colour code the fields according to ownership. Can they list the land owners in descending order of importance?

Some examples of tithe maps may lend themselves to making a colour-coded land use map. The particular example on photocopiable page 155 is shown as being largely under pasture but other maps will show more variation of land use: arable, pasture and meadows. Some plots of land will be largely domestic showing orchards, paddocks and gardens.

Suggestion(s) for extension
Some children may be interested to compare the tithe map for the area of their school with the first edition Ordnance Survey map. They could investigate the meanings of the field names, some of which contain clues about a much earlier period of history. Some children may like to make larger imaginary drawings of the landowners or occupiers who worked on the land in their tithe map area. The children could also include drawings of some of the farm tools or machinery that may have been used at that time.

Suggestion(s) for support
Some children may have difficulty in making connections between a tithe map and the modern environment. They should be helped to identify the different features that appear on a tithe map, such as roads, field boundaries and buildings.

Assessment opportunities
The children could identify changes that have taken place in land use for the area since the time when the tithe maps were made. They could also be asked to make connections with other sources they have studied in their work on local history.

Opportunities for IT
Children could create a simple database showing all the details for the fields on the tithe maps. This might include:

name of field	meadow leys
area of field	3.4 acres
owner	John Brown
land use	pasture
other information	close to river

This database would allow children to work out who owned most land or plot charts or graphs of differing land uses.

Display ideas

A reproduction of the tithe map for the school area will make a large, interesting classroom display. The children's own illustrated maps and drawings could also be displayed.

Reference to photocopiable sheets

The facsimile of the tithe map on photocopiable page 155 will give the children experience in using original source material. They will have to examine the photocopiable sheets carefully to understand how the information is presented and then use it to complete specific tasks.

ORAL EVIDENCE

To learn about the past using oral evidence.
†† *Whole class.*
🕐 *60 minutes.*

Previous skills/knowledge needed

Some knowledge of preparing questions about a specific topic or event, listening skills, note taking.

Key background information

Oral evidence is often under-used as a source of information and yet it is accessible to every school in which local history is studied. Parents, grandparents (increasingly great-grandparents!), older members of the community and teachers can all add to the children's knowledge about a variety of topics. For example, there will be many who remember the Second World War either as combatants or as civilians and who will come into school to talk about the war years. There are also likely to be those who, as children, experienced the wartime and post-war austerity and whose childhood memories will contrast sharply with the children's experience today. There may even be adults who were evacuated in wartime. The Coronation of 1953 will also be an event that adults of the same generation will be able to refer to in some detail. If the children are studying local industries that have recently disappeared or been transformed by modern technology, it will be helpful to draw upon the memories of people such as a dockworker who can describe the days before containerisation or a coal miner who can describe what it was like to work underground in seams which have now been abandoned. In some communities people with childhood memories of other countries and other cultures will be able to add a new dimension. For example, members of the local community who originally came from Jamaica and settled in Britain in the 1950s.

Preparation

Identify those members of the community who may be able to talk to the children and answer their questions about specific events or periods in the past. Arrange for the individuals concerned to visit the school and send them a list of questions that the children have prepared, in advance of the visit. The children should also have copies of the final list of questions that will be asked. Have available any source material such as information books, old photographs or video films about the events, activities or period of history that is being studied.

Resources needed

A prepared list of questions about a specific topic or event, information books, video films and photographs of related topics, a tape recorder, notebooks, pencils.

What to do

Visitors to the classroom could be asked to speak to the children about a specific topic or event, or their visit could take the form of an interview in which the children ask a list of prepared questions. If the latter form is chosen it is important that the children should prepare a list of questions prior to the visit. If possible, this list should be sent to the visitors before the interview so that they can prepare their answers and gather together any photographs or memorabilia to illustrate their responses.

The following topics could be considered and adapted, and used as the basis for specific interview questions about a particular event or period of time:

▲ local shops
▲ first job
▲ earliest childhood memories
▲ local characters (including itinerant salespeople)
▲ transport
▲ holidays, Sunday School outings
▲ clothes
▲ housing conditions
▲ food
▲ entertainment and leisure in the days before television
▲ work
▲ festivals
▲ school and education
▲ the position of women

The questions could be arranged into a logical sequence and different children allotted particular questions to ask. Each child should be prepared to take notes of the answers to their specific question. If possible the interview should be recorded on audio tape so that the children can replay it to check their notes to ensure that the whole interview is available for future study.

After the visitors have gone, it would be useful to discuss with the children ways in which the oral evidence has added new information to what they already knew. Did the children receive any unexpected replies to their questions? The children should be encouraged to see how such information is unique and cannot be obtained from any other source.

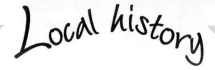

Suggestion(s) for extension
The children could work in pairs to transcribe parts of the interview from the audio tape. They could concentrate on the particular questions that they asked.

Suggestion(s) for support
It may be helpful to show the children a relevant video film or photographs in order to stimulate ideas for questions to be asked.

Assessment opportunities
The children could be asked how useful they think oral evidence is on its own or when used with other sources. Might there be any problems with using only oral evidence as a source of historical information?

Opportunities for IT
Children could use a word processor to write up and present the information they have learned from the interviews, or to type a transcript of the interview. Different pairs of children could be responsible for different parts of the transcript, saving the file each time a new section is added. Pictures could be added, taken from scanned photographs or the children's drawings, clipart or CD-ROMs.

Display ideas
The display could include the children's drawings and written work on the study topic, together with some written questions transcribed from the interview tape.

ARTEFACTS AND PICTURES
To find out how some Victorian and Edwardian artefacts might have been used locally.

†† *Pairs or groups of three.*

⏱ *60 minutes.*

Key background information
Many museums have loan collections which may include objects relevant to the period being studied here. Artefacts from the last century can still be purchased relatively cheaply from general bric-a-brac shops and some local markets. (Ideas may be obtained from the list of objects suggested on photocopiable page 157.) Old shopping catalogues from about 100 years ago are also a valuable source of information. (Harrods' catalogue for 1895 and Army and Navy Stores' catalogues have been printed in facsimile form in recent years.) If actual artefacts are unobtainable, collect a selection of pictures, photographs and pictures of engravings of different objects.

Preparation
Prepare one copy of photocopiable page 157 for the children

to share in pairs or groups of three. Collect about 10 or 12 artefacts which might have been used locally during the Victorian and Edwardian period, or pictures of different objects. Collect illustrated books, photographs and engravings which show the local area in the period. Facsimile pages from nineteenth-century shopping catalogues would also be useful.

Resources needed
Photocopiable page 157, artefacts, photographs, pictures of Victorian and Edwardian paintings and engravings, facsimile pages from nineteenth century shopping catalogues, paper for labels, sheets of paper with numbers for recording findings, pencils.

▲ Choose one object from this page and write its life story as if it were used by someone in your local area.

What to do
Distribute the artefacts so that children can work in pairs or groups of three. Allow each group to spend a few minutes looking closely at the artefact (or picture) they have been given. Each object should be labelled with a number. Each group should be given a piece of paper that has a list of the numbers relating to the labelled artefacts. The paper could be divided into columns so that an answer can be recorded for each of the questions suggested below. The children should be encouraged to ask questions about the artefact they have been given, for example: What is it made of? Is it complete? What kind of person might have used it? What do you think the object was used for? When they have finished, the children could be given a new object to examine in a similar way and then record their conclusions. When the children have looked at all the objects, discuss their written

conclusions. How many children made the same assessment about each object?

Then distribute copies of photocopiable page 157. Ask each child to choose one object from the page and to write its life history as if it were once used by someone locally. This activity could have more impact if the available objects are known to have a real history or if they are actually related to the local area.

Suggestion(s) for extension
The children could find out more about the sort of person who might have owned/used the artefact they have chosen to write about. They could draw a picture of the person with the artefact to illustrate their work.

Suggestion(s) for support
As an alternative to writing the life history of their object some children could make a large drawing of it instead. They could give it a face and draw a large bubble coming out of its mouth. A shorter version of the story told by the object could then be written inside the bubble.

Assessment opportunities
The children could be given an artefact or pictures of an artefact at random and asked to suggest ways in which their object might have been used in Victorian or Edwardian times.

Opportunities for IT
The children could use a word processor to write labels or questions for a display of the artefacts. Children could experiment with different fonts and layouts to make the display more interesting. Extended writing could include the children's ideas for the life history of the artefact.

Display ideas
A display could be made of the artefacts together with the children's stories, drawings and explanations.

Reference to photocopiable sheet
Photocopiable page 157 includes a selection of artefacts from a late Victorian shopping catalogue (1895). The information can be used to help identify other objects from that time.

VISUAL EVIDENCE

To use visual evidence to investigate changes in the local area across different periods.

†† *Pairs, followed by class discussion.*

🕐 *30 minutes.*

Previous skills/knowledge needed
Previous work on the interpretation of visual evidence. This activity will also build on any work on local history using sources such as maps.

Key background information
The availability of pictures will vary enormously from area to area but may include engravings and paintings of local views made in the eighteenth or nineteenth centuries. Before the growth of photography in the 1840s, these were the only visual means of recording what a landscape looked like and the appearance of old buildings. Old photographs, which are a rich source of information, often show rural communities that have long since been absorbed into modern conurbations or changed beyond all recognition. Photographs show not only how people lived, what they did, what they wore, etc., but they also provide a record of particular events. At a local level this could include weddings, funerals, celebrations, fairs and sporting events. However, it is important to remember when using photographs as historical evidence that they can only show one small part of an event and it is impossible to gain a full impression of what really happened from one shot; the camera can indeed 'lie'.

Preparation
Make a collection of visual material which shows the local area in different periods of the past. This could include: pictures of paintings, engravings, drawings, illustrated maps,

old photographs and old postcards. A similar collection of modern day visual material would be useful for reference.

Resources needed

Old photographs, photographic reproductions of paintings of the local area, illustrated maps, engravings and postcards. A collection of present day visual material of the local area, including a modern map for reference, writing materials.

What to do

Ask the children to consider what kinds of pictures might be available showing the area round the school and/or the local community as it was in the past. Remind the children that before the growth of photography in the 1840s people wishing to record a scene, a particular event or how someone looked either painted or drew a picture of what they saw.

Distribute the visual material so that each pair of children has at least one example to study. Ask them to discuss the image in pairs. They could be asked to make a list of questions they would like to ask before going on to suggest possible answers. Alternatively they might be asked to consider the following questions and make notes of their answers: What form does the visual material take? Was it a photograph? A painting using oil paints? etc. What does the picture show? (The children should describe in detail what they can see.) Is there anything in the picture that can still be seen today? If so, what changes have taken place? Is it possible to find evidence of these changes on old maps?

The children could exchange pictures and list things that have changed and those that look as though they are the same. A class discussion about the children's findings should follow. Then show the children the modern visual material of the local area. Ask them to describe the main changes that

have taken place. Reference should also be made to old and modern maps of the same location. Is it possible to see any of the changes that have taken place on the modern map?

Suggestion(s) for extension

The children could be asked to list the possible disadvantages of using paintings or drawings as historical sources. They could also be asked to consider whether there are circumstances in which a photograph might be unreliable.

Suggestion(s) for support

Some children could examine an old and a recent picture or photograph taken from a similar angle so that a comparison between the two will be easier.

Assessment opportunities

The children could talk about the usefulness of pictures and photographs as evidence.

Opportunities for IT

Children could use a word processor to write questions or commentaries about the picture they have studied. If the picture can be scanned into a digital format it can be loaded into a word processor, desktop publishing or drawing package and the labels or commentary added around it.

A useful long term resource for the school would be to create a bank of old pictures on a Kodak CD-ROM so that they can be used in any suitable computer program.

Display ideas

Pictures of the locality could be arranged in a timeline with a written commentary added by members of the class.

Photocopiables

The pages in this section can be photocopied for use in the classroom or school which has purchased this book, and do not need to be declared in any return in respect of any photocopying licence.

They comprise pupil worksheets and resource material for use by the children. Most of the photocopiable pages are related to individual activities in the book; the name of the activity is indicated at the top of the sheet, together with a page reference indicating where the lesson plan for that activity can be found.

Individual pages are discussed in detail within each lesson plan, accompanied by ideas for adaptation where appropriate – of course, each sheet can be adapted to suit your own needs, and those of your class. Sheets can also be coloured, laminated, mounted on to card, enlarged and so on where appropriate.

A Tudor family tree, see page 18

The Tudor family tree

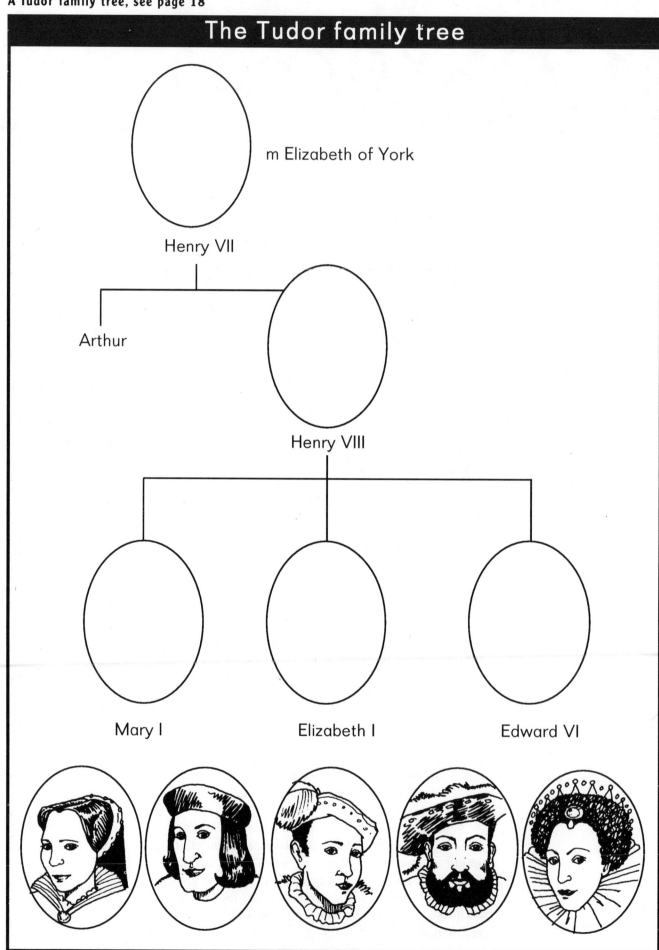

m Elizabeth of York

Henry VII

Arthur

Henry VIII

Mary I   Elizabeth I   Edward VI

Religious changes

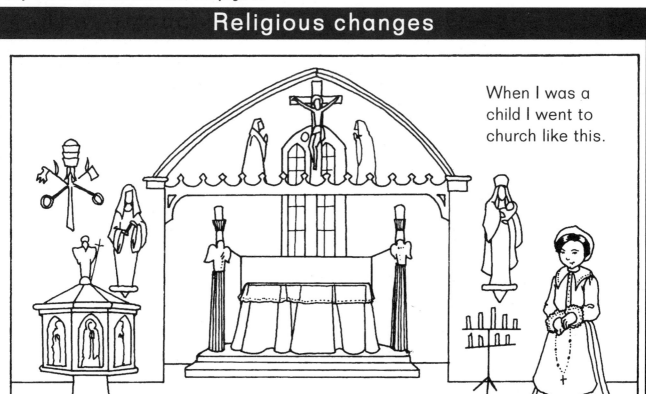

When I was a child I went to church like this.

By the time I had grown up, the church had changed and now looks like this.

▲ Look carefully at these two pictures of the church.
▲ Make a list of things that changed and things that stayed the same.
▲ Try to find out about why these changes took place.

Henry VIII and his accounts, see page 21

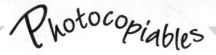

Accounts

▲ Translate the Roman numerals into Arabic numbers. Write out the amount of expenditure for each item in full using pounds, shillings and pence.
Key: **li**=pounds, **s**=shillings, **d**=pence.

Payment in April 1530

The xviii day paid in reward to the gardener of Hampton Court for bringing herbs	vi s viii d
The xx day paid to the garden at Windsor for one quarter wage due at our Lady Day	xx s
The xxii day paid to Walshe the gardener at Greenwich for weeding delving and for labourers	xx s

May 1530

To master Hennage for so much money by him paid to a servant of the Abbot of Gloucester for bringing a sturgeon to the King	x s
The xviii day paid to one in reward for bringing home Ball, the King's dog that was lost in the Forest of Waltham	v s
The xxi day paid to Walter Walshe for the cost of transport as well as the taylor and skinner for certain material and workmanship for my Lady Anne. As also to the printer for several books	lix li xviii s
The xxiii day paid to William Locke for certain silks and several other things on his bill	ccxxxii li x s iii d

December 1530

Paid v day to the clockmaker Vincent Keney for eleven clocks	xix li ii s vi d
Paid viii day to a poor man that had xiii children for their relief	iii li vi s viii d
Paid xxv day the Italian jeweller for certain pearls	ccclxxii li xi s iiii d

Dissolution

(Dorchester Abbey, 1530) The monks went off fishing and hunting.
They attended choir three times a year.

(Ramsey Priory, 1517) The prior is a bad tempered drunkard, who gets on well with his friends but is brutally hard with everyone else. The senior monks sent the junior monks off to say their office and then went off to play dice for money. As they played they swore hideously.

(Leicester Abbey, 1527) When the Abbot went to choir, he took his jester with him, who made quite a disturbance and laughter with his fooling and his songs.

The following items were sold from Brewood Nunnery, Staffordshire at the prices shown in pounds (**li**), shillings (**s**) and pence (**d**):

In the church – one table of alabaster, old forms and seats, ii partitions of carved wood, paving from the church and choir, panes of glass and one massbook *xx* **s**

In the vestry – ii pairs of green linen vestments, i old cope, i surplice, i altar cloth, i towel, i little bell and a brass censer *iiii* **s**

In the chapter house – iii panes of glass and two long forms *xii* **d**

Bells in the steeple – ii unsold bells are still in the steeple

The Hall – ii tables and a form *xii* **d**

The parlour – i folding table, i form, i chair, i cupboard and hangings of painted cloth *ii* **s**

The bailiff's bedroom, one matress, i coverlet, one blanket and one axe *xx* **d**

The buttery – ii ale tubs, i old chest, i board, i table cloth and ii brass candlesticks *xii* **d**

The larder – i trough and two little barrells *vi* **d**

The cheese loft – ii little tubs, two cheese racks, ii churns, i little wheel and ii shelves *viii* **d**

Waggons – i wain and i dung cart *xvi* **d**

Hay – *x* loads of hay *xv* **s**

Hunted priests, see page 24

Hunted priests

One Easter Monday, while it was still dark, the family were preparing for Mass when they suddenly heard the sound of horses' hooves on the drive. The next minute the house was surrounded. Upstairs, the altar which had been laid for Mass was quickly stripped. Hiding places were opened up and Father Gerard's papers and books and other belongings thrown inside. Mrs Wiseman, the lady of the house insisted that Gerard should hide under the chapel hearth, although there was no food or drink provided there. As the men hammered at the downstairs doors the priest was hastily passed a couple of biscuits and a little quince jelly as he was hidden away. They knew well that Father Gerard was inside the house. They knocked on the walls and floors of the different rooms measuring the widths of walls and they used candles to search in every nook and cranny, smashing open anything that they thought sounded hollow. They were determined to get him. For four days, Gerard had lain without sleep and starving. It was dark and cramped in the hiding place and he expected to be discovered any minute. Father Gerard continues:

'They had been in the room above and had examined the fireplace through which I had got into my hole. With the help of a ladder they climbed into the flue and sounded it with a hammer, and I heard one of them saying to another: "There might easily be an entrance at the back of the chimney." "Hardly," said the other whose voice I recognised... – "But there might easily be an entrance at the back of the chimney." As soon as he said this, he gave the place a kick. I was afraid he would notice the hollow sound of the hole in which I was hiding.'

▲ Can you continue Father Gerard's story? Your teacher will be able to tell you what actually happened to Father Gerard next.

Elizabeth I

"On her head she wore a great red wig. As for her face it is and appears to be very aged. It is long and thin and her teeth are very yellow and unequal. Many of them are missing so that one cannot understand her easily when she speaks quickly"

A description by a French ambassador in 1597.

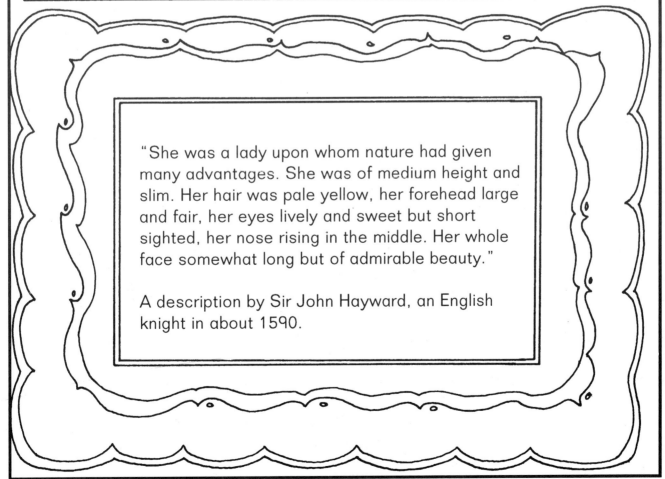

"She was a lady upon whom nature had given many advantages. She was of medium height and slim. Her hair was pale yellow, her forehead large and fair, her eyes lively and sweet but short sighted, her nose rising in the middle. Her whole face somewhat long but of admirable beauty."

A description by Sir John Hayward, an English knight in about 1590.

Tudor court (gifts)

This is a list of some of the gifts presented to Queen Elizabeth I on New Year's Day 1589.

By the Earle of Northumberland, one jewell of golde like a lampe garnesshed with sparks of diamonds and one oppall.

By the Lord Seymer, a confett box of mother -of-pearles, garnesshed with small sparks of rubies.

By the Barrones Lumley, a wastecoate of white taffety, imbrodered all over with a twist of flowers of Venis gold, silver and some black silke.

By the Barrones Shandowes Knolls, a stoole of wood paynted, the seate covered with murry velvet, ymbrodered all over with pillers arched of Venis gold, silver and silke.

By Sir Oratio Palavizino, one bodkyn of silver gilte, havinge a pendaunt jewell of gold, like a shipp, garnished with opaulls, sparks of diamonds, and three small perles pendaunt.

By Mrs Blaunch Aparry, one long cushion of tawny cloth of gold, backed with taffety.

By Mr John Stanhop, a large bagg of white satten, ymbrodered all over with flowers, beasts and burds, of Venis gold, silver and silke.

By Mr Doctor Bayly, a pott of greene gynger, and a pott of the rynds of lemons

By John Smithson, Master Cooke, one faire marchpayne, with St George in the middest.

By John Dudley, Sargeante of the Pastry, one faire pye of quinces orringed.

▲ What presents did Queen Elizabeth receive on New Year's Day?

▲ Which do you think she preferred the most?

▲ Which were the most expensive presents?

▲ Draw a selection of the presents which Elizabeth received on New Year's Day.

Law and Order, see page 28

Crime in Tudor times

Thomas Harman wrote about hookers in 1567. Hookers are thieves who '....vigilantly mark where or in what place they may attain to their prey, casting their eyes up to every window, well noting what they see there, whether apparel or linen, hanging near unto the said windows....They customarily carry with them a staff of four or five feet long, in which, within one inch of the top thereof, is a little hole bored through, in which hole they put an iron hook, and... pluck unto them quickly anything that they may reach therewith.'

William Fleetwood was recorder of the City of London and he wrote about a school for cutpurses in 1585.
'There were hung up two devices, the one was a pocket, the other was a purse. The pocket had in it certain counters and was hung about with hawks' bells, and over the top did hang a little scaring bell; and he that could take a counter without any noise was allowed to be a Public Foister: and he that could take a piece of silver out of the purse without the noise of any of the bells, he was adjudged a Judicial Nipper.'

This picture shows the art of picking locks.

This picture shows a young man gambling with dice.

This picture is of John Selman who was a well known cut purse. He was arrested on Christmas Day, 1611 during a church service and executed a year later.

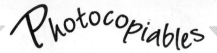

Sir Francis Drake and his voyages of exploration, see page 30

Sir Francis Drake

▲ Draw the route which Sir Francis Drake took on his voyage of circumnavigation on this map of the world. Design your own key to record the information.

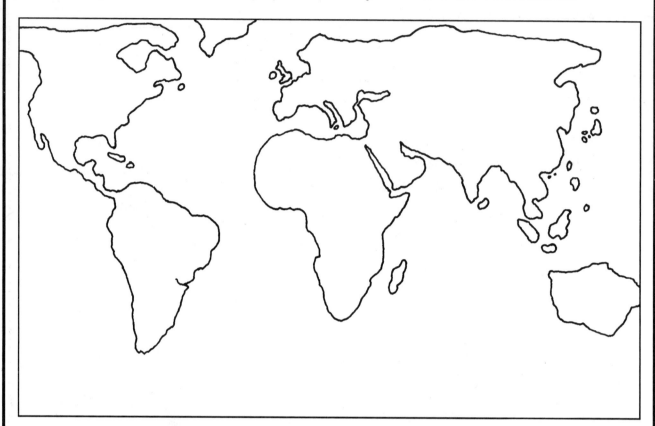

December 13th 1577 Drake leaves Plymouth.

June 18th 1588. Drake lands near Magellan Straits. One of his captains, Doughty tries to start a mutiny and Drake executes him.

August 20th 1588 Drake heads into the Magellan Straits.

September Drake's fleet emerges from the straits, but is scattered by gales.

October 7th 1588 Drake reaches the Chilean coast in the Golden Hind.

December 5th Drake captures 25,000 pesos of gold at Valparaiso.

March 1st 1579 Drake captures treasure ship Cacafuego with a load of Peruvian silver.

March 16th 1579 Drake reaches Nicaraguan coast.

April 16th 1579 Drake begins cruise up Californian coast.

June/July 1579 The Golden Hind overhauled and California claimed for Queen Elizabeth.

July/August 1579 Drake sets sail across the Pacific.

October 1579 Drake reaches the Moluccas and trades for cloves.

March 26th 1580 Drake sets off for Cape of Good Hope.

June/July 1580 Drake enters the Atlantic.

September 26th 1580 Golden Hind arrives back in Plymouth.

The Armada, see page 31

The Armada

▲ Drawing of the route of the Spanish Armada

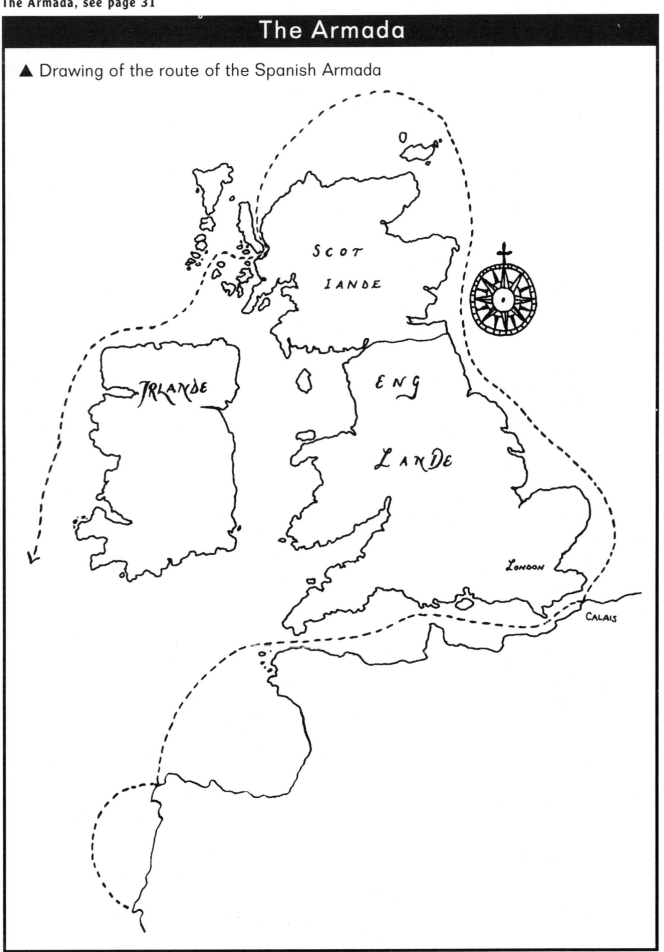

The Armada, see page 31

The Armada

▲ Cut out the pictures above and arrange in the correct order to tell the story of the Armada.

▲ Draw more pictures of your own to complete the sequence

Games and pastimes in Tudor times, see page 33

Games

This picture shows a variety of games and activities which were popular in Tudor times.

▲ Which activities can you recognise? Are any of these activities still popular today?

A hornbook

Education in Tudor times, see page 34

Dean Colet's Statutes for his Foundation

The Children

There shall be taught in the school children of all nations and countries indifferently to the number of 153, according to the number of seats in the school.

The master shall admit these children as they be offered from time to time, but first see that they can recite the catechism, and also that he can read and write competently, else let him not be admitted in no wise.

A child at the first admission once for ever shall pay 4.d for the writing of his name. This money of the admissions shall the poor scholar have that sweepeth the school, and keepeth the school clean.

In every form one principal child shall be placed in the chair, president of that form.

The children shall come unto school in the morning at 7 of the clock, both winter and summer, and tarry there until 11, and return again at one of the clock, and depart at 5, and thrice in the day prostrate they shall say the prayers with due tract and pausing, as they be contained in a table in the school, that is to say, in the morning and at noon and at evening.

In the school in no time in the year they shall use tallow candle in no wise, but only wax candle, at the cost of their friends.

Also I will they bring in no meat or drink, nor bottles, nor use in the school no breakfasts nor drinkings in the time of learning in no wise; if they need drink let them be provided in some other place.

I will they use no cockfighting, nor riding about of victory, nor disputing at St. Bartholomew's, which is but foolish babbling and loss of time.

Tudor buildings, see page 36

Timber framed buildings in Tudor times

▲ Look at these different buildings.
What materials are they made of? What were the buildings used for?

Moreton Hall

Grammar School

Guild Hall

Farmhouse

The Globe Theatre, see page 37

The Globe Theatre

▲ When you have listened to the story of one of Shakespeare's plays, retell the story in your own words for a visitor to the theatre. Decorate your programme for the play. Think carefully about the characters and other things you could draw.

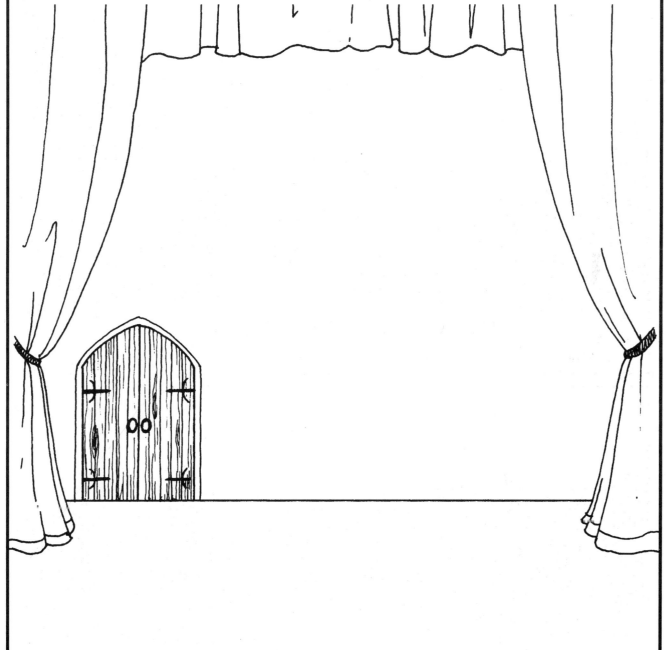

The railway revolution, see page 40

The railway revolution

How long did it take?

By stage-coach   By early steam train

▲ Find out the approximate distances in miles between the following cities:

Manchester to London _____   Bristol to Plymouth _____

Leeds to Birmingham _____   Newcastle to Leeds _____

London to Cardiff _____   London to Bristol _____

▲ How long would it have taken you to make these journeys by stage-coach (average speed 6 mph)? Now work out how long the same journey would have taken you by train (George Stephenson's *Rocket* could travel 18–20 mph).

▲ How would this have changed your life if you were a regular traveller in early Victorian Britain?

Photocopiables

The age of the steamship, see page 42

The age of the steamship

▲ Here are three ships designed by Isambard Kingdom Brunel. What differences can you see between the ships?

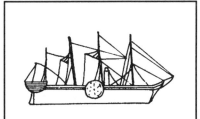  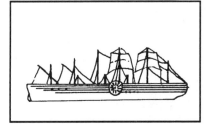

Great Western · Great Britain · Great Eastern

▲ Here is some information about the three ships. Use it to answer the following questions.

Which ship is the oldest?
What ship is the longest?
Which ship has no paddles?
Which ships had hulls made of iron?
Which ship had the most powerful engine?

Some particulars of the three ships as originally built			
	Great Western	Great Britain	Great Eastern
Date of launch	1837	1843	1858
Length overall	236 feet	322 feet	692 feet
Length between perpendiculars	212 feet	285 feet	680 feet
Breadth over paddles	59.8 feet		118 feet
Breadth of hull	35.3 feet	50.5 feet	82.5 feet
Depth to upper deck	23.2 feet	32 feet	58.0 feet
Draught laden	16.7 feet	18 feet	30 feet
Displacement at load draught	2300 tons	3675 tons	27380 tons
Hull material	Wood	Iron	Iron
Iron weight in hull		1040 tons	6250 tons
Propulsion	Sails and paddles	Sails and screw	Sails, screw and paddles
Design horsepower	420	1000	Paddles 1000 Screw 1600
Paddle diameter	28.7 feet	15 feet	56 feet
Screw: diameter	–	25 feet	24 feet
pitch	–	–	44 feet
blades	–	6	4
revolutions per minute	–	54	39

Religion, church and chapel, see page 44

Church and chapel

▲ Information I have found out about religion in Victorian Britain.

Church of England

_____

_____

_____

_____

_____

_____

_____

_____

_____

_____

_____

Non-conformists

_____

_____

_____

_____

_____

_____

_____

_____

_____

Victorian education and Ragged Schools, see page 46

Victorian education and Ragged Schools

Mary Carpenter was a teacher who lived in Bristol where she saw crowds of poor homeless children tattered and filthy begging for scraps. Some poor boys worked as crossing sweepers, donkey drivers or sellers of fire-wood. The girls sold oranges, watercress, matches or flowers. Like the sea birds in the harbour these children lived by scavenging what they could get.

In 1846, Mary Carpenter made plans to start a ragged school in a very poor slum district of Bristol. She rented a room in a tenement house and was given money by her local congregational church to help get the school started. She provided combs, towels and soap for the children to have a wash. When the school began Mr Phelps, the teacher, had a difficult time of it. He would go out into the gutter and invite boys in. The children pushed and shoved each other around. Benches were upset, books torn up and pictures ripped from the walls. At one stage, there was even blood on the floor and one boy shoved another's head through the window, shattering the glass and cutting his scalp.

Bit by bit things began to change. By the winter, local people were amazed to see a group of barefooted boys marching in twos with Mr Phelps, their teacher, as if they were on a Sunday school walk. The neighbours noticed that the streets were quieter and the local Mayor, who had said that the school taught them nothing but how to become thieves and rogues, had to say, when he called at the school, that he was pleasantly surprised. By Christmas, the school had become so successful that they needed a larger room. More than forty boys were coming in the day time and many more, including many girls, wanted to come if a night school could be held.

'Of 1,600 children in fifteen ragged schools, 162 had been in prison, 116 had run away from home because of ill-treatment, 170 lived in common lodging houses, 253 lived by begging, 216 had no shoes or stockings, 101 had no under linen, 68 children were children of convicts, 219 never slept in a bed, 306 had lost one or both parents.'
The Earl of Shaftesbury addressing Parliament in 1848.

▲ Imagine that you were going to Mary Carpenter's ragged school for the first time. What were the other children like? What did you learn? Describe your first day at school.

A Victorian census, see page 48

A Victorian census

▲ This is a page from the census taken in 1851 for one street in the parish of Henbury in Gloucestershire. Use this information to find out more about the people who lived there at that time. What differences do you notice from families today?

Name or No. of House	Name & Surname of each Person who abode in the house, on the night of the 30th March 1851	Relation to Head of Family	Condition	Age of Males	Age of Females	Rank, Profession or Occupation	Where born	Whether Blind or Deaf or Dumb
96	John Hathway	Head	Mar	54		Farmer of 80 Acres	Glostersh Westerleigh	✓
	Mary A Hathway	Wife	Mar		38	Farmers Wife	Somersetsh Portishead	
	Emma J Hathway	Daug	U		21	Farmers Daug	Glostersh Henbury	
	Henry Hathway	Son		17		Farmers Son	Glostersh Henbury	
	William Davis	Servant		40		Farm Labourer	Pembroke Sh	✓
97	William Smith	Head	Mar	51		Agricultural Labourer	Glostersh Alveston	
	Sarah Smith	Wife	Mar		42		Glostersh Alveston	
	William Smith	Son		12			Glostersh Alveston	
	George Smith	Son		7			Glostersh Alveston	
	Emma Smith	Daug			4		Glostersh Alveston	
98	Richard Willis	Head	Mar	58		Farmer	Glostersh Henbury	✓
	Grace Willis	Wife	Mar		57		Glostersh Barnstaple	
	George Willis	Son	U	18		Farmers Son	Glostersh Henbury	
	Charlotte Roberts	Daug	Mar		31		Glostersh Henbury	
	Richard Roberts	Grandson		8			Glostersh Henbury	
99	Hester Allen	Head	Wid		65		Glostersh Henbury	
	Eliza Allen	Daug	U		26		Glostersh Henbury	
	William Allen	Son	U	23		Fisherman	Glostersh Henbury	
	Elizabeth Britton	Aunt	U		67		Glostersh Henbury	✓
	Charles Anstice	Servant	U	16			Somersetsh Pill	
100	Edwin Webb	Head	Marr	29		Beer Retailer	Glostersh Henbury	
	Maria Webb	Wife	Marr		27		Glostersh Henbury	
	Edwin Webb	Son		3			Glostersh Henbury	
	Robert Webb	Lodger	U	29		Agricultural Labourer	Glostersh Henbury	
	Henry Collins	Lodger	U	36		Agricultural Labourer	Glostersh Littleton	
101	George Parker	Head	Marr	42		Farm of 90 Acres	Glostersh Almondsbury	✓
	Sarah Parker	Wife	Marr		42		Somersetsh Norton	
	Samuel Sharp	Servant	U	20		Farm Labourer	Glostersh Stoke	
	Charles Deer	Servant		15		Farm Labourer	Glostersh Henbury	
102	William Gregory	Head	Marr	56		Farmer of 74 Acres Employing 2 Labourers	Hampshire Hatten	✓
	Dinah Gregory	Wife	Marr		61		Staffordshire Boddington	✓
	Mary A Powles	Grandaug			11		Glostersh Henbury	
	Hannah Horner	Servant	U		18	House Servant	Glostersh Henbury	
	Henry Wheeler	Servant	U	25		Farm Labourer	Glostersh Henbury	

A Victorian Christmas and entertainment at home, see page 50

A Victorian Christmas

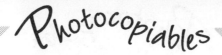

Conditions in factories, mills and mines, see page 52

Working conditions

Here is part of a report which shows you how few children attended school in one part of South Wales in 1839. Can you suggest why this was so?

▲ Look at the total number of children compared with the whole population in each Welsh town.

▲ What differences do you notice? Which town has the poorest school attendance?

Parish	Elementary schools	Dame schools (2–5 year olds)	Total at school	Total Population
Merthyr	15	8	1,322	34,000
Bedwelty	13	10	825	20,000
Aberystwyth	2	4	300	8,000
Trevethin	13	7	638	16,000
Mynnyddyslwynn	4	4	223	7,000
TOTALS	47	33	3,308	85,000

In his report on the miners and iron workers of Bedwelty and Merthyr Tydfil in 1839, Seymour Tremenheere recorded the following account about school attendance:

'(Children) are taken away whenever their father has not earned as much as usual, or has spent more. They think instruction of any kind very little necessary for girls, whose assistance at home they are unwilling to dispense with. The boys are taken into the coal or iron mine at eight or nine years old, often earlier. The value of the labour of the youngest is about 6d a day.'

These are the average weekly wages for boys who worked down the mines.
▲ How do these wages compare with your pocket money?
Boys from 7 to 9 years of age – 3s to 5s per week (3s = 15p; 5s = 25p)
Boys from 9 to 16 years of age – 6s to 12s per week (6s = 30p; 12s = 60p)

Within your group find out:
▲ What is the total number of adults who live in your homes? (Your group only)
▲ What is the total number of children who live in your homes? (Your group only)
▲ What is the total number of adults who live in your homes? (All the class)
▲ What is the total number of children who live in your homes? (All the class)

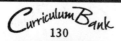

The growth of towns, see page 54

The growth of towns

Here is a picture of an industrial city in the early Victorian period. What do you think it would be like to live there? Describe some of the houses and factories.

This is how a Frenchman called Alexis de Tocqueville described Manchester at the beginning of the Victorian period:

'The **wretched** dwellings of the poor are scattered **haphazard** around them. Round them stretches land **uncultivated** ... and still without the **amenities** of a town. The soil has been taken away, scratched and torn up in a thousand places, but it is not yet covered with the **habitations** of men. The land is given over to industry's use. The roads which connect the still **dis-jointed** limbs of a great city, show, like the rest, every sign of hurried or unfinished work... Some of these roads are paved, but most of them are full of ruts and puddles into which foot or carriage wheel sinks deep. Heaps of dung, rubble from buildings, **putrid**, **stagnant** pools are found here and there among the houses and over the bumpy, pitted surfaces of the public places...

A sort of black smoke covers the city. The sun is seen though it is a disk without rays. Under this half daylight 300,000 human beings are **ceaselessly** at work. A thousand noises disturb this damp, dark **labyrinth**, but they are not all the sounds one hears in great cities.'

▲ Find out what the words in bold letters mean. Read the description again and make your own picture of life in an industrial city during the early Victorian period. Underneath, describe some of the things that you have learned.

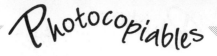

The growth of towns

It took a long time for conditions in Victorian towns to improve. Life for the old and the poor was terrible. Men like the Earl of Shaftesbury had to work hard to change things. Here are some of the changes that the Victorians made to improve life in Britain's biggest towns.

▲ Match the boxes on the left with those on the right. On the left are conditions in early Victorian towns; on the right are changes (or reforms) that were introduced by Parliament.

Lack of good water supply and sewers: people died of cholera and typhoid	Public Health Acts result in proper sewers
People made to work long hours in factories Women and children sent down mines	Schools are set up for all to attend
Enormous number of the population have no opportunity to be educated in school	Working conditions are improved
Housing for many is overcrowded and unhealthy Little attempt at careful town planning	The opportunity to vote in elections is extended
Crime is widespread in the streets of big cities	An improved police force and better law and order Street lighting using gas manufactured in the towns
Poor people have no say in how they are governed	Better city planning and better housing conditions The first public housing

The workhouse, see page 56

The workhouse

This is a description of a workhouse written by Friedrich Engels in 1844:

'The food is worse than that of the most ill-paid working man while employed and they work harder... The food of criminal prisoners is better, as a rule, so that the paupers frequently commit some offence for the purpose of getting into jail. For the workhouse is a jail too; he who does not finish the task gets nothing to eat; he who wishes to go out must ask permission, which is granted or not, according to his behaviour or the inspector's whim; tobacco is forbidden, also the receipt of gifts from relatives or friends outside the house; the paupers wear a house uniform... the men break stones... the women, children and aged men pick oakum.'

(These were jobs that were usually done by prisoners in jails. Oakum was ship's rope, stiff with tar which had to be broken down into small pieces for making ships' timbers watertight.)

▲ Imagine that you have just visited a workhouse and are very unhappy with the conditions that you have seen. Write a letter to the Board of Guardians who control the workhouse. Tell them some of the things that you saw and suggest what could be done to improve conditions.

Architectural styles and public buildings, see page 57

Victorian architectural styles

▲ Using a pair of scissors, carefully cut out each of these buildings and mount them on a sheet of card. Underneath each building write your own caption, stating what you have been able to find out about it.

Photocopiables

Mechanisation comes to farming, see page 60

Mechanisation comes to farming

	By 1850s	By 1950s	By 1990s
Milking			
Ploughing			
Harvesting Grain			

▲ Look at the pictures carefully. Describe in your own words the developments that had taken place in agricultural methods by the 1950s.

▲ Make your own drawings in the boxes on the right of modern farming methods in the 1990s or write about some of the changes that have happened since the last century.

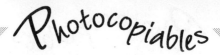
The development and impact of the motor car, see page 63

Development of the motor car

Here are some of the problems that developed as the motor car became more and more popular. The solutions are mixed up.

▲ Match the problems to their correct solutions.

Problem	Solution
1934 Concern about speeding	Mini Minor introduced in 1959
1939–45 Petrol in short supply, priority given to war effort	Government plan to introduce drink/drive law
1955 Increase in traffic volume	Government introduce 30 mph limit in towns
1955 People are worried about cost of fuel	Councils plan to build urban motorways
1960 Enormous expansion of motoring	Government plan to build motorways
1965 Alarming number of road accidents	Government plan to axe uneconomic railways lines
1966 Traffic jams in large cities	Petrol rationing introduced

One Man's War, see page 65

One Man's War

▲ Look carefully at each of the items on this page.
What does each one tell you about Frank Jackson?

This is a photograph of Frank Jackson with his daughter. He carried it with him when he went off to war.

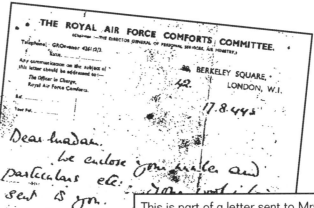

This is part of a letter sent to Mrs Jackson enclosing wool for making 'comforts' for service men. Comforts were woollen articles which did not form part of a serviceman's regular kit, but were made by volunteers. Mrs Jackson loved knitting and was keen to help the war effort by making woollen clothing for servicemen. As the letter suggests, the wool was supplied by the RAF Comforts Committee.

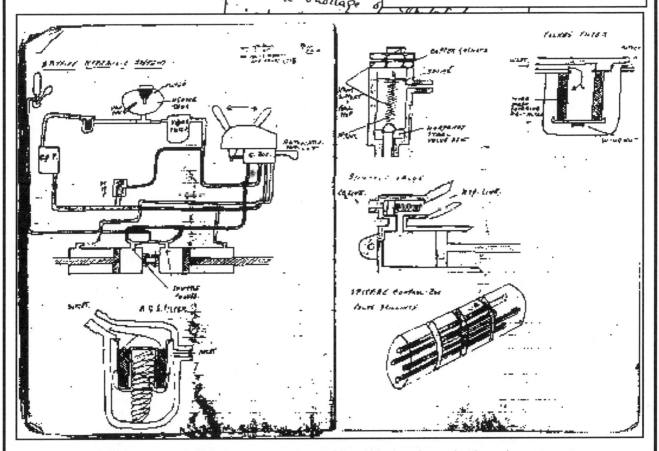

Right: This is a drawing from a page in one of Frank Jackson's notebooks on how to repair aircraft. Frank filled several exercise books with notes and diagrams to help him with his work. The information includes how to repair bullet holes in the wings of aeroplanes.

One Man's War, see page 65

One Man's War

Management
HUMAYAN THEATRES LTD.
House Manager
JOHN D. EDEN
E.N.S.A. Entertainments
for H. M. Forces
By Arrangement with Canteen Services (India)
present
"THE ENSA
WELSH CHOIR"
IN
A CAVALCADE OF SONG
"From Folk Song to Grand Opera"
Under the Direction
OF
LIONEL ROWLANDS
Commencing Monday, 14th January, 1946, at 9 p.m.
CALCUTTA

This is a programme of entertainment provided in India for HM Forces. ENSA, which the forces called Every Night Something Awful, was the government organisation responsible for arranging entertainment for the forces overseas.

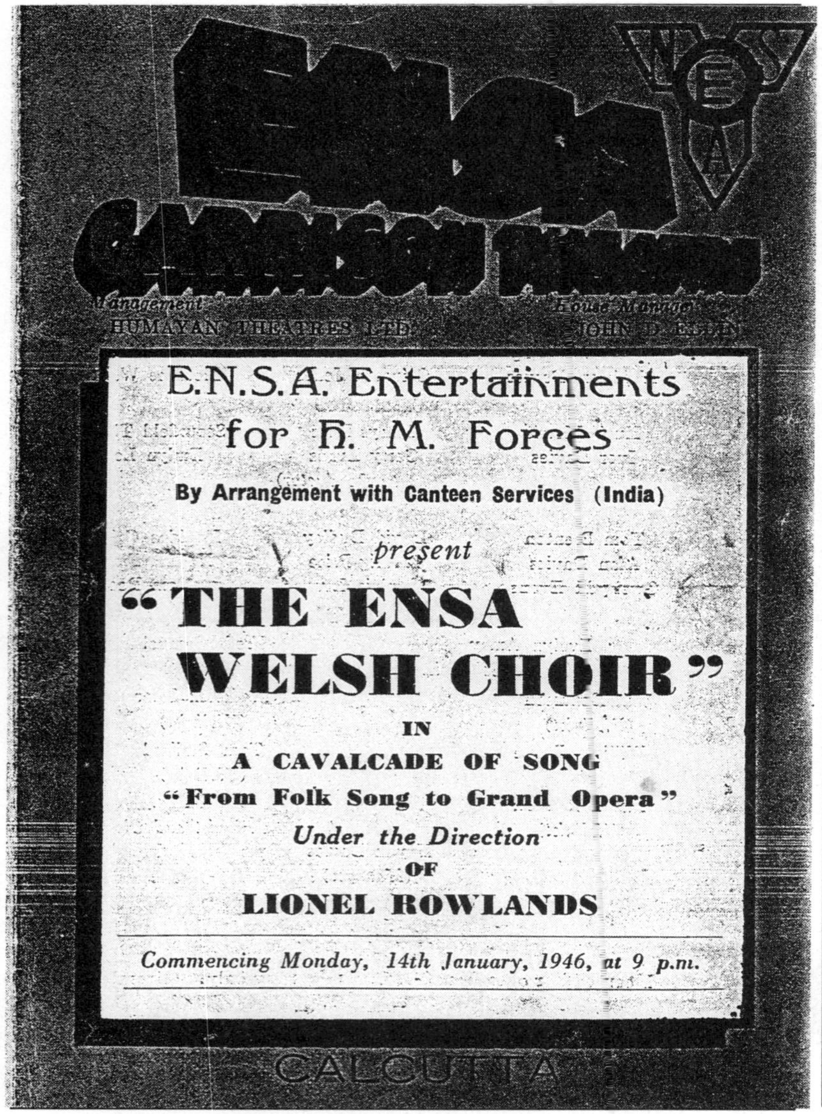

LIST IF ITEMS TO BE WITHDRAWN AT UNIT BEFORE DAPARTURE TO WORLI.

1 Officers. W.O.'s and N.C.O. Aircrew.

All items on form 667. Flying Clothes Card, except Boots Mosquito. (to be withdrawn by B.R.D. Worli.) and items detailed in appendix 11. Form 667B are to be retained by the individual. Officers who desire to read in their Caps Kits may do so in accordance with ACSEA Order 160/45.

11. Airmen W.O.'s and N.C.O. Aircrew.

Sec/Ref.	Description	Denom.	Qty.
21E SD13	Dhurries small.	Each.	1
SD19	Lines Bedding	"	1
378	Sheets cotton.	"	12
22B 27	Knives clasp.	"	1
29	Lanyards.	"	1
35	Towels Hand.	"	1
23 221	Helmets Crash (M/Cyc only.)	"	1
157	Helmets Steel.	Each.	1
10 or 230	Whistles (aircrew or police.)	"	1
191	Nets Camouflage.	Each.	1
22G 587	Gloves M.T. L.H.(M.T.Drivers only)		1
590	" " R.H. "	Each. "	1
22H 236	Armlets Geneva cross MEC. Only.)		1
578	" Police, Police only.)		1
23A & 23B	Allpersonal Anti Gas Equipment.		
	All personal webbing equipment except the following items :-		
	Bottles Water		
	Carriers Water bottle.		
	Haversacks.		
	Braces left.		
	Braces right		
	Bags ration.		
	Tins mess.		
	Belts Waist. (W.OL and N.C.O. aircrew only.		
	Holsters pistol.	----------do----------	
	Pouchers Ammo.	----------do----------	

Flight or Section Commanders are to ensure that the above items are returned to store by personnel on clearing for release. 664B action is to be ititiated by Flight or Section Commanders for any deficient items.

Above: Equipment list

Post-war reconstruction, see page 68

Post-war reconstruction

Here is a list of questions that could be asked about life in Britain at the end of the war and the immediate post-war years, and then about life in Britain after 1950.

The end of the war and conditions in post-war Britain

What were you doing during the war?

Where were you living when the war ended?

How did you celebrate the end of the war?

Did you move house during the war or soon after the war ended?

What was rationing like and how did you manage?

Do you remember eating bananas for the first time after the war?

What do you remember about the general election of 1945?

What were the effects of the bitterly cold winter of 1947?

Please describe anything you can remember about it.

What were fashions like at this time? Did you use clothing coupons?

Can you remember having to pay for a visit to the doctor or dentist?

Did the introduction of the National Health Service make any difference to you? If so, how?

After 1950

Did you have a radio? If so, what were your favourite programmes?

What were your favourite toys?

What can you remember about the Festival of Britain of 1951?

What books, newspapers, and comics did you read?

When did you first see television?

When did you get your first TV set?

Can you remember any early programmes on TV?

Did you see any events such as the Coronation on TV?

Did your family have a car by 1950? If not, when did they get one?

Do you remember getting your first washing machine?

How was washing done in your house before then?

Photocopiables

The Coronation

'Then, at last, we saw the flash of bright helmets and we knew that the long-awaited pageant had begun. So for almost an hour we watched wonderful bands, superb marching, RAF, Navy, Royal Marines and the Army mostly in its blue uniforms ending up with the Brigade of Guards in vermilion coats, with their great bearskins on their heads. More rain at this moment and the bearskins were bedraggled and dripping with water... Then the rain stopped in time for the carriage procession to pass...

At last came the great golden coach with its glorious trappings, riders and horses. We focused our eyes intently on the lovely creature sitting bolt upright in her seat smiling with a serene dignity at her excited people. Beside her sat the smiling figure of the Prince in his lovely gold braided uniform. It was like something out of a fairy story.... an artist would have the greatest difficulty in capturing the delicacy of the rose and white complexioned Queen with her smiling blue eyes and glorious robes and crown.'

Here are some of the items (called regalia) that Queen Elizabeth used during her Coronation ceremony. Can you match the labels with the pictures?

▲ Choose two items and explain why they might be important.

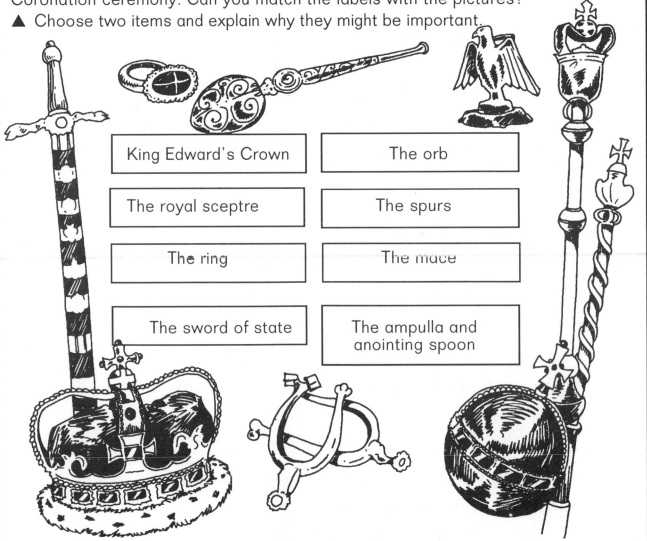

King Edward's Crown	The orb
The royal sceptre	The spurs
The ring	The mace
The sword of state	The ampulla and anointing spoon

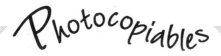

The development of aircraft, see page 72

Development of aircraft

This is a list of important events in the development of aircraft.
Choose three events and find pictures and information about each one.
Use your research to describe how flying has changed since 1903.

1903	USA, Wilbur and Orville Wright fly the first powered aircraft
1909	Louis Blériot, a French aviator, crosses the English Channel
1914–18	Aircraft used to drop bombs during the First World War
1918	The Royal Air Force is formed
1919	John Alcock and Arthur Whitten-Brown, fly non-stop across the Atlantic
1924	Flights from Britain to Canada and South Africa begin
1930	Amy Johnson flies to Australia
1939–45	Bombers, fighter bombers and fighter planes play a big part in World War II
1941	First flight by a plane powered by a jet engine
1952	The first British jet airliner (the *Comet*) goes into service
1969	The world's first supersonic airliner (*Concorde*) makes its first flight
1970	The first American 'jumbo jet' carrying 370 passengers goes into service

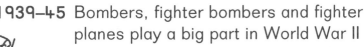

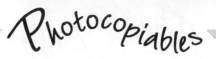

Changes in how we do our shopping

These items would have been sold in a grocer's shop in the 1950s.

▲ How many do you recognise? Look at the weights and prices.
▲ How much would the same items cost in present day money?

Package holidays to Europe, see page 80

Package holidays to Europe

Mr and Mrs Woods joined a coach tour to Spain organised by Overground Tours in August 1957. You will be able to find the places they visited or passed through on a map of Europe. Mr Woods kept a diary of the holiday and these are some of the things that he noted down.

Mon 12th Aug We left Victoria Bus Station in London before 8 am and travelled on an East Kent bus arriving in Dover about 3 hours later. We caught the ferry and had a smooth crossing from Dover to Calais. We joined our tour bus and began the long drive into Normandy. We arrived at Rouen after dark but we saw the cathedral flood-lit.

Tues 13th Aug After rolls and coffee for breakfast (no tea!), we travelled via Chartres where we only had time for a quick look at the cathedral. At Tours we had lunch though there was no time to see anything and at Poitiers, all we saw were railway yards. We travelled through beautiful wine growing country and reached Angouleme by dark.

Wed 14th Aug Left Angouleme very early. Just outside Bordeaux, the bus broke down. Hours later we drove on to the Pyrenees, Tarbes and Lourdes. Lourdes was packed with pilgrims for a special festival. Many of our group had to share beds or sleep in a different hotel. After dinner we saw the torch-lit procession.

Thurs 15th Aug Spent the day in Lourdes. Some of the party went on the cable railway but saw nothing because it was cold and misty.

Fri 16th Aug An early start. We crossed the Pyrenees via Pau. At the Spanish border we were delayed for an hour, but we had a glorious drive through mountain scenery, along some hair-raising passes. Then we found the Spanish sun. The coach was very hot and there was nothing to see but scattered olive trees. At Huesca we couldn't find the cathedral. Then we went on to Saragossa.

Sat 17th Aug Leaving Saragossa, we drove to Madrid. We arrived at our hotel in the evening. It was in the poorer part of the city and it was noisy. We had ancient tramcars crashing past our window. But we were so tired we managed to sleep a bit.

Sun 18th Aug Had a coach tour of Madrid. We only had an hour in the Prado, one of the finest art galleries in Europe. Then some of the group went off to a bull fight, but we took the metro into the city. The train was antique and very full. Spanish prices weren't as cheap as we had been told to expect. When we got back, the group had returned from the bullfight. They hadn't enjoyed it and we were very glad we hadn't gone.

Tues 20th Aug We left Madrid without regret and made for Burgos. This was a lovely drive! We crossed the Guadarrama Mountains stopping for a good lunch at a pretty chalet. At Burgos, a real pot of tea was awaiting us!

Wed 21st Aug We travelled via Vitoria to San Sebastian to stay by the seaside. Our hotel was in a small fishing port near to the town.

Thurs 22nd Aug We spent all day in San Sebastian. The weather was chilly and dull. There were no deck chairs, no sea trips, no coach trips and sun bathing was prohibited. There very little for people to do except walk about. And this is Spain's major seaside resort!

Fri 23rd Aug We crossed the frontier at Irun into France on our way home. On to Bordeaux where we had the world's worst cup of coffee and then to Angouleme again where we stayed the night.

Sat 24th Aug After going through Poitiers and Tours, we reached Paris in the early evening. After dinner we went on a coach trip round the sights: the lights of Montmartre, the Moulin Rouge, Notre Dame, the Eiffel Tower, the Champs Elysee and the Place de la Concorde (very lovely).

Sun 25th Aug Made a terribly early start hoping for a good crossing. But there were gales in the Channel and the crossing from Calais was very rough. But we were only ten minutes late arriving at Dover. We returned home to sleep off the effects of the most exhausting holiday of our lives.

Exploring space, see page 82

Exploring space

▲ Here are some pictures of events from the history of space exploration, but they are in the wrong order. Cut out each of the pictures, place them in the correct order and glue them on to a separate sheet of paper.
Write some information about each event beneath each picture.

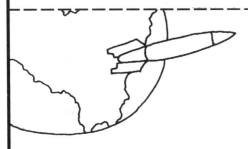

1961 Yuri Gagarin, the first man to make a space flight around the earth, it takes 108 minutes.

1969 Neil Armstrong and Edwin Aldrin became the first men to land and walk on the moon.

1995 USA, space probe descends to surface of Jupiter.

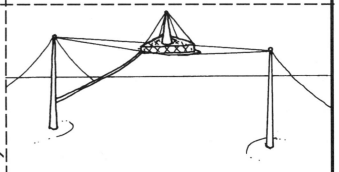

1955 Radio telescope completed at Jodrell Bank.

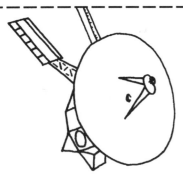

1990 Hubble telescope is launched into orbit as the world's largest space telescope.

1981 USA launches *Columbia* shuttle, first re-usable spacecraft.

Britain and the EU

▲ Colour in the map to show the order in which different countries joined the European Union. Use a different colour for each group.

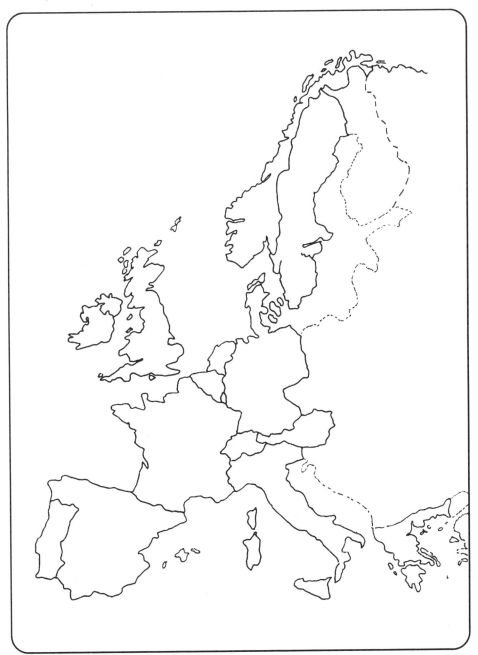

1958   West Germany, Holland, Belgium, Luxembourg, France, Italy.
1973   The Irish Republic, the United Kingdom, Denmark.
1981   Greece.
1986   Spain, Portugal.
1995   Austria, Finland, Sweden.

Use the map to mark on other things you have found out about the different countries.

Prehistoric and Roman sites, see page 89

Prehistoric and Roman sites

▲ Here is a list of the main periods of the early history of Britain.
▲ Design your own symbols for some of the things that have been found at the historical sites in your area and write a brief description of them.

PERIOD	MY SYMBOL IS	FINDS MADE
Old Stone Age (Palaeolithic)		
Middle Stone Age (Mesolithic)		An arrowhead
New Stone Age (Neolithic)		
Bronze Age		
Iron Age		
Roman		

Anglo-Saxon, Viking, Norman, Mediaeval and Tudor sites

▲ Here is a list of the main periods in the history of Britain from AD 400 to 1600.
▲ Design your own symbols for some of the things that have been found at the historical sites in your area and write a brief description of them.

PERIOD	MY SYMBOL IS	FINDS MADE
Anglo-Saxon 5th to 11th centuries		
Viking 8th to 11th centuries (in the North and Midlands, Danelaw)		
Norman and early Mediaeval 1066–1272	(church symbol)	Church
Plantagenet 1272–1399		
Late Mediaeval 1399–1485		
Tudor 1485–1603	(cross symbol)	Monastery

Design features of local housing, see page 92

How to identify types of houses from different historical periods

▲ Here are some pictures of houses from different historical periods.
Use these pictures to help you identify the period of houses in your area.

Tudor
Half-timbered lattice
windows

18th century
Classical Greek features
Casement windows, small
rectangular window
frames

Victorian 1870
Terraced houses
straight onto street

Late Victorian 1885
Large detached houses
bay windows and larger
window panel

1930s
Mock tudor with
garage space

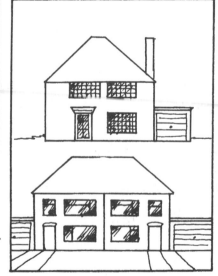

Post war
Detached and semi-
detached

Looking at old buildings, see page 95

Old buildings

Here are some of the buildings which can be seen in a Bristol street.
Use the key to help you identify the age of each building.
Choose a different colour for each century.

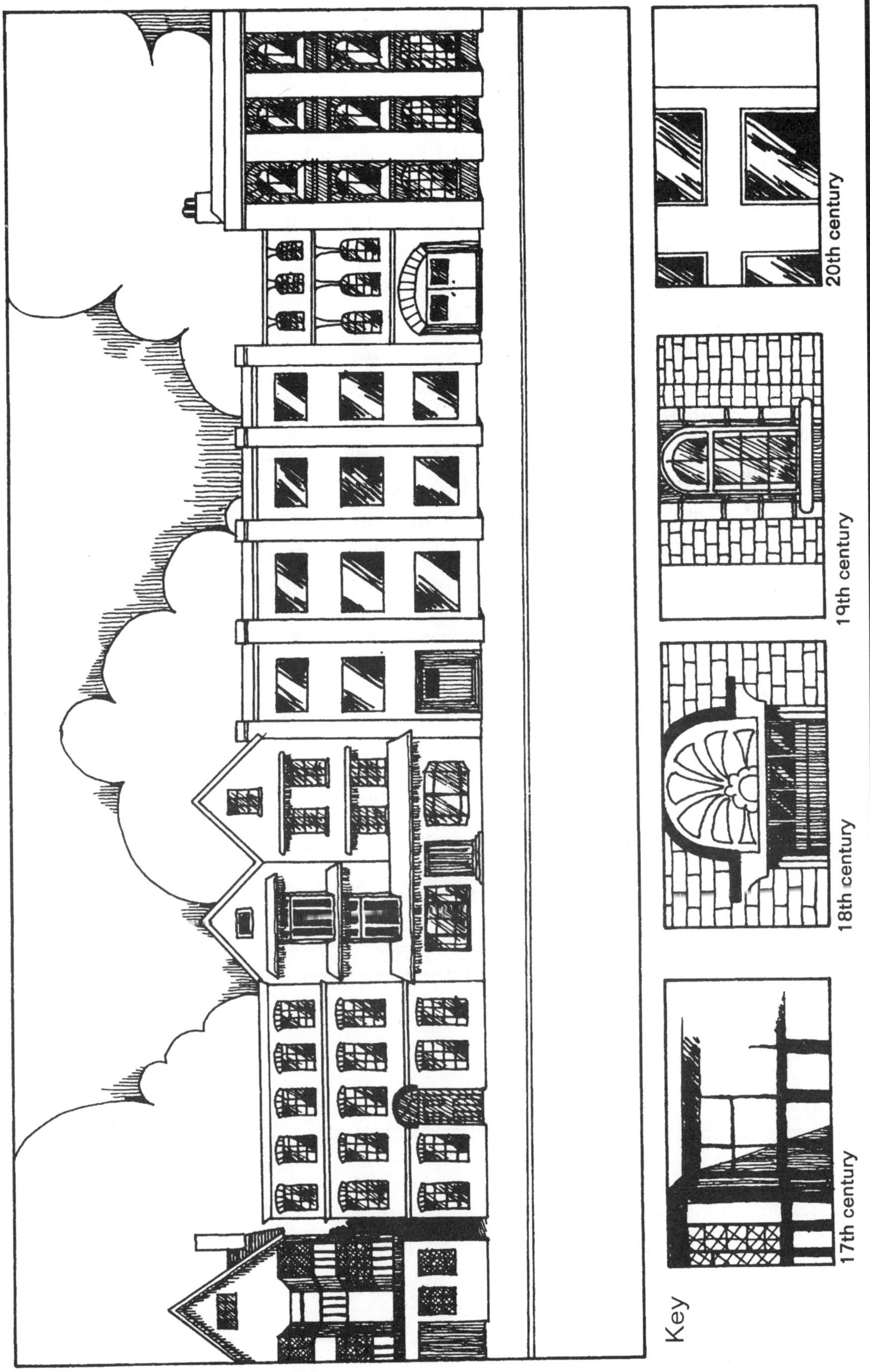

Key

17th century

18th century

19th century

20th century

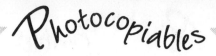
Market Day

▲ Read this description of a market in Bristol 200 years ago. Choose one or two items that are being sold and make a drawing of them on the market stall.

An eighteenth century view of Bristol

A market is also held on Back every other Wednesday where the Welsh boats, arriving at spring tides, discharge the produce of their country for sale; fine salt-butter, poultry of all kinds, roasting pigs and geese ready for the spit; fruit as apples and pears, etc. The great brewhouses and malthouses, the bakers and cornfactors, are furnished with corn and flour by water carriage from the West Country and the fertile vale of Evesham, and the counties of Hereford, Monmouth, and Worcester, which is landed on St. Austin's wharf, at the head of the Quay, out of the trows; or on the Back, where convenient markethouses are built for securing it when landed from the weather, and there exposed to sale every spring tide: here also landed great quantities of cyder.

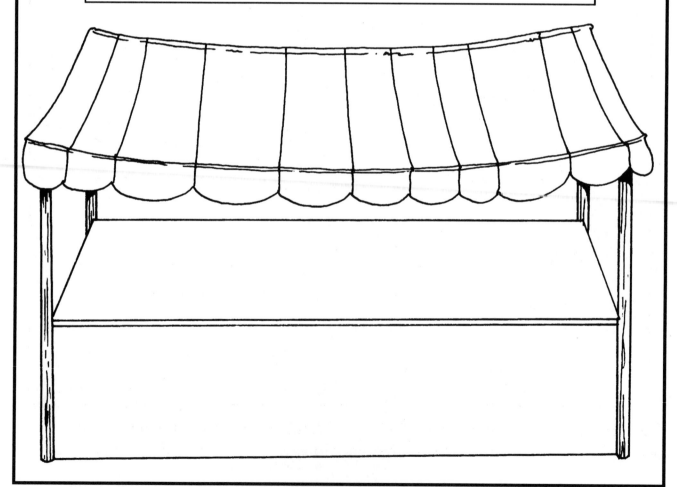

19th century map of local area

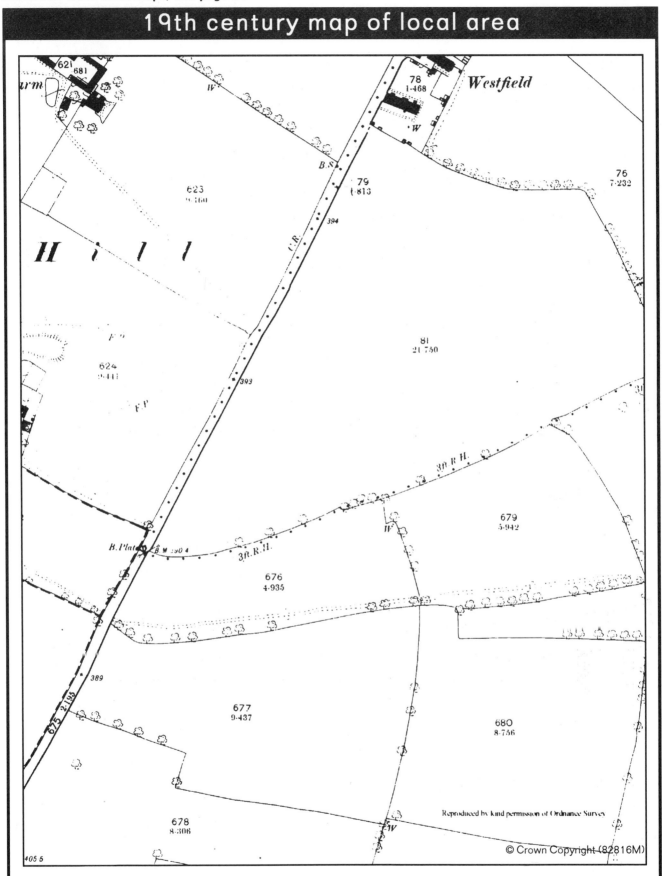

▲ This is a map of an area in 1883. Look carefully at the road and the field pattern. Compare this map with the one of the same area in 1989 on page 152.

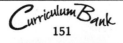

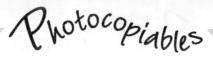
1989 map of local area

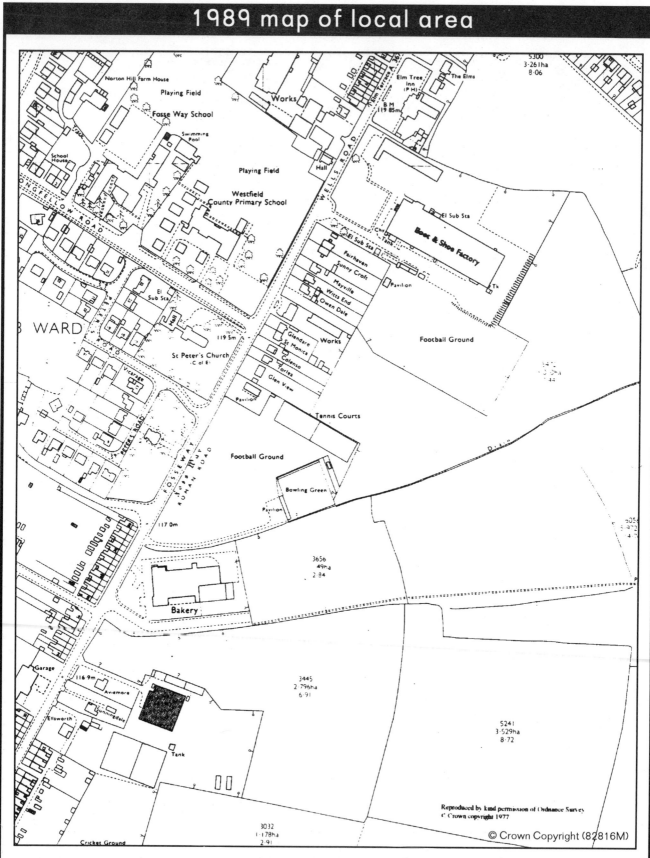

© Crown Copyright (82816M)

▲ This is a map of an area in 1989. How does it compare with the Victorian map on photocopiable page 151? How far do the lines of the modern streets follow the pattern of the old fields? How many things have stayed the same?

Changes to Whiteladies Road

1878	1894
140 A. Mogford & Sons, oil & colorman	140 Albert Mogford and Sons, house decorators
138 William Pidgeon, greengrocer	138 Mrs Sarah Sealy, greengrocer
136 George H. Fear, pork butcher and dairyman	136 Geo. H. Fear, dairyman and pork butcher
134 Lloyd & Son, fishmongers & poultr'	134 Cleal & Nash, drapers
132 James Morrell, baker	132 James Morrell, baker
130 Mrs M. Hughes, butcher	128 & 130 Lloyd & Son, fishmongers and poulterers
128 Supply Co., grocers	
——Wellington Park intersects	——Wellington Park intersects
126 Robt. J. Troake, chemist & druggist	126 Robt. J. Troake, chemist & druggist
124 Thomas H. Partridge, waiter and greengrocer	124 Mrs E. A. Partridge, greengrocer
122 Thomas Gregory, tea dlr. & grocer	122 J. M. Highnam. artist's colourman and picture frame maker
120 G. W. Isaac & Co., chemists	120 G. W. Isaac & Co. pharmaceutical chemists
118 Joseph Edward Betts; boot and shoe warehouse, Northampton hs Globe Express Office	118 Mrs Emily Betts, boot warehouse Globe Parcel Express Recvn Office
114 A. E. Pring & Co. grocers, etc. London house	116 Jno. Palmer, furnishing ironmongr
112 Edward R. Batchelor, wine and spirit merchant	114 E. A. Pring, grocer & tea dealer
110 Alfred Darby, grocor, etc	112 Ed. R. Batchelor, wine merchant
108 Geo. Clark, poulterer & fishmongr	110 Alfred Darby, grocer, etc
	108 Redland Fish Supply

▲ Use the street directory above to help you to write out the names of the owners and the type of shop in the list.

Shop in Whiteladies Road		1878 Name of the owner and the type of shop	1894 Name of the owner and the type of shop
	108		
	110		
	112		
	114		
	116		
	118		
	120		
	122		
	124		
	126		
	128		
	130		
	132		
	134		
	136		
	138		
	140		

▲ Colour in all those shops which by 1894 had changed. Describe some of the changes on the back of this sheet.

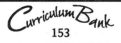

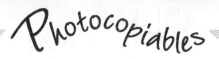

Victorian census

▲ Make up a list of questions to help you find out about the people who lived in Etloe Road in 1881 (taken from Census Enumerator's book, 1881).

© Crown Copyright Public Records Office

Road, street No or name of house	Inhabited Y N	Name	Relation to Head of family	Con-dition	Age M	Age F	Occupation	Where born
		Ethel STONE	Dau	–		2		Bristol
		Annie WEARE	Servant	Un		24	General Servant	do
1 Etloe Road	1	Frederic JONES	Head	Mar	27		Colliery Agent	Bristol
		Mary JONES	Wife	Mar		25		Bristol
		Henry JONES	Son	–	3			Bristol
		Lilly JONES	Dau	–		2		Bristol
		Ethel JONES	Dau	–		1		Bristol
		Beatrice CHAPLIN	Sister-in-law	Un		16		Bristol
2 Etloe Road	1	John BUTLER	Head	Mar	51		Dairy Man	Northamptonshire
		Jane BUTLER	Wife	Mar		46		South Wales
		Mary BUTLER	Dau	Un		21	Milliner	South Wales
		Elizabeth BUTLER	Dau	–		13		Stoke Bishop, Glos
		Albert BUTLER	Son	–	11		Scholar	do Glos
		Florence BUTLER	Dau	–		7	do	do Glos
		Anne BUTLER	Visitor	Un		60		Northamptonshire
3 Etloe Road	1	John PRING	Head	Mar	32		Builder	Somerset
		Mary PRING	Wife	Mar		32		Flaxley, Glos
		Frederick PRING	Son	–	9			Bristol
		Charles PRING	Brother	Un	24		Mason	Somerset
		Robert PRING	Brother	Un	21		Carpenter	Somerset
4 Etloe Road	1	George MAWDITT	Head	Mar	36		Builder	Devonshire
		Eliza MAWDITT	Wife	Mar		46		Hertfordshire
		George E MAWDITT	Son	Un	13		Office Boy	Westbury, Glos
		Georgina MAWDITT	Dau	–		11	Scholar	do Glos
		Georgina E MAWDITT	Sister	Un		40	Domestic Servant	Devonshire
		Alice FOSTER	Visitor	–		12		Somerset
5 Etloe Road	1	Thomas HOLBROOK	Head	Mar	46		Mason	Somerset
		Catherine HOLBROOK	Wife	Mar		48		Westbury, Glos
		Grace HOLBROOK	Dau	Un		18	Dressmaker	do
		Thomas HOLBROOK	Son	Un	14		Mason	do
		William HOLBROOK	do	–	12		Scholar	do
		John HOLBROOK	do		8		Scholar	do
		Nancy HOLBROOK	Dau	–		5	Scholar	do
6 Etloe Road	1							
7 Etloe Road	1	John QUICK	Head	Mar	31		Labourer	Devon
		Sarah QUICK	Wife	Mar		33	Laundress	Somerset
		Matilda QUICK	Dau	–		14	Laundress	do
		Charles QUICK	Son	–	10		Scholar	do
		Aaron QUICK	do	–	8		Scholar	Bristol
		Mary JOHNSON	Visitor	Un		21	Domestic Servant	Somerset
		Ernest JOHNSON	Visitor	–	15		Farm Labourer	Somerset
		Wallima JOHNSON	Boarder	–	13		Page Boy	do
		Rosey QUICK	Dau	–		4	Scholar	Bristol
		Ada MASON	Wife	Mar		30	Laundress	Bristol
		Henry MASON	Son	–	2			do
		Mabel MASON	Dau	–		1		do
		Ada HOWARD	Niece	–		12		do
Wallcroft Cottage	1	William ROBERTS	Head	Mar	37		Gardener	Wales
		Susan ROBERTS	Wife	Mar		38		Somerset
		Ada ROBERTS	Dau	–		10	Scholar	Bristol

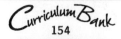

Tithe apportionment map

▲ Write the name of each field on the map. Shade in each of the following using a different colour: Arable land
Pasture
Meadows

▲ Who owned the most land? How was most of the land used?

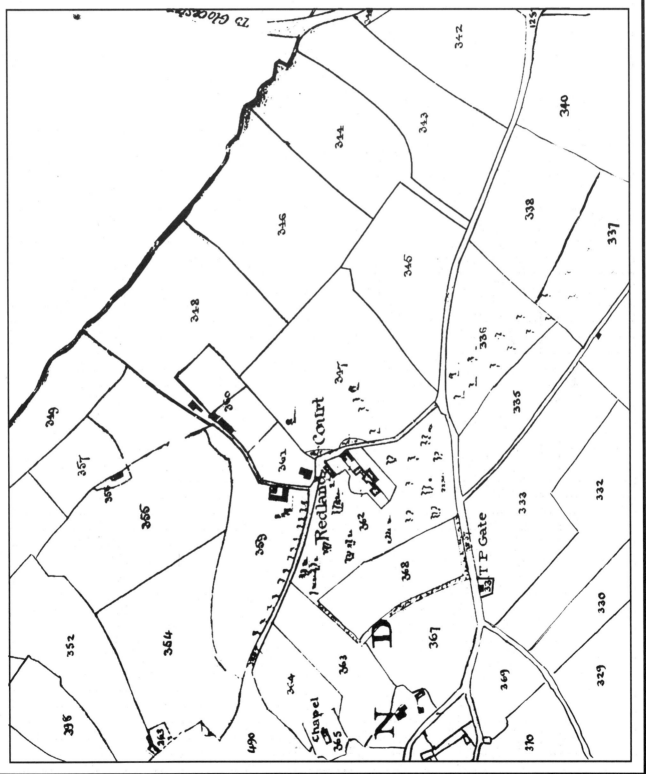

Tithe apportionment map

Landowners	Occupiers	No	Name/description of lands and premises	State of Cultivation	Acre	Rood	Perch	£	s	d
James Ewan Baillie Esquire	William Creed	316	Arch Field	Pasture	7		39	2	7	6
	Elizabeth Tripp	317	Close	Pasture	4	2	25	1	10	6
	Thomas Iles	318	Close by lane	Pasture	8	1		2	14	
		336	Lower Hilly Close	Pasture	4	1	37	1	7	6
		337	Upper Hilly Close	Pasture	4	3	15	1	9	6
		338	Fennell Close	Pasture	5		14	1	13	8
		340	Clots hill	Pasture	7	1	22	2	8	8
		341	House Garden and Shed			1	22		2	8
	Thomas Lamocrale	345	Clotts Paddock & Long Meadow	Pasture	5	1	39	1	16	4
		346	Lower Meadow	Pasture	8	2	27	2	13	10
		347	Upper Meadow	Pasture	8	2	6	2	16	6
		348	Lower Meadow	Pasture	7	2	6	2	9	9
	William Edwards	359	Close and shed	Pasture	5	1	3	1	12	2
		360	Gardens and Cottage		2		19			
		361	Laundry and Plantation		1		8		15	10
		362	Redland Court Offices							
			Building Yards Pleasure Grounds and Lane adjoining		7	3	26	2		3
		368	Close adjoining	Pasture	3	1		1	1	6
		368a	Plantation	Pasture	1	1	6		1	10
	Robert Isles	349	Long Mead	Pasture	4	1	27	1	7	
		350	Little Mead and Hop Yard	Pasture	3		31		16	3
		351	Cow House Yards etc			1	23		2	
		352	Great Wood	Pasture	6		24	1	14	11
		353	House and Garden				31		1	
		354	Outward Brookridge	Pasture	6	2	14	2		2
		355	Inner Brookridge	Pasture	7	1	37	2	5	8
		356	Cow House and Barton				17			6
	Thomas York	357	Little Wood	Pasture	2		11		11	2
		358	Calves Leys	Pasture	2	1	31		13	
		499	Five Acres	Pasture	5	1	31	1	10	3
		500	Coppice and Plantation	Wood	3	3	11		1	3
		501	Three acres	Pasture	3	3	5		19	2

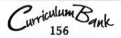

Learning from artefacts and pictures

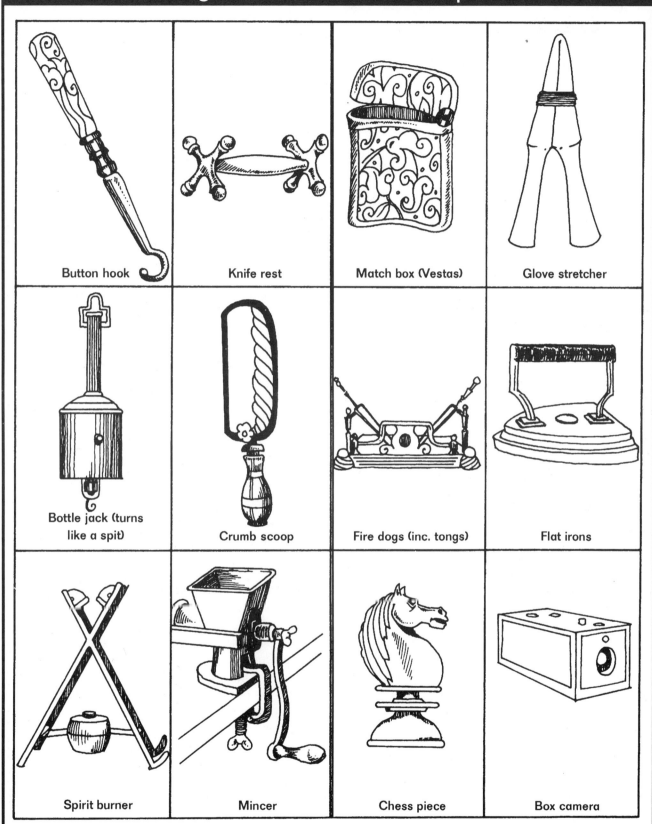

Button hook

Knife rest

Match box (Vestas)

Glove stretcher

Bottle jack (turns like a spit)

Crumb scoop

Fire dogs (inc. tongs)

Flat irons

Spirit burner

Mincer

Chess piece

Box camera

▲ Choose one object from this page and write its life story as if it were used by someone in your local area.

INFORMATION TECHNOLOGY WITHIN HISTORY

Many different areas of IT have been identified in these activities. As the use of multi-media authoring software and CD-ROMs is becoming more widespread they have been specifically highlighted below.

CD-ROMs

There are an ever growing number of CD-ROMs available which have been designed to complement History Study Units at Key Stage 2. They vary in quality and suitability so it is worth evaluating specific CD-ROMs before purchasing them. CD-ROMs fall into three broad categories.

The first are those which provide an encyclopaedia type of environment. The CD-ROM will contain text and pictures; some of the more up-to-date include moving pictures and sounds such as music, sound effects and speech. Children can access the information in a number of ways. They may be able to do a simple search on a specific topic by typing the words *Queen Victoria*, for example. This will take them to the relevant part of the CD-ROM. When they read the page they may find some of the words highlighted in a different colour. By clicking on these words they will be taken to another section of the encyclopaedia which has more, or 'linked' information. Moving from one part to another via these 'hot links' is called browsing.

It is often possible to save the text from searches or pictures from the CD-ROMs. However, when children save large quantities of text from the CD-ROM, it is important that they sort it to find the key points that are relevant to the topic being studied. Make a printed copy which children can use away from the computer, marking the key points with a highlighter pen. They can then load the text into a word processor and edit it to present the useful information.

CD-ROMs usually contain such a vast quantity of information that it is important to try any new CD-ROM in advance of its use with children. Check the quality and relevance of the information, the readability of text, where and how the information can be found and whether it is possible to extract pictures or text for use in other work. It is often useful to set up some simple questions to direct children's use, as they can spend a lot of unproductive time browsing in areas which have no relevance to the work being undertaken.

A second form of CD-ROM is an interactive one, where children make a decision that takes them to another part of the CD-ROM. These types may be in the form of adventure games or interactive stories. *Frontier 2000* which looks at the area around Hadrian's Wall is probably one of the better known in this category. There are many 'living book' type CD-ROMs that the children either read for themselves or hear the words read to them. They can re-listen to a section

by clicking on the sentence or individual words. There are often animated pictures and sound effects which make these more interesting.

The third type of CD-ROM is usually a large collection of pictures or other resources that can be used within the children's own work. There may, for example be collections of 'clipart' or photographs of artefacts and other documentary evidence linked to particular topics such as Britain since the 1930s.

Multi-media authoring software

This software is a relatively recent addition for most schools but is proving to be a very versatile and powerful medium. It combines many of the features of a word processor or desktop publishing package but its main benefit is that the different pages of a child's work can be linked together. Depending on how the links are created, children can move to different parts of the presentation by simply clicking on a symbol, word or picture with the mouse. Such presentations usually begin with a title page which allow the user to move to different chapters in a story, or sections of the presentation.

An important feature is the software's ability to handle a range of information including text, pictures from art and drawing packages, digitised pictures from scanned images, icon cameras and video cameras, sounds from audio CDs or sound samples moving pictures taken from a CD-ROM or captured using a video camera. Some of these latter areas require specialised equipment but the mixing of text, pictures and simple recorded sounds can be undertaken with a minimal amount of equipment. The data files created by such work can be very large and a computer with a hard disk and large memory is needed. If the final presentation is to be moved to other computers via a floppy disk this will also limit the number of pages and amount of pictures and sound bytes that can be included.

Work with authoring packages is best undertaken as part of a longer project, with children working collaboratively. A class presentation can be split amongst several groups with each one preparing the text and pictures for their section and deciding how the pages are to be laid out and linked. Children will need support when they first start to putting ideas into the computer. They will need to know how to create frames, alter text styles, add colours, import graphics and sound files from other disks and make the links between the pages. A structure can be set up in advance by the teacher, giving a starting point for group work. The teacher should spend some time familiarising themself with the software and hardware before embarking on a multi-media project with children.

History provides teachers with abundant opportunities to use IT both to develop children's IT capability through communicating information, modelling and simulations and to enrich children's historical knowledge and understanding.

IT links

The grids on this page relate the activities in this book to specific areas of IT and to relevant software resources. Activities are referenced by page number rather than by name. (Bold page numbers indicate activities which have expanded IT content.) The software listed is a selection of programs generally available to primary schools, and is not intended as a recommended list. The software featured should be available from most good educational software retailers.

AREA OF IT	SOFTWARE	ACTIVITIES (PAGE NOS.)			
		CHAPTER 1	CHAPTER 2	CHAPTER 3	CHAPTER 4
Communicating Info	Word processor	**21**, 27, 29, 31, 32, 34, 35	42, 43, 45, 47, 52, **57**, 58	61, 63, 65, 67, 70, 74, 79, 81, 84	90, 104, 105, 106
Communicating Info	DTP	21, 29, 32, 34, 35	**57**, 58	65, 74, 79, 81, 84	90, 106
Communicating Info	Drawing package	19, 29, 31	52	**74**, 79, 81, 84, 86	106
Communicating Info	Framework software	37			99
	Timeline software	21		65, 74, 79, 84	
	Mapping software		42		94
Communicating Info	Authoring software	28		63, 84, 86	
Information handling	Database		**49**, 55, 58		90, **94**, 99, 101, 102
Information handling	Spreadsheet		53, 55	65, **77**	
Information handling	Graphing software		49, 53, 55	65	
Information handling	CD-ROM	27, 28, 29, 31, 32, 34	43, 58	63, 65, 67, 79, 81, 84, **86**	104, 106
Modelling	Simulations	28			

SOFTWARE TYPE	BBC/MASTER	RISCOS	NIMBUS/186	WINDOWS	MACINTOSH
Word processor	Pendown Folio	Pendown Desk Top Folio	All Write Write On	Word for Windows Kid Works 2 Creative Writer	Kid Works 2 Easy Works Creative Writer
DTP	Front Page Extra	Desk Top Folio Pendown DTP Bearword	Front Page Extra NewSPAper	Creative Writer NewSPAper	Creative Writer
Framework		My World		My World	
Drawing package		Draw Picture IT		Claris Works	Claris Works
Multi-media authoring		Magpie Hyperstudio Genesis		Genesis Hyperstudio Illuminat us	Hyperstudio
Database	Grass	Junior Pinpoint Find IT KeyNote	NewSPAint	Sparks Claris Works Information Workshop	Claris Works EasyWorks
CD-ROM		Children Micropedia Hutchinsons		Encarta 96 Children's Micropedia Grolier	Encarta 96 Grolier
Timeline	Timelines	Timelines Time Traveller		Timelines	
Simulations		Landmarks		Landmarks	
Map software		Map Importer Aegis 2		Aegis 2	

	ENGLISH	MATHS	SCIENCE	GEOGRAPHY	D & T	IT	ART	MUSIC/PE	RE
LIFE IN TUDOR TIMES	Reading. Discussion. Role-play; drama. Writing. Story writing. Extracting information. Archaic words and spellings. Stories from Shakespeare.	Using pre-decimal coinage and Roman numerals. Calculating position at sea.	Tudor ships.	Drake's voyages. Voyages of exploration (Americas and Africa).	Priest holes. Navigation. Building construction.	Timelines. Representing a Tudor court using CD-ROMs/newspapers/books. Scanning pictures. Different fonts/styles.	Portraits. Family trees. Church interiors. Drawing from written accounts. Ruffs. Framing pictures. Concertina books. Medals. Modelling houses.	Tudor musical instruments. Singing and dancing. Outdoor games.	Reformation. Dissolution of monasteries. Persecuted priests. Religious festivals.
VICTORIAN BRITAIN	Discussion. Using reference books; recording; investigating. Writing imaginative accounts. Poetry; recitation. Charades and alphabet games. Spelling bee. Reading from Dickens/Kingsley. Writing plays.	Comparative times/distances by road/rail. Comparison & specifications of steamships. Population statistics. Averages. Statistics for children at school and population.	Steem-powered ships. The elements game. Pollution in Victorian towns.	Map work using 1" OS. Journeys by land and by sea. Census data for streets. Places of birth. The elements game. Victorian cities.	Paddle wheel. Building construction.	Computer-based OS maps. CD-ROM info. Writing letters. Creating/working with a census. Rules for games. Graphing software for school children/growth of towns. Desktop play writing.	Collage. Wall displays. Christmas cards and trees. Drawing buildings.	Party pieces. Carols. Music Hall. Street cries.	Victorian church and nonconformity. Victorian churches. Homelessness. Christmas tide.
BRITAIN SINCE 1930	Writing letters. Discussion. Role-play. Written accounts. Writing scripts for broadcasts. (H G Wells) space fiction and comics. Reading.	Road and car statistics. Shopping. Pre-decimal coinage and weights.	Electricity. Petrol combustion. Safety precautions. Broadcasting. Astronomy. Public health.	Road transport. Map of theatre of war. Climate/environment and their impact. Route of Coronation procession. Imperial trade (food). Package tours mapping route.	Mechanisation. Electrification. Industries. Internal combustion engine. Design of cars & construction. Aircraft – their development and repair. Radio/TV.	Recording findings using CD-ROM timelines. Word processing. Drawing package spreadsheet.	Displays of Blitz. One man's war. Coronation regalia. Modelling and drawing aircraft/mobile. Posters. Modelling TV/radio sets.	Wartime entertainment and songs. Coronation music.	Coronation ceremony. Foreign churches/religions.
LOCAL HISTORY	Discussion. Brainstorming. Writing; recording; listing. Listening. Interviewing. Reading texts. Imaginative writing.	Census statistics. Bar charts. Using census data. Comparative popularity of names.	River boats. Artefacts: what are they made of/used for?	Making maps. Distribution of sites/finds. Housing; land use. Trade via river. Evidence from maps. Census data. Occupations/place of birth.	Prehistoric technology. Transport/storage of grain etc. Surveying. Farm tools and machinery.	Data bases for finds/sites and place names. OS maps in digital format. Concept keyboard. Census files.	Frieze of houses. Architectural styles. Market collages. Table top models. Drawing. Painting. Costume.	Local festivals.	Places of worship. Church ownership of land.